College Grad Job Hunter
The guide that has launched thousands of college grads on the path to career success!

More praise from recent grads for **College Grad Job Hunter:**

"Why didn't they teach this stuff here at college? I put more than $75,000 into my education, yet your book taught me things that put the 'book learning' of my classes to shame. They should start teaching a class here in Jobs 401 with your book as the textbook."

—*S.T., University of Massachusetts*

"This book blows away all the others. I've read several books on job search and this is the only one that really covers the entry level hiring process in detail."

—*D. M., Jackson State University*

"Your book has helped me organize in my mind the sometimes overwhelming process of getting a job. It was the only book that I found that met my exact needs. It covers the entire job process instead of just one aspect or another."

—*D. K., Oklahoma State University*

"The career techniques and tactics you've revealed in your book are absolutely incredible . . . Not only did I get the job I wanted, I used the salary negotiation techniques to get the salary and perks I wanted. Actually more than I wanted. Your book has easily been worth more than $5,000 to me."

—*J. S., University of California—Berkeley*

"As a foreign student, this book helped me understand how you really get hired in the U.S. job market. I got a great job offer and I start the week after graduation."

—*P. K., Ball State University*

"I was beginning to feel sorry for myself and thinking I'd never find a good job when my roommate gave me your book to read. Wow! I went from no offers after 12 interviews to 4 job offers from my last 5 interviews—all just by using your Personality Matching Technique. Now the hardest part is deciding which one to accept."

—*M. B., Fresno State University*

"Just a note of thanks to you for a wonderful summer . . . while all my friends worked at McDonald's and Wendy's, I landed a job with Shearson Lehman . . . and they've already offered me a job after graduation if I'm interested."

—*W. C., University of Florida*

"Your book is an honest look at the 'real world' and, at the same time, very inspirational. It's been very helpful to me in my job search. Thanks for a great book!"

—*C. L., North Carolina State University*

"Your section on evaluating the job offer helped me remain calm, cool, and in control. As a result, I received vital information concerning future raises and negotiated an excellent salary along with benefits. Thanks!"

—*S. J., Texas Tech University*

More praise from hiring managers for **College Grad Job Hunter:**

"There is a difference between 'getting a job' fresh out of college and getting 'the right job.' The right job becomes the catalyst to a career that progresses in an exciting yet logical fashion, rather than a career filled with stops and starts. *College Grad Job Hunter* is just what the doctor ordered to help in identifying and attaining 'the right job.'"

—Dan Anhalt, Technical Resource Manager, Compuware

"You have tapped into many of the techniques that it has taken others a lifetime to learn, and then capsulized them into a highly workable format. I would strongly encourage anyone seeking a true competitive advantage to take full advantage of the contents of your book."

—Justin Strom, President, The Overton Group

"*College Grad Job Hunter* truly hits the mark for the college student of the '90s. This book should be in the hands of every college student who is serious about finding a great job and every parent that wants to help with the process. It helps the student with specific strategies to jumpstart their job search. And it helps the parents understand what steps need to be taken and what they can do to help. Your concepts of how to get started and then how to carry the search through to successful completion provide a tremendous opportunity for the student. Highly recommended."

—Tom McElwee, Director — Quality Performance, MGIC Investment Corp.

"I have taken the opportunity of reviewing your book, College Grad Job Hunter, and want to compliment you on a job well done. The book offers an outstanding map for job seekers to follow as a means of securing that 'just right' position. It should be a godsend to any and all recent graduates at any level to help them prepare for the selection process . . . Again, congratulations on your efforts."

—Robert Hutchison, Senior Vice President, Human Resources, First Bank

"Your book is the best affordable tool I have found that will give today's college grad the win! win! results to connect with top level positions in today's highly competitive professional job market. I have started circulating your book between my three grandsons, who will all be graduating in the next four years."

—Richard Sovitsky, Former President, Everbrite Company

"As a professional writer and former marketing consultant, I concur with your techniques, tips, and tactics. Your suggestions are the best I've seen in terms of marketing individuals—which is really what obtaining a job is. The details, suggestions, and research are evident throughout every page. This is the best book on the subject I've ever read."

—Sharon Goldinger, President, PeopleSpeak

COLLEGE GRAD
JOB HUNTER

4TH EDITION

COLLEGE GRAD
JOB HUNTER

*Insider Techniques and Tactics
for Finding a Top-Paying Entry Level Job*

Brian D. Krueger, CPC

Adams Media Corporation
HOLBROOK, MASSACHUSETTS

Published by
Adams Media Corporation
260 Center Street, Holbrook, MA 02343

ISBN: 1-55850-841-4

Printed in Canada

J I H G F E D C

Library of Congress Cataloging-in Publications Data
Krueger, Brian D.
College grad job hunter : insider techniques and tactics for finding
a top-paying entry level job / by Brian D. Krueger.
—4th ed., completely rev.
        p.   cm.
Includes index.
ISBN 1-55850-841-4
1. Job hunting. 2. Résumés (Employment.
3. College graduates—Employment. I. Title.
        HF5382.7.K78   1998
        650.14—dc21   97-47078
                                            CIP

This book is available at quantity discounts for bulk purchases.
For information, call 1-800-872-5627 (in Massachusetts, 781-767-8100).

Visit our home page at http://www.adamsmedia.com

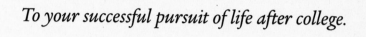

To your successful pursuit of life after college.

CONTENTS

Introduction xi

SECTION 1: Preparing for Your Job Search
Chapter 1: Job Search Prep 3
Chapter 2: Real-World Experience 19
Chapter 3: Best College Resumes 29
Chapter 4: Best College Cover Letters 45
Chapter 5: Best College References 53
Chapter 6: Job Search Central 59
Chapter 7: Your Career Development Office 69

SECTION 2: Finding Hiring Companies
Chapter 8: Network Intelligence Gathering 77
Chapter 9: Employer Research Strategies 99
Chapter 10: Internet Job Search Strategies 115
Chapter 11: Job Fair Success 135
Chapter 12: Setting Up On-Campus Interviews 149
Chapter 13: Getting Inside Hiring Companies 155
Chapter 14: Getting the Off-Campus Interview 167
Chapter 15: Guerrilla Insider Techniques 179

SECTION 3: Interviewing Success
Chapter 16: Competitive Interview Prep 197
Chapter 17: Mastering the Interview 213
Chapter 18: On-Campus Interviewing Success 245
Chapter 19: Phone Interviewing Success 251
Chapter 20: Company-Site Interviewing Success 255

SECTION 4: From Interview to Offer to Job
Chapter 21: After the Interview 269
Chapter 22: Successful Job Offer Negotiation 275
Chapter 23: When the Offer Does Not Come 297
Chapter 24: Graduation and Still No Job 303
Chapter 25: New Job Preparation 313

Appendix A: Guidelines for Successful Interview Dress 323
Appendix B: Fifty Standard Entry Level Interview Questions 325
Appendix C: Illegal Interview Questions 327

Index 328
Software Offers 336
About the Author 338

INTRODUCTION

All our dreams can come true—
if we have the courage to pursue them.
—Walt Disney

Dear Friend,

I am looking forward to helping you in your job search. I am a strong believer in the fact that there is a job out there that is just right for you. It is waiting for you to find it. Your job will be to find and secure that job. This book is my way of reaching out to guide you as we walk down that path together.

As you look forward to life after college, your first priority should be to focus on the importance of securing an outstanding first job. That first job, whether it lasts twelve months or forty-five years, will start you on the path to your future life. This book is designed to serve as your personal advisor in seeking out and finding that critical first position. The pages that follow are filled with literally hundreds of techniques and tactics that will guide you in your quest.

> YOUR JOB SEARCH SHOULD BECOME YOUR #1 PRIORITY IN YOUR FINAL YEAR OF COLLEGE.

I realize that this book contains far more techniques and tactics than any one person could use during the course of a single job search—or even in a single work lifetime. Why are there so many? Because some techniques will work for you—and others will not. That's right. Some of the information will not apply to your specific circumstance, and other information will need modification to fit your personal style. The key is that each person who uses the appropriate techniques will gain a true competitive edge by putting this information to use.

Does each technique presented work every time? Obviously not. But these techniques can assist you in opening new doors that might have been previously impassable. They can assist you in getting into a company that is not officially hiring. They can assist you in finding an opportunity that no one else is aware of. They can assist you in succeeding in the interview when you might have otherwise failed. In short, this book can assist you in reaching your full employment potential. Remember, I am only here to assist you. You are the one who has to actively put the information to work.

Please look at this information as a diamond in the rough, a gem requiring polish to bring forth the shine and brilliance contained within. These techniques have all been field-tested and have been highly successful for others. But they will require an element that no book can give: your personal touch. The best job search tactics are those that allow for modification to fit your personal style and needs. That has been a central focus in developing this book: giving you the tools you need, while retaining your individual personality. So make this book your own and adopt these techniques and tactics by putting your personal "spin" on them.

What This Book Is About

As you review the techniques contained within this book, it is important that you understand in advance what this book is and is not.

> THE TIME YOU INVEST NOW IN YOUR JOB SEARCH WILL PAY BACK DIVIDENDS FOR THE REST OF YOUR LIFE.

First, what this book is. It is a compilation of unique techniques, tactics, methods, tips, and approaches specifically designed for the entry level job market. The great majority of information in this book is not available in any other book. This book was developed to give college grads a true competitive edge in the entry level job market of the '90s and into the new millennium.

Second, what this book is not. It is not a one-size-fits-all formula. It requires your interaction and your personal touch. And it is not a job offer. Properly used and applied, it will lead you to the job offer. But there is a great deal of personal effort that you will need to provide in between. Never underestimate the amount of time necessary to find the very best position. You have invested a large amount of time and money in your education.

Now, as the payoff nears, do not sell yourself short in this, the all-important final lap.

Finally, this book is written specifically for the entry level college grad market. While much of the material is applicable across all levels of job search, from entry level to management, from clerical to professional to technical, the techniques are written specifically for your job market. That said, however, you will find that many of the techniques are truly timeless and will be useful to you for the remainder of your professional life.

Plan to read this book with a pen in hand. Feel free to mark, underline, highlight, fold back page corners, or whatever it takes to prompt you toward actually using the information. It is entirely up to you what you make of the material contained in this book. These techniques have proven successful with hundreds and thousands of others, but will do nothing for you until you actually use them. Don't just say, "Hmm, that's interesting." Do it! Make it happen!

One final opening note: if you are looking for the "standard textbook answers" on entry level job search, you are reading the wrong book. The information I am giving you is not a collection of ideas from other books—in fact, much of what you will read is not in other books and often contradicts what the other books say. And with good reason. Most of the books on job search either do not apply specifically to entry level college grads or, worse yet, are just plain wrong. There are too many "job search handbooks" written by professional writers who have never hired—or been hired—in their entire life.

But if you are looking for honest, solid advice from someone who has been there, get ready for a whirlwind tour of everything you ever wanted to know about entry level job search. By the time you finish this book, you will be well-equipped to be a standout in the entry level employment process.

In the pages ahead is the adventure of your lifetime. I look forward to being your guide on this adventure. Happy hunting!

Section 1

PREPARING FOR YOUR JOB SEARCH

Chapter 1

JOB SEARCH PREP

Choose a job you love,
and you will never have to work
a day in your life.
—Confucius

Finding a job and finding a good job are two different things. If you want to be successful in your job search, you should focus on finding a *good* job. An important key to accomplishing that goal will be to spend the time necessary to properly prepare yourself for your job search. It's not enough to sign up for a few on-campus interviews, take your best shot and hope for the best. An offer may come, but it may not be for the type of job you are truly seeking. Or, worse yet, an offer may not come. To prepare yourself fully for your job search, you will need to understand more about the job search process. You need to understand

> NO ONE OWES YOU A JOB. YOU HAVE TO PUT FORTH THE EFFORT TO FIND IT.

what is happening on the other side of the resume read. You need to understand what is happening on the other side of the job fair booth. You need to understand what is happening on the other side of the interview desk. You need to understand what is happening on the other side of the telephone. You need to understand the process.

Job search is a process. Actually, it is a multiprocess, with many concurrent processes (based on multiple employer contacts) taking place at the same time. To reach the next level of the process, you need to successfully pass the previous level. So start your job search on a solid foundation by understanding how the process works and work your way successfully through each level toward your ultimate goal.

THE JOB SEARCH PROCESS

Your ultimate goal is your new job. Yet there will be several steps of completion required along the path to this goal. Following are the basic steps in the job search process:

➤ **Establish your career objective**
- Self-assessment
  - Personality
  - Aptitude
  - Interests
  - Values
  - Identify skills and abilities
- Career exploration
  - Researching career types
  - Researching industries
  - Researching geographic locations
  - Understanding the career requirements
- Career preparation
  - Academic—major, classes, projects
  - Extracurricular—activities, clubs
  - Experience—work, internships, volunteering

➤ **Prepare job search tools**
- Resume
- Cover letter
- References, letters of recommendation

➤ **Find hiring companies**
- Identify on-campus employers
  - On-campus interviews
  - On-campus job fairs
- Identify off-campus employers
  - Building and activating a career network
  - Utilizing employer research materials
  - Off-campus job fairs
  - 1Prospecting and following up on referral leads

➤ **Secure the interview**
- Make contact
- Request and confirm interview

➤ **Interview**
- Prepare for the interview
- On-campus interviewing
- Phone interviewing
- Company-site interviewing

➤ **Offer**
- Post-interview follow-up
- Job offer negotiation
- Accept and begin new job!

Seems simple enough, right? Just follow the yellow brick road to job search success. Unfortunately, what the process flow does not show is the iterative nature of the job search process. There will be failures along the way, and you will be repeating many of the steps (from "Find Hiring Companies" on) for each employer you are pursuing. And, being a linear process, it is subject to time and timing. That is, you may find yourself at square one with Employer #1 at the same time you complete the process and have an offer in hand from Employer #2. Worse things can happen in your job search, but this type of timing situation does provide a dilemma of its own. Overall, seek to master each step so that each employer interviewing process will continue to a potential offer, and you can choose. Mastering the job search process will result not only in a job offer, but in the right job for you. This book is not just about getting a job. It is about getting the right job.

Notice that the process closely mirrors the chapters and materials contained in this book. And for good reason. This book is designed as a guide. It will provide you with the information you need (and then some) for each step in the job search process.

> **THIS IS NOT A SPRINT; THOSE THAT WIN ARE THOSE THAT KEEP ON RUNNING.**

CAREER PLANNING

Remember when you were a kid and everyone would ask you, "What do you want to be when you grow up?" It is interesting that in Western society we usually stop asking that question of our children after age ten or so. So our last response was usually in the doctor/lawyer/President-of-the-U.S. category. For many, the subject of career selection does not arise again until college graduation (and an uncertain future thereafter) is staring them in the face.

Spend the time necessary to analyze both yourself and the job market. In analyzing yourself, consider utilizing a combination of testing instruments and career counseling, both of which will likely be available to you for free (or minimal cost) at your campus Career Development office. The specific tests you should consider taking include the following:

> ➤ **Personality:** Myers-Briggs Type Indicator (MBTI), the Kiersey Temperament Sorter, and others; analyzes your personality type and compares it with various careers.

➤ **Aptitude:** Structure of Intellect (SOI) and others; analyzes your aptitude for particular careers.

➤ **Interest:** Strong Interest Inventory (SII) and others; analyzes your personal interests and how they correlate with those of others who have been successful in a variety of careers.

➤ **Values:** System for Interactive Guidance and Information (SIGI) and others; examines your value system and how the priority of your values may work with (or against) you in a variety of careers.

In taking these tests, you will see a pattern of career paths emerging, although it is unlikely there will be a single career recommendation. Combine your test results with career counseling and career exploration to assist you in deciding on career paths to pursue. *The Occupational Outlook Handbook,* updated biennially by the Bureau of Labor Statistics, provides information on more than two hundred occupations, including hiring trends, type of work, training requirements, typical earnings, and future job outlook.

It is vitally important to know what you want to do before you go out and try to find it. In seeking a job, seek out one you will love. There are far too many people in today's work world who are grinding away at work they detest just to earn a big paycheck—and leading lives of quiet desperation in return. Do what you love and the paycheck will follow. And if the simple satisfaction of a good day at work is not enough for you, consider the longevity factor: a Duke University study of human longevity listed work satisfaction as the number one predictor of long life, even more important than good health habits or good genes. Live long and prosper.

THE REALITY OF SUCCESSFUL JOB SEARCH

The reality of successful job search is straightforward and simple: to be successful, you need to sit on the other side of the desk. The simple key to success is to market your product (yourself) according to the needs of your intended market (potential employers in your field). Yet very few graduates actually do this. Most job searches are conducted from a "here I am" and "this is what I want" perspective. However, the reality is that most companies do not really care about what you want until you are able to demonstrate that you can provide what they want. They care about what you can do for them. It is only after you have shown what you can do for them that they will begin to take note of what they can do for you in return.

DEVELOPING YOUR MARKETING STRATEGY

Do you consider yourself a good salesperson? If yes, good for you—you will be putting your skills to work throughout the job search process. If not, get ready to become one—because in order to be effective in your job search, you have to become effective at marketing.

Your "product" is you and your "market" is the segment of the employment marketplace that is a potential purchaser of your product.

Remember these two key points:

1. No one knows your product better than you.
2. No one can make the sale other than you.

If you don't market you, who will? Successful job search is not just a matter of taking a couple of on-campus interviews and waiting for the offers to roll in. You need to fully prepare yourself for a highly competitive entry level job market.

No matter what your major, no matter what field you intend to enter, you must be ready, willing, and able to market yourself. Just as it is difficult to market a product you do not truly believe in, it is difficult to market yourself if you do not believe in yourself. First and foremost, you have to believe in you. Do not expect me to believe in you if you don't.

> **YOUR COMPETITION IS SITTING NEXT TO YOU IN CLASS EVERY DAY.**

How can I be expected to "buy in" if you don't buy in first?

Take a long hard look in the mirror. Don't look for the bad—look for the good. Look for all the good points. Look for all the aspects about you and your background that make you an outstanding job candidate. Those are the attributes that I want to see when I meet with you.

The reality is, it's easy to market yourself into a job or company that you love. If you are enthusiastic about your work and your ability to complete the necessary tasks and activities, you will not even think of it as marketing. But if you are doing it "just for the bucks," then you are just selling your services to the highest bidder. And eventually it will burn you out.

In preparing to meet the needs of the marketplace, make sure you are comfortable selling your talents and skills to that market. The reaction from the other side of the desk to true enthusiasm will almost always be positive.

Sit on the other side of the desk. Imagine interviewing yourself for the position you most desire. Would you hire you? If not, why would anyone else? Work on yourself, your appearance, your attitude, your enthusiasm, your product, *before* you bring your final product to market.

You never get a second chance at a first impression. Make sure your first impression is right on the mark.

MARKETING YOU IN THE EMPLOYMENT MARKETPLACE

You will have to become a salesperson in order to sell yourself in the employment marketplace. And you will have to learn to sell yourself according to the way your customer buys. Meet customer needs first in order to meet your personal needs.

The first step in the customer-driven marketing process is to understand the market in general and what potential customer needs may be. It does no good to have a super product if there is no market for it. There has to be an established need or want in the job market that is satisfied by what you are intending to sell.

Do you know what your market is?

Who are your potential customers?

What are the specific needs of customers in your market?

THE STEPS YOU ARE NOW TAKING IN YOUR JOB SEARCH WILL CHART YOUR COURSE FOR THE FIRST SEVERAL YEARS OF YOUR CAREER.

The next step in the customer-driven marketing process is to develop the product. It should be developed to meet the needs of the marketplace. Have you developed your product for a specific market? Unfortunately, most students end up taking a major with little or no thought about their intended market.

While it is not the purpose of this guide to go into the entirety of career planning, I will forewarn you that if you are not able to: (1) identify your market, and (2) identify your product in relation to that market, you will fail either totally or partially in your job search. So consider yourself forewarned— you need to have a road map, an automobile, and a full tank of gas before you start on your trip. Most of us plan our vacations better than we plan our careers. The first step in your job search is to plan the direction you will take toward the type of career you will be seeking. If you have no plan for where you are going, any road will take you there. Don't start off your life blindly or in a random direction. Please make sure you know where you are going before you start your journey of a lifetime.

DEVELOP A PERSONAL CAREER MISSION STATEMENT

The business world is always attaching itself to the latest "in" topics and buzzwords. In the '80s everyone was talking about the "paradigm shift." And in the '90s, every company, large and small, has developed a company mission statement. Not that they did not have a mission before. Just that it was usually never published or publicly articulated. A mission statement is a short, descriptive statement of the common objective and focus of the organization.

> PLAN OUT AS EARLY AS POSSIBLE WHAT YOUR MISSION IN LIFE WILL BE. DO NOT ABDICATE THIS RESPONSIBILITY TO ANYONE ELSE.

In developing your personal career focus, take the time to prepare your personal career mission statement. Not because it is the "in" thing to do, but because it will help you in crystalizing your vision of who you are and where you want to go in your career. Keep your career mission statement limited to no more than three sentences and no more than thirty words. Begin your statement with the words, "My personal career mission is..." and finish with qualifying words and phrases to describe your mission. Following are some examples:

"My personal career mission is to become a world-class aeronautical engineer in the commercial aviation industry."

"My personal career mission is to gain experience in the public accounting field toward earning my CPA designation."

"My personal career mission is to master the leading GUI software development tools and gain greater understanding of business applications development."

Your personal mission statement should be tightly focused toward the first three to five years of your career. You can give specifics about job type and/or industry, as appropriate. This personal career mission statement will form the foundation of your career focus and will guide you toward successful completion of your entry level job search. The material developed here will be utilized again in the development of your resume and cover letter, in interviewing, and in all future job search contacts.

A mental conception of your personal career mission statement is not enough. You must write it down on paper and put it up on your wall. Ideally, where you can see it every day. And if it needs to be changed or modified over time, so be it. But keep your career mission statement in sharp focus in your mind. As you zero in on your larger goal, your short-term goal will become clearer.

THE GAP ANALYSIS TECHNIQUE

This is an excellent technique for planning out the initial stages of your career and focusing your job search toward areas of positive change. Do a survey of the want ads from at least two or three major newspapers. Clip out all the ads for positions you might want to have someday. Take it all the way up the line to VP and President, if that is your mission. Then, on three separate pieces of paper, accumulate the following information from these ads:

> Page #1: List all of the job responsibilities, duties, tasks, and functions.
>
> Page #2: List all of the experience, skills, and knowledge required.
>
> Page #3: List all the keywords or industry buzzwords.

In analyzing the information, note where you are now in relation to where you want to be in the future. Take note of any and all gaps, present or future. Checkmark all the gaps you can close before you enter the job market and lay out detailed plans for how to close those gaps. If there are buzzwords you are not familiar with, make sure you find out what they are. Keep your gap analysis information for future reference and update it as your career progresses.

Work on closing the gaps as much as possible between your academic career and the career you are seeking. The closer you are, the easier the decision will be. For you and the employer.

PREPARE TO MAKE AN INVESTMENT

I have heard literally hundreds of college students talk about how they are going to "coast" in their final year right up to graduation. Your class load may be down, your work load may be lower, and in general, you are finally ready to start living the good life. Hey! Have you forgotten something? If you don't have a job yet, your number one priority should be finding that job. Yet, many students end up spending their final year hitting all the parties, developing a flourishing romance, or just "taking it easy." And then they talk about how they were "too busy" to look for a job when they come up empty at graduation.

Sorry to crash your party, but until you have landed a job, you still have work to do. In fact, more work than you have done to this point. If you want to be a success in your career, you have to be prepared to make an investment—now!

> **THE INVESTMENT IN YOUR EDUCATION WILL ONLY PAY A PROPER RETURN IF YOU FIND A JOB WHERE YOU ARE HAPPY AND FULFILLED.**

First of all, you need to invest your time. You should plan on dedicating a minimum of five hours and sometimes as much as fifteen hours per week to your job search. I know that sounds like a lot of time, but get ready—there is even more. You should also plan to use your fall, winter, and spring breaks for full-time job searching. Your breaks are nonrefundable time that should be banked directly to your job search account. I realize I may be stepping on a lot of Florida-party-animal toes by recommending New York or Chicago over Daytona, but this is the time for a reality check. One week in the sun could end up burning you badly come graduation. Don't make the excuse that you cannot possibly fit anything else into your "crowded schedule." If you are taking more classes than you need to, drop them. If you are attending more social engagements than you need to, avoid them. Stop volunteering for everything that comes along. You only have a limited number of minutes and hours in each day, so make sure you spend your time productively. Make time on your schedule now or you may end up with an overabundance of time come graduation.

Second, you will need to invest your money (or somebody else's money if you are truly penniless). Conducting a successful job search costs money. Whether it is developing your job search materials, making long distance phone calls, buying an interview suit, or making weekend and spring break trips, they all cost money (I didn't say you could not travel over spring break, just not to Daytona—and no, I do not think there are very many entry level positions open in Daytona). No money left? Used it all up? This is a good time to tap into the parent bank. "Mom and Dad, you have helped me get this far, I would hate to see it all wasted for lack of a few hundred bucks more." Whatever you do, do not shortchange your career due to a simple lack of funds. Hit on rich old Aunt Sally if you have to. Use your parents' calling card for making phone calls. Remember, your future credit is good, assuming you use the money wisely toward your job search and securing a good job. Besides, Mom and Dad will spend a whole lot more money if you are unsuccessful in your job search because you will probably end up moving back home and mooching off them. And we know that is a conclusion that all concerned would like to avoid. Time to move on with your new life.

Last, you will need to invest your energy. There is no way to cram the night before, walk in bleary-eyed, and ace your "job search final." You have to be ready at all times to put forth your very best. Which means you have to be focused on your job search. What has your focus been for the last several years? Grades? Let them slide a little—remember, no one cares what your grades are for your last semester, unless you manage to actually flunk a class. Employers are only looking at your official GPA to date. Has your focus been social? Let it chill for now—you will have zero social life if you end up in the ranks of the unemployed. Has your focus been athletics? Now is the time to let others carry the torch. In summary, don't be afraid to say "No." Don't be afraid to say, "I have some work that I need to get done." Make your job search your number one priority in your life and devote yourself to it.

As a side benefit, if you devote yourself totally to your job search and secure a great job early, then you can go back to your other diversions. In fact, securing a job early is the very best thing that can happen to you in both your professional and personal life.

MODIFY YOUR CLASS SCHEDULE TO YOUR ADVANTAGE

One effective means of creating more available time in your schedule is to adopt a Tuesday/Thursday or Monday/Wednesday/Friday class schedule in either or both of your last two semesters. The absolute best schedule is a T/Th schedule of two classes in the morning, two classes in the afternoon, and a night class on Tuesday or Wednesday evening to round things out. This leaves long weekends for interview trips and focused blocks of time to dedicate to your job search. This scheduling allows you to be totally devoted to your studies on certain days, while totally devoted to your job search on the other days. You are now in the mode of part-time student and part-time job seeker. Check into modifying your schedule to allow for your new dual role in life.

THE BEST COLLEGE COURSE FOR JOB SEARCH PREP

Although a course in "Jobs 101" would be popular with most students, most colleges offer little in the way of direct job search help as part of the regular course offerings. There is, however, an excellent course to prepare you for job search success. Nearly every college and university offers it in some form or shape. That course: Speech 101. The dreaded "stand up in front of others and embarrass myself" course that most students try to avoid. If you have not taken it yet and still have some electives left, this is an outstanding course to take. It will give you the uncommon experience of expressing yourself eloquently to a group of strangers—excellent preparation for the interviewing process that lies just over the horizon.

> PUBLIC SPEAKING EXPERIENCE WILL BENEFIT YOU IN YOUR JOB SEARCH AND THROUGHOUT YOUR CAREER.

An alternative to this type of course (or as a continuation of developing your speaking ability) is to join a local Toastmasters International club. You can find them in the phone book, or call their national headquarters at 800-993-7732 to find out more about a club near you.

By the way, if you are interested in having an actual course in Jobs 101 taught at your college or university, contact me at bkrueger@collegegrad.com. I am currently in the process of developing a model curriculum for use at colleges and universities throughout the United States and Canada.

JOB SEARCH TIMETABLE

Following is a job search timetable for each year of college. It is not meant to frustrate Seniors, who have no way to reach back into the past. It is meant to provide a best-case layout for your college years. Those at two-year colleges should simply compress the time frame. Those in graduate school should seek to cover previous tracks as much as possible and sync the final-year activities with those listed for the Senior Year. And unemployed graduates should review all the information to see if there are any new steps that could be completed to enhance their job search. Keep in mind that it is never too late (or too early) to start.

➤ **Freshman Year**
  • Take a wide variety of classes to broaden your exposure to potential career paths.
  • Focus on good grades from the start; if you fall behind, it's difficult to recover.
  • Begin career exploration through your campus Career Services and Planning center to find out more about how your aptitudes, interests, personality, and values match with potential career paths.
  • Develop your first resume and continue to refine it by adding content and focus throughout your college years as your experience and vision increase.
  • Join a campus organization or club in an area of professional interest and attend the meetings regularly. In addition to providing valuable vocational information, you will develop your teamwork and leadership skills. Be a joiner throughout college.
  • Target working in an industry or occupation of interest in a support/clerical position part-time during the school year and/or full-time during the summer.

➤ **Sophomore Year**
  • Choose your major based upon your career planning and eventual career focus.
  • Focus your coursework within your major. Don't use up all of your elective credits early.
  • Ask recent graduates for the names of the professors and classes that most benefitted their career.
  • Information interview with several employers to better understand the career field and what you can be doing now to prepare for it.
  • Begin to build and develop your personal network, following the techniques outlined in later chapters in this book.
  • Continue career planning with a greater emphasis on understanding the profession and the needs of employers for entry level talent. Plan and develop your work experience and classes to match this profile.
  • Develop a relationship with the Career Development office, including assistance with preparing for work after graduation and internship experience during college.
  • Target working in a low-level co-op, internship, or research position within your chosen field part-time during the school year and/or full-time during the summer.

➤ **Junior Year**
  • Keep your grades up; the classes will begin to get more difficult, so continue to focus on excelling in your studies.

- Develop relationships with the leading professors and department heads in your major. They will be contributors to your job search, both directly as a referral source and indirectly as companies inquire about the leading students in the major.
- Run for lower-level offices (Secretary, Treasurer, etc.) in your extracurricular activities in preparation for the higher-level offices next year.
- Contact professionals in your chosen field with whom to conduct informal informational interviews in order to learn more about the profession.
- Begin planning for your final year with the Career Development office to ensure your preparation is on target for meeting the needs of potential employers.
- Target an assistant level or professional level co-op or internship within your chosen field part-time during the school year and/or full-time during the summer. Attempt to locate a position as close as possible to the type of work you would like to be doing after graduation.

➤ **Senior Year**
- Keep your grades high, yet shift your focus toward the direct applicability of your coursework to your chosen profession. This year will be your greatest preparation for the world of work.
- Complete as many courses within your major as possible. Use available electives to further your educational experience within your chosen field.
- Continue to pursue professional level work experience part-time during the school year, but look only at full-time entry level work for after graduation.
- If you have not yet acquired work experience in your chosen field, offer your services as a volunteer. Volunteer experience is still experience.
- Direct any special projects within your major toward your chosen field or profession.
- Fine-tune your resume for graduation.
- Prepare for your job search early, with all of the prerequisite materials (resume, transcripts, etc.) on file at your campus Career Development center no later than one month into your final year.
- Utilize the counseling resources at the Career Development center to further broaden your job search.
- Activate your personal network, enlisting their support in your job search.
- Begin interviewing as early as possible in your final year. Many of the best positions are filled before the end of the first semester.
- Make it your goal to find your new job as early as possible in your final year.

THE SCARLETT O'HARA SYNDROME

In reviewing the above timetable, you might feel somewhat overwhelmed, especially if you are already in your final year having done little in the way of job search preparation. It can be very easy to get caught in the daily procrastination of the Scarlett O'Hara Syndrome—"I'll think about it tomorrow."

Every day that passes is a day that could have been (and should have been) invested in your job search. While there is nothing you can do now about yesterday, and tomorrow is always one day into the future, you have full control over today.

Don't put off your job search until the last minute. The longer you wait, the more difficult it will become. Take control of your life right now and begin to do the preparation for your job search.

Don't get caught in "analysis paralysis." You will never find perfection in your job search, so make your start when you are ready to give it your best. Your best is the best that you have to offer. No one (including yourself) should ever expect anything more from you. Nor should you settle for anything less.

This book is your starting point. Begin putting the techniques and tactics into action in your life.

JOB PREP PROVERBS

Following are some initial thoughts for you to consider as you prepare for your job search:

- ➤ Only you can find your dream job. Do not depend on anyone else to hand it to you on a silver platter.

- ➤ Your college owes you nothing other than a great education. Your diploma does not come with a guarantee for a great job. That is something you will have to secure on your own.

- ➤ Seek work you love. You will be spending the greater portion of your life working. Make it an enjoyable experience.

- ➤ You are infinitely better off making $15,000 and being happy than making $50,000 and being miserable. No, the extra $35,000 is really not worth the misery. Happiness is priceless.

- ➤ Extracurricular activities count. Whether a club or athletics, it shows you are a well-rounded person. And it may be your best opportunity to exhibit leadership skills.

- ➤ Experience is experience. You gain new experiences every day. You do not need to be paid for it to make it valid experience.

➤ Grades do matter. If you are reading this early, keep your grades high. If late, you will have to provide a very good reason if they are not at least a 3.0 or above.

➤ Keep your ethics high and it will soon become your most admired quality. For very few have stayed honest to their ethical standards. Do not let yours down. Be the exception rather than the rule.

➤ Don't be afraid to ask questions. There are many people willing to help. But first you must be willing to ask for their help.

➤ Develop the key computer skills for your field or industry of interest. If you are not sure what they are, check out the classified ads.

➤ Thoroughly research each employer you pursue. It is not enough just to show up for the on-campus interviews and hope for the best.

➤ The best person does not necessarily get the job. The person with the best job search skills will typically get the job over the most qualified person.

➤ Job search is a game, complete with a defined set of rules. You need to play by the rules. But to win, you will need to stretch those rules to the limits.

➤ Remember that managers hire people who are like them. Do your best to fit in.

➤ Always think about meeting the needs of others. This is the only way to meet your own personal needs.

➤ Nervousness is common and to be expected. It helps you stay on your toes.

➤ You are unique. There is no one else out there exactly like you. Learn to recognize your unique strengths so that you can communicate them to others.

➤ A smile will carry you a great distance in your job search. A warm, friendly attitude will always get you further than coarse insensitivity.

➤ What you lack in experience, compensate for with enthusiasm.

➤ The better you get at your job search, the easier it becomes. And when you have mastered the process, it is over. But it is a life skill that you will return to again and again.

Chapter 2

REAL-WORLD EXPERIENCE

*Only those who risk going too far
can possibly find
out how far one can go.*
—T. S. Eliot

A recurring theme in entry level job search is the lack of experience factor. "Where do I get experience if no one is willing to hire me?" Army? Navy? Air Force? Marines? Possibly for some, but there are other alternatives.

Many students focus exclusively on seeking paid work experience as their only alternative. Be careful not to box yourself into this limited focus. As a Hiring Manager, I look at any and all experience you may have accumulated to date, whether full-time or part-time, paid or unpaid.

Work experience makes you more marketable as a job candidate; it also gives you the opportunity to gain greater understanding about your chosen field. You will be able to find out in advance what many of the positives and negatives are, and truly enter your field with your eyes wide open. Or step back early from what could have been a major career mistake.

So as you approach the task of gaining real-world experience, do it from a "sponge" perspective—be ready to soak up every bit of information that comes your way. Full-time or part-time. Paid or unpaid. Worker or observer.

> EXPERIENCE IS A HARD TEACHER. YOU GET THE TEST FIRST AND ONLY THEN DO YOU GET TO LEARN THE LESSON.

INTERNSHIPS

An internship or a co-op is nirvana to the college student seeking work experience. The original "co-op" idea—combining classroom study with practical work experience—has evolved over the past decade into a universally accepted program for gaining work experience. The experience gained in an internship/co-op can be the key differentiator for many new college grads. Make no mistake—a successful internship can be your ticket to locking down a job offer (or several job offers) early in your final year. But it can come at a price.

> THERE ARE MANY WAYS TO GAIN REAL EXPERIENCE. AND ANY EXPERIENCE YOU GAIN WILL MAKE YOU A STANDOUT IN THE ENTRY LEVEL JOB MARKET.

Most schools offer classroom credit for formal internships, usually six or nine credit hours; not the standard fifteen-plus that most students require per semester to graduate on a "normal" schedule. In addition to standard work hours, you may be required to write formal term papers to report on your internship/co-op experience. The net effect of the lower number of credits earned while school is in session may require many interns to go an extra semester or through a summer session to make up for the lost credit hours.

Another adaptation of the "internship" term is to refer to summer employment as an "internship." This experience in the field also plays well in your job search, although you should not be concerned with finding summer work specifically listed as an internship. In fact, if you ask an employer if they offer summer internships, the answer is often "No." However, when you ask if they offer summer jobs in your field, the answer may be "Yes." Why the difference? Because most employers consider internships to be formal training programs in preparation for real work, while summer jobs are simply doing the real work. Which would you rather do? The real work is always the best experience.

WHAT THEY NEVER TELL YOU ABOUT INTERNSHIPS

While an internship can be the single best differentiator for you in achieving job search success, it does come with some attached baggage. Namely, why would you want to work anywhere other than with the company you interned with?

The opportunity usually exists to work for the company you interned with after graduation. That is, if you were a good employee. While accepting a position with your intern company can make your job search infinitely easier, it also limits your scope of opportunities to just one company. Would you consider marrying the first and only person you ever dated? Probably not. Yet that is what many students are doing when they go to work for the company they interned with. If the company is everything you ever wanted, if they provide you with opportunities for growth and advancement, if they are the realization of all your hopes and dreams—go for it. But then why are you reading this book? Probably because you want to know if there is something better out there.

For most students, the company you interned with is just one of many potential employers to consider in the job search. Yet other employers will wonder why the intern chose not to work for the company you interned with. You will need to have a ready answer to this question, or you may end up looking like the unwanted leftover from another company's internship program. If there is an offer to return full-time after graduation, make sure you mention this fact in your correspondence (written, verbal, and during the course of the interview) and why you decided to consider other companies.

The strongest hand to play is when you have an open offer from your intern employer to return as a full-time employee after graduation. It will provide you with an offer in the bank, which can only be beaten by better offers, and it will intensify the competition for you as a prospective employee. Use your time wisely while the offer is still open, but do not put off a decision beyond the requested response date.

THE VOLUNTEER INTERN TECHNIQUE

So what do you do if you missed the internship boat first time around? The Volunteer Intern Technique is a great technique for college students who still lack "real-world" work experience. If you missed the opportunity to formally intern or gain work experience in your field during your earlier years of college, you still have a chance to get that experience, even up to (and after) graduation. To gain that experience, you will need to volunteer. Yes, volunteer. Gratis. No pay. Why? Because as a volunteer intern you will be getting as much as you are giving (and sometimes even more). Whereas some of your friends may have been sharp enough to land a paying internship during the preceding years, your best choice, if you are into your final year, is to give up some of your free time and volunteer. By volunteering, you have flexibility that might not otherwise be available to you. If you volunteer during the school year, try to put in at least eight hours per week (two mornings, two afternoons, two evenings or one weekend day per week is usually the minimum required for gaining experience that can later be referenced).

Most companies will be very willing to take you on as a volunteer intern. If you are unable to find volunteer work with a for-profit company, there are plenty of not-for-profit organizations (schools, government agencies, associations, community service groups, etc.) that would appreciate your offer of service. The key is getting into a position where not only are you doing work, you are also working under someone else. Shadow them, learn from them, and use the internship as a period of training for your upcoming professional life.

The net result is twofold: first, it will provide you with a very valuable experience listing on your resume, one that will pay back monetarily many times the dollar amount you "lost" by volunteering. Second, you may have your potential future employer right in front of you. You are now on the inside—so if you are interested in working for the company after graduation, let them know! Even if they do not have something in that particular department, they will usually feel a debt of gratitude and may be willing to help you find other job possibilities within the company.

A recent grad used this technique to go from being a very average job seeker to being one of the most sought after in his class. He had worked at manual labor his entire college career until the second semester of his Senior Year, when he signed on as a Networking Intern with the Telecommunications Department at the college. He worked there only three months, yet parlayed that experience into the resume experience he needed to compete for meaningful work. He got a job with a company that "wasn't hiring at the entry level" as its new Network Administrator. Remember, with his experience, he was no longer entry level. Pay doesn't matter. Experience does.

This technique can even be used after graduation to keep moving forward in gaining experience. Not only will you avoid lapses of time in your resume, you will have real experience to show for the time you have invested.

No experience? This is a quick and simple solution to the problem. A small sacrifice now, even late in your college career, can pay handsome rewards for years to come.

THE SPECIAL PROJECT TECHNIQUE

Another excellent technique for filling in the gaps in the Experience section of your resume is the Special Project Technique. It works especially well if you can dovetail in a large project for one of your classes with a company you have a specific interest in.

Choose a project that not only will fulfill the requirements of a class project assignment, but will also serve as a real-life simulation of work in the field. If there are no special projects on your class docket, you might want to try talking one of your professors into using this as a substitute for your final, or as extra credit, or you might seek approval of the Department Chair to make it an Independent Study project. Choose the company you have your strongest interest in and then contact them to gather as much basic information as possible. You have an open door for researching the company that no other student has access to because you are studying the company as a special project.

> "I am in the process of completing a special project for my _____ class and have chosen your company to research. Could you please provide me with some information?"

Your academic approach to the company will have the words flowing forth from otherwise tight-lipped employees. In the process of gathering company in-formation, you will also gather names and ti-tles of key individuals in the organization. Because you are likely the only college student to be using the company specifically as the focus for a special project, you will put yourself in good standing for any job openings that might occur. You already have the inside track.

The net result is that you have killed three birds with one stone: you have met your academic needs via the project, you have greatly improved your resume (and your ability to talk about "real-world" experience), and you have gained access to a company that you have an interest in. It's win-win-win in all three areas!

A recent grad used this technique in his Senior Financial Management class and did a case study on the role of a partic-

> ACADEMIC "PROJECTS" ARE OFTEN THE BEST WAY TO COMBINE THE WORLD OF SCHOOL WITH THE WORLD OF WORK. YOU CAN GAIN BOTH WORK EXPERIENCE AND CLASSROOM CREDITS AT THE SAME TIME.

ular investment banking firm in the recently completed merger of one of its clients. He developed an entire case study from what he felt would be the client's perspective in the merger, including an exploration of all potential concerns. Then he developed answers for each one for the investment banking firm. As it turned out, his uncanny knack for research scored a direct hit with the firm, and eventually they offered him a job after graduation in the Mergers and Acquisitions Group.

THE TRYING-ON-FOR-SIZE TECHNIQUE

Have you ever bought an expensive outfit without first trying it on? Certainly not. And yet the standard in career selection is to pour thousands of dollars into

> ## You will never fully understand your profession until you have experienced the reality of 8 to 5 (or 7 to 6).

training and schooling for an anticipated career without first trying it on for size to make sure it is a good fit. Seems rather silly, yet this is the process that millions of students stumble through, year after year.

Your best opportunity for truly understanding a particular job or industry is to try it on for a day, a week, a month, or a year. How? By temping in the field. Working through a temporary help agency will give you the opportunity to develop real-world work experience while trying on your chosen field for size.

There are plenty of opportunities to work through temp agencies. The key is to be specific about your preference for positions within your chosen field. Be specific, yet not picky. Working at the desk next to your target position is often just as profitable as sitting behind that desk. Temping often works best over summer break, but can also be used during fall, winter, and spring break. And if you are extremely productive, you may be given the opportunity to continue part-time while classes are in session.

This is a classic win-win situation. You have the opportunity to view your chosen field from the inside. The employer has low-cost, temporary labor to fill in the gaps. And in the best of all possible worlds, you may find your future employer.

THE SHADOWING TECHNIQUE

Even if you are not able to gain specific, referenceable experience in your field, you can still access information to help you make decisions about post-graduation job planning and gain some valuable network contacts in the process. The most efficient way to do so is by the Shadowing Technique. Locate a person in your chosen field or occupation (friends, relatives, or friends of friends are best, or anyone within your personal network) who can connect you with someone at their company who works in your area of interest. This person will serve as your company sponsor. Please note that your sponsor does not have to be a Hiring Manager—in fact, it is usually better to work with someone at or just above the job level you are seeking. When you have found a sponsor, ask that person to designate a day or half day that would be a good example of work in that field. It's important to communicate that it will require no extra time from the sponsor—just the opportunity for you to "shadow" them while they are working. Then show up at the company dressed as you would if you were in the position. Bring a notebook with you and take plenty of notes. If your sponsor is open to talking about the work they are doing, feel free to ask questions. If you are spending a full day, treat them to lunch—ideally in the company cafeteria, where you can get even more "touch and feel" information on the company and its people. Lunch is also an excellent time to ask the questions you have been noting throughout the morning. When the day is over, make sure you send a very personal "thank you" note to your sponsor.

By using the Shadowing Technique, you will be able to gain information firsthand from someone who is actively working in the field. By seeing the inside of the company you will get a true feel for what it is like to work there yourself. You will have direct access to company information and be able to develop potential network contacts.

The Shadowing Technique is greatly preferred over the acclaimed informational interviewing technique (which I usually do not recommend, for reasons that follow). Shadowing gives you a hands-on feel for the position and company; it also requires little additional time on the part of the sponsor. The sponsor does not feel used because his or her business day is not interrupted artificially.

P.S. "Take Your Daughter/Son to Work Day" is based upon this same type of shadowing. You may have already done some shadowing in your earlier years. Now it is time to extend this technique to your chosen career.

INFORMATIONAL INTERVIEWING

While we are on the subject of getting on the inside of potential employers, let's clear the air on a very common misperception among college students. Starting in the late '80s, there has been a plethora of books written on the subject of informational interviewing and on using it as a wedge to get into a hiring company.

Let's get this straight—if you use informational interviewing as a ruse (i.e., lie, deception) for getting information, you should be put up against the proverbial wall of ethics and shot. Strong words? Maybe. But I have seen the scores and scores of abuses in this area and there seems to be no end in sight.

The problem is this: many career authors (often with little or no personal real-world work experience) are unknowingly setting up college students for the wrong use of informational interviewing. There is a right use of informational interviewing: namely, to speak with someone in a career you are considering to help you decide whether to pursue that career path. The wrong use of informational interviewing is when you already know what career path you intend to pursue and use informational interviewing as a wedge for talking to someone on the inside of a company you want to work for. Let's call it what it is—dishonest and unethical. Any fool that gives in to your informational interviewing ruse will be a fool no longer when you get to the closing line (and true ulterior motive): "Your company sure sounds interesting. Do you know of any way that I could get a job here?"

When I was at IBM, no one in our department would even consider going through an informational interview—even if we thought it was valid. Why? Because the technique was so abused that we had become calloused to its usage in any form. And you will find the same response at many large companies.

My advice: don't do it. If you are an underclassman sincerely seeking information on which career to pursue, informational interviewing is valid. But there should be no job strings attached. On the other hand, if your true motivation is to get an interview with the company, do not lie about it. Be up front. And use the following technique as an honest and ethical way to get on the inside.

THE COMPANY INTERVIEWING TECHNIQUE

Instead of rusing your way into a company by saying you are "informational interviewing," be honest and let them know you want to work for them. Then seek out a person who is willing to be interviewed in a "company interview," that is, an interview where you interview that person about their company. This does not have to be a formal interview setting; in fact, it does not even have to be face to face—over the phone is usually sufficient. The key is to choose your potential interviewee wisely. They should not be a potential Hiring Manager, and not someone in Personnel or Human Resources. Ideally, they should be a contact you have generated through your personal network, someone who has a personal desire to help you. Your "network" is your personal connection with others who can help you in your job search. The subject of networking will be fully covered later in the Network Intelligence Gathering chapter. Next best is a member of a professional association of which you are a student member.

The key questions you should be asking are:

"What type of person does your company typically hire?"

"What is the hiring process and who is involved?"

In addition, ask your contact questions about why they joined the company, why it is a good company to work for, and what the company culture is like. You need to be careful in asking your questions so that you are not asking the person to give out "Confidential" or "Internal Use Only" information. For example, it would be inappropriate to ask for a company phone directory or a copy of internal correspondence. But if you build a rapport with this person, you can usually get not only the broad overview of the company, but also the basic information identifying the specific steps taken in the internal interview process. Then you will be prepared to proceed through those steps with advance information already in hand.

USING COMPUTER EXPERIENCE TO YOUR ADVANTAGE

There is one area of experience where you will likely outshine the great majority of the working world: computers. You have grown up with computers throughout your school years and have a level of comfort shared by few in the work force.

> AN UNDERSTANDING OF COMPUTERS AND TECHNOLOGY IN GENERAL IS ESSENTIAL FOR ALL PROFESSIONALS IN THE 21st CENTURY.

Take advantage of this experience by highlighting your proficiencies on your resume and within the context of your interviews. Just having user-level knowledge of some of the popular PC packages will greatly increase your potential value for most companies. Most companies are looking to hire people who bring practical skills to the position, and computer literacy is a very practical work skill in almost every profession. It is a mistaken impression that computer knowledge is important only in technical professions. It is also important in nontechnical professions, where any level of knowledge over the current work force will produce an even larger experience gap in your favor.

If you still have time before graduation, seek to learn the software programs and packages that are most common within your target profession or industry. Not only will it prepare you well for your eventual work, it will prepare you well for scoring points during your job search.

HELP WANTED IN TWELVE DIFFERENT FLAVORS

Consider the following to be a comprehensive (although not all-inclusive) listing of possible avenues for gaining further experience:

1. Internships
2. Summer jobs
3. Campus jobs
4. Entrepreneurial/self-employed jobs
5. Temporary work
6. Volunteer work—school, church, club, not-for-profit organizations
7. Special projects
8. Research papers
9. Certification courses
10. Campus activity positions
11. Fraternity/sorority/social club positions
12. Extracurricular or sports leadership positions

Review the above list. Use it as your checklist. Don't ever again fall into the trap of saying that you don't have any real experience. If you haven't found or experienced it yet, create it or make it happen on your own. Remember—experience is number one on nearly every employer's list of preferred attributes for entry level hires. Somewhat ironic, since we are still talking about entry level jobs. But experience is number one on their list. Make sure it is also number one on your list.

And if it is late in the year (or already past graduation) it's still not too late to generate real-world work experience. But first be sure to look back on what you have already accomplished. You may have already gained real experience that you have not fully recognized. And your future is still wide open for additional experiences. Keep it focused toward your goal and do everything within your power (and then some on top of that) to reach your goal.

Chapter 3

BEST COLLEGE RESUMES

The greatest thing in this world is not so much where we stand,
as in what direction we are moving.
—Oliver Wendell Holmes

Most college students utter an audible grunt the first time the "resume reality" hits them: "Uugghhh. I gotta do that resume thing." Do you really need a resume? Yes, you really need a resume. It will not get you the job, but you will not get the job without it. Anyone who tells you that you do not need a resume is out of touch with the entry level job market. Don't depend on it to magically perform the required steps for you, but know that anytime you make a serious job contact (including networking and interviews, both on campus and off), it will be a requirement.

Don't procrastinate on this important activity. The tendency is to wait until a resume is required before going further in the job search process. Then it is often cranked out with just the basics in hopes that it will free the student to go on to the more important steps. If you properly understand what the resume is and where it fits into the entry level hiring process, you will see that it requires a great deal more thought and preparation than just "cranking it out."

Your resume is a professional reflection of you as the potential product: professional resume, professional product; sloppy resume, sloppy product. Take the time to develop your resume as the very best reflection of you.

A NEW PERSPECTIVE ON RESUMES

From the perspective of the hiring company, your resume is your initial marketing brochure. Period. Nothing more and nothing less. Once you start looking at the resume from a marketing perspective, you are on your way toward developing one that is more effective. It cannot "make the sale" any more than a marketing brochure can sell you a car—there still has to be the test drive, a look under the hood, a chance to kick the tires. If the marketing brochure is effective, you are already sold before you enter the showroom. Same for resumes.

THE VERY BEST WAY TO CREATE YOUR RESUME

Most resume books tell you, as the first step, to "take a piece of paper and begin listing all your positive attributes," or something to that effect. Why? I thought you wanted to write a resume? If you want someone to produce an exhaustive list of all your positive attributes, go ask your mother—moms are great in the "positive attribute listing" category. This practice in "positive attribute development" futility might be okay for little Johnny about to graduate from high school who wants to figure out what he wants to do with his life, but hey—are we not college grads? Why don't we take that quantum leap forward and just start putting together the actual information on disk in resume format where it can be used?

> A GREAT RESUME WILL NOT GET YOU THE JOB. BUT A POOR RESUME CAN KEEP YOU FROM GETTING THE JOB.

Successful resumes generate information as they are created. Think about it. Do you ever write a term paper from scratch? Not usually (unless you are using a typewriter—any typists still out there?). You use either a template file with all the information and codes already set up (like the standard format for the bibliography section that comes at the end of every term paper), or you reuse the basic information from a previous paper (that is why you handed in your Psych paper with last October's date on it).

The same principle applies to resumes. The very best way to create your resume is on-line—on the screen, right in front of you, capturing information as you go and updating as necessary over time. No PC of your own? This is a good time to make your pilgrimage to the campus computer lab. Take two blank disks with you—one to use as your working copy and one as your backup for that inevitable point in the future when you accidentally destroy the first disk. Usually when you need it most.

But do not waste your time using one of the commercial resume software packages. Reason? First, they artificially force you into their format, which may or may not be correct and most definitely cannot be fine-tuned to your specific needs. Second, they are not portable—meaning that the output file can only be modified with that package. So the next time you want to update your resume, you either have to locate (or buy) the same package or you are out of luck. You are better off working with a standard word processing package (such as WordPerfect or Microsoft Word) and creating your own.

An excellent way to get a jump start on your resume development is with Quickstart Résumé Software (available direct for readers of this book), which contains preformatted resumes for over thirty different majors (from Accounting to Zoology). Quickstart Résumé does not require you to learn an entirely new software program, nor does it force you into a rigid format. If you can use a word processor you can use Quickstart Résumé. Simply add your own content to customize your personal resume. Readers of this book can get a copy of Quickstart Résumé for just the shipping and handling fee. See the last page of the book for the ordering form.

> STORE YOUR RESUME IN A FORMAT WHERE YOU CAN CHANGE AND MODIFY IT AS YOU MOVE FORWARD IN YOUR JOB SEARCH.

The following page contains a sample format for a successful resume. It provides you with the basic features you need for developing a solid resume structure.

Tracy Q. Graduate

Campus:
456 College Hall
Normal, IL 67890
(111) 222-3333

Permanent
123 Main Street
Anytown, NY 12345
(777) 888-9999

Objective: Auditor position in the public accounting field in the Chicago area.

Summary:
- More than two years of progressive accounting and auditing experience
- Auditor internship with Arthur Andersen in New York City
- Magna Cum Laude graduate with BBA in Accounting
- Proficient with Excel, Lotus 1-2-3, Windows 95/3.1, Word, Power-Point, and Netscape

Education: **Bachelor of Business Administration in Accounting, May 1998**
Illinois State University, Normal, Illinois
Graduated Magna Cum Laude with a GPA of 3.6 on a 4.0 scale

Courses taken included:
Managerial Accounting	Corporate Audit
Intermediate Accounting I & II	Financial Management
Accounting I & II	Internal Audit
Accounting for Not-For-Profits	Managerial Economics

Experience: **Auditor Internship, May 1997 to August 1997**
Arthur Andersen & Company, New York, New York
- Participated in the annual audit of Zephyr Megalithic Holdings, including development of the final certification report.
- Participated in quarterly audit of Alpha Bank Corporation, including identification and correction of over twenty major accounting errors.
- Developed several Excel spreadsheet macros currently in use for reducing entry time and automatically cross-referencing for errors.
- Received Employee of the Month award twice—first intern ever to win the award

Accounts Payable/Bookkeeping Clerk, May 1995 to Present
Anytown Tax and Bookkeeping Service, Anytown, New York
- Assisted (via remote) with payroll, tax, and account processing.
- Developed automated monthly sales tax payment system.
- Implemented Rapid Tax Refund service for individual customers.

Activities:
- Vice President, Student Accountancy Chapter, 1997–1998
- Treasurer, Phi Beta Kappa honors society, 1996–1997
- Dorm Resident Assistant, 1996–1998

After reading the sample resume, you might find yourself somewhat intimidated. "How could I ever compete with someone like that?" For those of you who are near graduation, don't worry—very few have a background that strong (and if they do, Andersen has probably already hired them). For those of you who have time remaining before graduation and have yet to fully form your end product, you can still change your work experience so that you will look strong on paper.

Remember, looking good on paper is only the first step. The sample resume is provided primarily for formatting purposes. Even someone with a mediocre background will look much stronger by following that tight, concise format and structure. The resume is only your start. You still have a long way to go.

THE MOST IMPORTANT FEATURE OF YOUR RESUME

Employers' number one complaint about entry level resumes? Lack of a specific objective. This is by far the most important feature of an entry level resume. Without it, you are destined to languish in the sea of mediocrity, swallowed up by your own lack of direction. I do not mean the wishy-washy "Position with a progressive organization that will fully utilize my talents and skills..." objective that tells me absolutely nothing about what you are looking for. Your objective has to be clear and concise. If someone told you not to include an Objective section because it is too limiting, that person is obviously out of touch with the reality of the entry level job market. If you are not specific and directed, you lose. Plain and simple.

> THE FIRST THING AN EMPLOYER LOOKS FOR IN A RESUME IS THE SPECIFIC FOCUS. YOU HAVE TO COMMIT YOURSELF ON PAPER TO WHAT YOU REALLY WANT TO DO IN YOUR CAREER.

The key to writing a successful objective is *focus*. Remember putting together your personal mission statement in Chapter 1? This personal mission statement is the basis for putting together a successful resume objective. But instead of utilizing the flowery language of the broader career mission statement, you will be focusing sharply on what type of position you are specifically seeking. Restrict your objective by any or all of the following three areas:

1. Job type (such as Accountant, Electrical Engineer, etc.)

2. Industry (such as Retail, Banking, Insurance, etc.)

3. Geographical area (such as Pacific Northwest, Oregon, Portland area, etc.)

Examples:

Staff accountant position in the public accounting field in the Houston area.

Retail management position in the New York City metropolitan area.

Reporter position with a major news daily-open to relocation.

Marketing position with a computer software vendor in the Chicago area.

Electrical engineering position in the silicon industry in California.

Multimedia development position—open to travel and/or relocation.

Note that a well-written and well-focused Objective section is often what sets you apart when your resume is compared to those with no objective or a wishy-washy one.

THE SECOND MOST IMPORTANT FEATURE OF YOUR RESUME

What next? The section that is almost always missing on entry level resumes: the Summary section. This section is the ten-second "sound bites" section that immediately follows the Objective section of the resume. It provides the high-level support for the objective and draws the reader into the remainder of the resume, which provides further detailed support (Education, Experience, Activities, etc.). This section is crucial in the "high-speed resume review" world that we live in. Make sure it is there and bulleted—three or four one-liners about who you are.

THE BEST RESUME—THE BUZZWORD RESUME

Want to have a truly outstanding resume? Then get to know and use the buzzwords that apply to the job type or industry you are seeking. If you merely list the "features" of your background from a product-driven approach, you will most likely fail. Make sure you take a customer-driven approach and list what is important to your customer. What are the buzzwords? They are the industry or job-defined words that have special meaning to those within that particular industry or job type. Acronyms are used in almost every industry. Information systems is a prime example. To list the following under the Summary section of the resume of an Information Systems major would be entirely appropriate:

➤ Programmed Java front-end utilizing Oracle as the back-end RDBMS.

Or within Manufacturing Management, the following might be an example:

➤ Developed JIT Inventory Control system using A-B-C hierarchical FILO process.

Buzzwords solidify your standing as an insider. By using them correctly and in proper context, you communicate that you understand the terminology of the field and are able to speak the language fluently. In addition, most electronic resume searches are based on buzzwords. If you have properly included them, you will be found. If not, you may never surface. Note that the words do not have to be acronyms or technical specs to qualify as buzzwords. Every industry and job type has its own set of commonly used buzzwords. Get to know them via your coursework or other

> **THAT CRITICAL FIRST SCAN OF YOUR RESUME IS WHEN THE BUZZWORDS SHOULD JUMP OFF THE PAGE AND CAPTURE THE ATTENTION OF THE READER.**

college resources. Or subscribe to one of the leading industry trade magazines. Start to acquire the "language" of the field you are entering. Buzzwords in resumes is just the start—you will find them used throughout the job search process.

One final note on buzzwords—please do not use them just because they "sound good" but do not actually apply or, even worse, you have no idea what they mean. Make sure you know what terms (especially the latest buzzwords) really mean before you use them. Proving your ignorance via inappropriate use of specialized terms quickly moves you into the "no interest" category when hiring decisions are being made.

THE NOTABLES TECHNIQUE

If you are having difficulty filling in the details contained in the bullet points of the resume, ask yourself this question: "What did I do that was notable?" Ask this question for each section, for each major heading, and for each activity listed on your resume. As you do, you will begin to formulate the detail that will begin to build an outstanding resume. Were you the youngest person ever hired by your employer?

➤ Youngest person ever hired by this upscale fashion store.

Did you receive any special awards or recognitions in your academic program?

➤ Received the Johnson Award of Excellence, which is given to the top three students in the Journalism degree program.

Did you accomplish anything of note in your extracurricular activities?

➤ Captain of the first school wrestling team to ever win the regional title.

Think about the notable accomplishments in your life. Think about what you might tell your parents or grandparents about notable accomplishments at school over the last semester or last year. These notables will provide you with excellent detail for your resume. They are what set you apart from the crowd. They are what I look for in deciding whom to interview. And they are the basis for many of the compelling stories told in interviews that lead to eventual offers.

Note your notables. Build them into your resume. And build them into your job search vocabulary as the foundation for showing what makes you truly different.

LISTING YOUR GPA ON YOUR RESUME

To list or not to list? The answer to the question is rather simple, yet often ignored. If your overall GPA is 3.0 or higher, list it on your resume. If your major GPA is 3.0 or higher, while your overall GPA is below 3.0, list it as your "Major GPA" on your resume. You can list both if they are above 3.0 and your major GPA is at least three tenths higher than your overall. And always round the number to the nearest tenth. I know the Registrar's Office provides it to the hundredth or even thousandth, but this is not an exercise in higher math. Besides, 2.951 rounds up very nicely to 3.0.

And yes, I am fully aware that if your resume lacks your GPA, it likely means that you missed the coveted 3.0. You better be prepared with a very good reason why you fell short. And if you are an undergrad, you may still have time to make up for your earlier carelessness.

USING A RESUME SERVICE

As you venture out into the great unknown of preparing your resume, be aware that there are a variety of resume services out there that will try to convince you to turn over the entire process to them. They will offer to do everything from writing your resume and cover letter to generating a mass mailing, including digitizing your signature at the bottom of the cover letter and mailing out a couple hundred resumes for you. A note of caution: the great majority (95+ percent) of resume services will do nothing more than take your data and crunch it into their cookie cutter format, then try to sell you on their fancy paper and a variety of worthless additional services. If you have solid writing skills, you are much better served by writing your own resume. Follow the sample format in this book.

For those of you who need assistance in developing content and finessing it into the proper style and format for an entry level resume, do not just head off to the nearest resume service and hope to find one of the 5 percent that are truly different (they all say they are). My recommendation is to get in touch with Strategic Résumés, a nationwide resume service which works in conjunction with Kinko's copy centers throughout the United States to deliver high-quality resumes. They will interview you over the phone to fully develop your resume and highlight your most marketable skills, abilities, and experience. Your formatted resume is then downloaded to Kinko's within twenty-four hours for final printing. Strategic Résumés also provides free resume changes for a year and permanent storage of your resume (or you can have it sent to you on disk for personal storage and access). Their service does come at a cost (their one-page resume is $49.50), but if you lack strong writing skills or simply would like to upgrade your resume image, it may be money well spent. I have personally spoken with Grant Cooper at Strategic Résumés about their service in relation to entry level resumes and feel they are an outstanding choice. They have agreed to provide readers of this book (mention *College Grad Job Hunter* when you call) with a free standard cover letter as an added bonus. You can reach Strategic Resumes toll-free at 800-700-9748. Or you can fax them your current resume at 800-440-2053 for a free evaluation and critique.

THE GREATEST RESUME MISTAKE

Every year, I see resumes from students who try to "stretch the truth" in order to sound more desirable on paper. Resume inflation. This lack of honesty, when discovered, becomes an instant knockout factor which disqualifies that person from further consideration. Corporate Recruiters are paid to screen people out, and the quickest and surest way to do so is when a "white lie" (it is still a lie, white or black) or exaggeration is found.

> YOUR RESUME IS A REFLECTION OF WHO YOU ARE. MAKE SURE YOURS IS YOUR VERY BEST.

A recent graduate attempted to show experience in a computer language by placing it on his resume. It generated calls, but it also generated rejection letters when it became apparent that he did not really have a foundational understanding of the language. Doors were shut that might have otherwise been open to him.

Remember, the resume is not a work of fiction. While it should emphasize the positive, it should never emphasize what does not exist.

HOW TO GET YOUR RESUME NOTICED

Use colored paper. Not a flashy neon, but a conservative pastel. It has to be a light, soft color, since anything too dark may not copy well. My favorites (in order of preference) are salmon, light blue, and light blue-green, always using a high-quality bonded paper. A colored resume will always stand out in the sea of whites and ivories. It will also identify you as someone who is yearning to be noticed. And you will be.

THE VERBAL PROOFING TECHNIQUE

When you feel confident that your resume construction is complete, take time to read it aloud several times through. Grammatical mistakes and faulty sentence construction are often most obvious when you hear them. Errors such as missing words or doubled words tend to jump out when read aloud. If the sentence does not flow when spoken, it will not flow on paper. Many on the receiving end of your resume will be verbally oriented people—even to the point of quietly reading your resume "aloud" (you have probably noticed people who read aloud to themselves or at least move their lips ever so slightly—that's the verbal-oriented crowd).

THE INDUSTRY PROOFING TECHNIQUE

And when you think you are finished with your resume, you still have some work to do. Actually, it is work required of others, but you need to solicit their input. The key to having your resume successfully reviewed is to ask someone who is actively working in your chosen field. They can provide you with a resume review in relation to the correct usage of buzzwords and industry terminology. Content critiquing is important when doing an industry proofing. Try to avoid format reviews, though, since ten different people will have ten different formatting preferences. It's best to stick with the conservative format outlined in this chapter.

> PROOF YOUR RESUME AT LEAST THREE DIFFERENT TIMES. IT'S AMAZING HOW MUCH STILL NEEDS TO BE CHANGED AFTER THE THIRD PROOFING.

After they have reviewed your resume, they also can provide you with a key jump start in your job search as one of your first network contacts. Ask them, "What are the top five companies you would recommend for me to contact in my job search?" Two birds, one stone.

THE FIFTEEN-SECOND PROOF TECHNIQUE

After you have gone through the initial resume review and revision, use this technique to verify the final results. Provide your resume to a group of reviewers, ranging from professors to industry contacts to friends. But restrict them to only fifteen seconds. Ask them to take just fifteen seconds to review the resume, then ask them what they remembered about it.

> YOU HAVE FIFTEEN SECONDS OR LESS TO CAPTURE MY ATTENTION. IF YOU HAVE NOT, I AM ON TO THE NEXT ONE.

You will often be surprised what jumps off the page in those fifteen seconds. Keep in mind that fifteen seconds is usually the maximum amount of time your resume will be given in the initial screen. If the key facts and points do not make their impact, you may need to change the ordering or emphasis to ensure that they do. It is only when your resume is able to pass this fifteen-second proof that it is truly ready for prime time.

WHERE TO DELIVER THE FIRST COPY OF YOUR FINISHED RESUME

To the Career Development office at your campus. Ideally, you should do this as early as possible in your final year—beginning of the first semester of your final year is best. Why? Three reasons. First, most Career Development offices put together a paper or electronic resume collection which they send out to prospective employers. Second, they will send out your resume individually to those employers requesting resumes for prospective graduates in a particular major or career focus, including those who are prescreening potential candidates for on-campus interviews. And third, usually you cannot begin to sign up for on-campus interviewing until this step is complete.

RESUMES ARE NEVER COMPLETE

A little play on words here, with an intended dual meaning. First, resumes never provide the full story of who you are, nor should they. Resumes are meant to be your introduction toward gaining a face-to-face interview with a prospective employer. They will never serve as your life history or as the starting document for your autobiography. So keep the resume in its proper perspective as an initial marketing brochure.

> MASS MAILING YOUR RESUME IS ONE OF THE MOST INEFFECTIVE METHODS OF JOB SEARCH. IF THAT IS ALL YOU ARE DOING, YOU ARE BARELY LOOKING.

Second, now that your resume is "finished," do not assume it is complete. You should continue to modify and update your resume as your search progresses. Gain new experience? Add it to your resume. See a better way to state your education? Modify your resume. Find out that a point in your background could be viewed as a negative? Remove it from your resume. Keep your resume as a living document which can be updated and changed to suit your specific needs.

RESUMES WORK BEST UNFOLDED

How to keep them unfolded? By mailing in a 9x12 envelope? Even better—keep them unfolded by not mailing them at all. The best use of the resume is when it is passed hand to hand. Resumes have a place in the process, but it is not in the form of the "cross my fingers and mail it out and hope I get a response" mailing that most people use. Mailing the resume gives us a false sense of security that we are actually doing something. In reality, very few people are hired through this passive approach. You are much more productive making direct contact (by phone or in person) with the employer.

But if you must mail out a resume, the 9x12 envelope is a sure eyecatcher. For even greater impact, consider the $3 Priority Mail envelope from the post office. You get a free cardboard envelope (with its bold red, white, and blue colors), which will arrive in two or three days and will be screaming out its in-basket importance until it is opened.

Then always make sure you follow up by phone. You will greatly increase your odds by this simple act. Woefully, more than 95 percent of mailed resumes are from the "cross my fingers" crowd. Take the simple step toward standing out from the crowd.

Refer to later chapters in this book for how to make active use of your resume in generating interviews.

HOW TO MAKE YOUR RESUME IRRESISTIBLE

> A RESUME IS JUST A PIECE OF PAPER WITH WORDS. IT IS WHAT YOU DO WITH THAT PIECE OF PAPER THAT WILL MAKE THE DIFFERENCE.

Have you ever received a free computer disk in the mail or as an add-on to a magazine? Free disks still hold a certain fascination for most people, in spite of the recent onslaught of disks from America Online and other on-line services. There is something inside us that just will not allow us to discard the disk until we have fully examined the contents. The front office receptionist at our company had difficulty when I told her it was okay to discard the America Online disk that was sent to me because I already had America Online installed. "But what if there is some sort of new information on this disk?" She just couldn't do it. I finally took it from her and threw it in my own wastebasket, although I have to admit that even I cringed at the thought of a diskette sitting there in the trash. There is just something sacrilegious about discarding a diskette, free or not. The "diskette mystique" is alive and well in corporate America.

For those seeking employment, this diskette mystique can work very nicely to your advantage. When used as the format for presenting your resume, it can turn an otherwise plain and drab piece of paper into a truly irresistible personal presentation. While most resumes arrive in a standard #10 envelope and are relegated to mass review and filing, a resume on disk arrives in a nonstandard-sized diskette mailer. And I guarantee it will receive special attention when being passed through the internal mail process.

We recently hired a college student into our entry level training program based largely on his method of introduction—putting his resume on disk. The disk arrived in my in-basket along with the rest of the daily mail, but it was the first one opened. I was drawn in by the simple instructions:

1. Insert Disk
2. Enter — "HIREME"

The rational side of my brain told me it was probably "just another resume," but the creative side knew it wasn't. It was quite different. I set my work aside to take a look. The resume was viewable through a slick graphical interface with full color, sideline graphics, and even sound clips. When one of the references was selected from the drop-down menu, I was presented with a picture of the person giving the reference and a short sound bite of the person talking about the student. Very cool!

So what did I do? I called at least four or five other managers into my office to view "the multimedia resume" on my system. Two other managers installed it on their PC to watch it personally. The phone call invitation for an in-person interview at our office went out later that afternoon.

We interviewed. We tested. We grilled. And we hired. He came to be known as "the person who did the multimedia resume" when the personal introductions were made. And all the staff who had seen or heard about the resume gave their obligatory "Oooh!" response.

Here is the key: this student attended a college that was not on our circuit of schools where we did on-campus interviewing. We would never have met but for the unique way his resume was packaged and prepared. We still do not have that college on our preferred list and may never actively seek out anyone from that college. But this person found us and allowed us to find him by his unique technique for showcasing his talents. Interestingly, this person was hired far ahead of our scheduled on-campus visits, so we already had one in the bank by the time we got to the regularly scheduled schools. For those students who patiently waited for us to arrive at their campus, the odds of being hired had just been reduced by one filled slot.

The resume on disk is successful because it is unique. If you have the technical talent to create your own version of the resume on disk, do it.

Don't worry that "no one else is doing it that way." It is your opportunity to stand out and be noticed in your field. And not just for technical fields—

nearly all Hiring Managers have a PC on their desk. It can actually work best for nontechnical fields, since it is even more unique. In a few years, this technique may be more commonplace. But for now, you will truly be a standout.

> Be creative in your job search. The worst that can happen is that you will be rejected one more time. All you need is one "yes."

If the thought of having your resume on disk appeals to you, there is a quick and inexpensive way to have one developed professionally. Avalanche Multimedia Ltd., a multimedia software development company based in Vancouver, British Columbia, will convert your resume into a personalized interactive resume on disk for copying and sending out to potential employers. Avalanche has agreed to lower the $49 normal price for their Graduate Interactive Résumé to just $35 for readers of this book, but you must mention *College Grad Job Hunter* when ordering.

To take advantage of this offer, send your resume in any word processing format (you should also save it in ASCII format to make sure they can read it) and any graphics (such as photos or portfolio shots) in .GIF or .JPG format (you can have them scanned at Kinko's or a local service bureau), along with your check for $35 to:

Avalanche Multimedia Ltd.
309-425 Carrall Street
Vancouver, BC Canada
Phone: (604) 687-0169
Fax: (604) 687-1781

Or you can submit your resume and graphics electronically through their Website located at: http://www.avalanche.bc.ca. Be sure to specify whether you want PC or Mac format. Production time varies from one to two days. Once you receive the executable resume, you may copy and distribute it as many times as you like. Avalanche can also do custom work, such as personalized 3D animation, narration, and customized clip arts, at an additional charge.

If you are truly looking for a way to stand out from the crowd, this is a sure way to do so!

RESUME CHECKLIST

Use this checklist to ensure that your resume is complete:

❏ One page only, unless you have significant previous experience

❏ Word processor generated, with full spell check and proofing

❏ Times Roman or other Serif font, 10 point to 12 point size

❏ No more than two fonts or two sizes

❏ Margins no less than .75" and no more than 1.5"

❏ Quality bond paper, 8½ x 11 inches

❏ Contact information clearly stated; campus and permanent addresses both listed if appropriate

❏ Clear, focused objective

❏ Summary of your top three or four skills listed as bullet points

❏ Degree listed first, college/university second

❏ GPA listed if over 3.0

❏ Major GPA listed if over 3.0 and overall GPA under 3.0

❏ Graduation date listed, even if you have not yet graduated

❏ Experience section listing most notable accomplishments

❏ Descriptive (not actual) job titles

❏ Industry buzzwords and keywords included

❏ Activities section listing your most notable extracurricular activities

❏ No personal data or potentially discriminatory data

❏ Spell-check and grammar-check your resume—twice; then have at least one other person do it for you again.

Chapter 4

BEST COLLEGE COVER LETTERS

The most valuable of all talents
is that of never using two words when one will do.
—Thomas Jefferson

Take everything you have ever heard, read, or seen about cover letters and throw it out the window! That's right, 99.44% of the information about cover letters is useless. Contrary to some of the more fashionable books on job search, no one ever got a job because of a spiffy (or "perfect") cover letter. Cover letters are extremely limited in value, even when properly used.

THE REALITY OF COVER LETTERS

Why are cover letters limited in value? Three reasons. First, most people assume that the cover letter is actually read before the resume. Wrong. Just ask those who spend any portion of the work day reviewing resumes—they go past the cover letter directly to the resume and only look at the cover letter if they are still interested after their initial resume review. In my review of more than twenty-five thousand resumes, I have probably read only five thousand cover letters. It is actually rather amusing to watch a Hiring Manager reading a newly arrived resume. The cover letter and resume are pulled from the envelope, the cover letter is immediately placed behind the resume, and the resume is scanned first, then read. And you know there is interest if they finally make their way back to the cover letter.

Second, most people assume that the cover letter should be about you. Wrong again. It should be about the company, your prospect, your target. Your resume will tell them everything they need to know about you (if it is well written). If you are interested enough in the company to make an initial contact, take the time to fully reflect your understanding of the company and how you may be able to meet their needs in your cover letter.

Third, and most important, many college students end up using the cover letter/resume mass mailing as a crutch to convince themselves that they are actually doing something in their job search. "But I sent out over two hundred resumes!" In reality, all they are doing is generating rejection letters. Mass mailing of your cover letter and resume has extremely low odds for success in today's job market.

Understand that at the entry level a resume and cover letter on their own do little good. Most larger companies have established college recruiting programs which serve as the focal point of entry level hiring. Therefore, unsolicited entry level resumes are usually ignored, or at best filed away. Most small and medium-sized companies do not have the internal resources necessary to train entry level hires, so the entry level resume is ignored. The best you can hope for in a blind mailing campaign is that you will be filed away and perhaps miraculously resurrected at some future date. Very unlikely.

THE BEST USE OF A COVER LETTER

So when should you use a cover letter? Only as part of a limited, targeted campaign to reach employers. Take the time to research and understand a company before committing yourself on paper as a potential employee. If you have no idea what the company does, do not just send your resume and cover letter in the blind hope of making a match. If you are not willing to invest time and energy to find out whether a match is possible, why would you expect me as the Hiring Manager to do so?

A successful cover letter should be specific and personal. It should be clean, neat laser copy, yet not mass generated. Each letter should refer to a specific person at a specific company and provide a specific next step that you will be taking. If you wait for them to call you, your odds of contact decrease dramatically. It usually requires a proactive response on your part to move the process forward to the next level. The "Squeaky Wheel Theory" (i.e., the one that squeaks the loudest gets the grease) is alive and well in the employment marketplace. If you make the effort to contact me, I will respond to you. If you passively wait for your phone to ring, do not expect me to call. If you wait for your resume and cover letter to magically produce results, you will likely find yourself buried underneath reams of other resumes. Be the one who stands out.

The cover letter should cover two important points: (1) what your product can do for your customer (the company), and (2) what your customer will need to do to buy your product. If that sounds like marketing mumbo-jumbo, consider that most marketing people miss that point. They spend time telling about their "great" product, when they really should be concentrating on telling how it will benefit the customer.

If you have no idea how you can benefit that customer, then you may be wasting everyone's time (including your own) in even attempting a reasonable job search. Ask any astute marketing person the following question: "What is your competitive advantage in the marketplace?" If that person is good, you will get a quick and ready answer. You should also have a ready answer to the very same question. If you are just another player in the already very crowded entry level job market, you will not be noticed.

If you are not sure what differentiates you from the rest of the market, find out! Research your background and make note of the areas where you excel. And make that your number one focus in writing the cover letter.

A basic formula for cover letters is as follows:

Standard business letter address format—prospect name, title, company, address—top left

Salutation (yes, it should be to a real person—take time to know who your target is)

First paragraph—why you are writing? To meet that company's specific need(s)!

Second paragraph—briefly state two or three top skills (from the Summary section of your resume), then immediately follow with benefit after benefit these features (and you as a person) will provide to the company

Third paragraph—close! Not just the ending of the letter, but the "sales closer" to the letter. Close the sale. Give your target contact a specific action to take and a backup action you will take if you do not get a response.

That's it! For an example of this format, refer to the sample cover letter that follows. But remember—what is right for one person can sound canned or contrived for the next. Take the time to write a basic cover letter structure you feel comfortable with, then customize it to the specific needs of the specific customer (or at least the industry).

456 College Hall
Normal, IL 67890
February 16, 1998

Ms. Jane Doe
Partner-In-Charge
Big Public Accounting, Inc.
123 N. Michigan Ave.
Chicago, IL 12345

Ms. Doe:

I was referred to you by Mr. Dave Zbecki, a Partner with your New York office, who informed me that the Chicago office of Big Public Accounting is actively seeking to hire quality individuals for your Auditor Development Program.

I have more than two years of accounting experience, including interning as an Auditor last year with the New York City office of Arthur Andersen. I will be receiving my BBA this May from Illinois State University, graduating Magna Cum Laude. I am confident that my combination of practical work experience and solid educational experience has prepared me for making an immediate contribution to Big Public Accounting. Having interned with a leading Big Six firm in the public accounting field, I understand the level of professionalism and communication required for long-term success in the field. My background and professional approach to business will provide your office with a highly productive Auditor upon completion of your Development Program.

I will be in the Chicago area the week of March 16. Please call me at 217-222-3456 to arrange a convenient time when we may meet to further discuss my background in relation to your needs. If I have not heard from you by March 9, I will contact your office to inquire as to a potential meeting date and time. I look forward to meeting you then.

Sincerely,

Tracy Q. Graduate

Tracy Q. Graduate

This type of cover letter will pay back far greater returns than the simple "introduction to me" letter that most people use. Remember that a successful cover letter is a marketing tool used to move your customer one step closer to buying your product. Customers do not buy features, they buy benefits. So make sure you drive home your benefit to the customer!

And keep in mind that many employers look to the cover letter as an example of your written communication skills. Resumes are often written and proofed by others, but cover letters are often yours alone. Make certain your cover letter is spell-checked, grammar-checked, and proofed by someone other than yourself.

> YOUR COVER LETTER SHOULD ALWAYS BE PERSONALIZED. "TO WHOM IT MAY CONCERN" IS AN IMMEDIATE TURNOFF.

I realize that no matter how many times or ways I say it, people will copy the example cover letter almost verbatim. If you do, you will be spotted as having used a canned letter. Take the time to do it right.

THE POSTSCRIPT TECHNIQUE

If you want to add an extra splash to your cover letter, consider adding a P.S. at the end. This works especially well in focusing on your most marketable attribute. An example would be: "P.S. I was the first intern ever to receive the Employee of the Month award at Andersen's New York office. And I won it not once, but twice. I am looking forward to bringing that same level of personal work commitment to you at Big Public Accounting." And if you truly want maximum impact, handwrite your P.S. I guarantee it will be the first thing read.

THE WORST USE OF THE COVER LETTER

Now that we have covered the basics of how to write a proper cover letter, please do not fall into the trap of using the cover letter as a crutch—"I have this great cover letter and resume. Now all I need to do is send it out to fifty (or one hundred or two hundred) different companies and sit back and wait for things to happen." This is the wrong use of the cover letter. The cover letter should only be used in directed marketing, not in blanket coverage marketing. Take the time to use it right.

Read the following chapters throughout the book for information on how to take a targeted approach in your job search and when and where to use your cover letter and resume.

THE TESTIMONIAL COVER LETTER TECHNIQUE

A unique, highly effective way to get your message across to a prospective employer is to add testimonials to your cover letter. Testimonials add credibility to your presentation. They provide more than the "I think I'm great" viewpoint by showing that someone else also thinks you are great.

There are three ways to incorporate this technique into your cover letter. The first is to place the testimonial quote within the body of the cover letter, along with the person's name and phone number. The testimonial can be provided as a separate paragraph or can be incorporated into the text of the skills/benefits paragraph. The second is to actually use a testimonial letter as a full cover letter. The third is to include a copy of one of your testimonial letters along with your resume. The following chapter includes examples of testimonials and letters of reference.

Testimonials can provide expansive power to your personal presentation. Make sure you take full advantage of them whenever the opportunity presents itself.

THE REPLY POSTCARD TECHNIQUE

If you want to greatly improve your odds of receiving a reply to your resume and cover letter, try using reply postcards. Using 4" x 6" or 3½" x 5½" standard postcard stock, on one side include your name, return address, and a 20-cent (as of late 1997) return stamp. On the other side, provide a series of follow-up questions for the employer to fill out. An example would be to give the employer several "outcome options" and a place for the name, title, and phone number of the responding contact.

The Reply Postcard Technique will greatly increase your chances of further contact with a prospective employer. Not only will they be more likely to respond to you, they are usually more likely to review your materials in the first place because they feel at least some guilt and obligation for the extra effort you have put forth. Following is a sample format for this technique.

_____ Please call me to arrange an interview.
_____ Please call me to further discuss your background.
_____ We will contact you within _____ months to follow up.
_____ We currently have no interest for the following reason:

_____

Name: _____

Company: _____

Title: _____

Phone: _____

You can have the above information printed onto postcard-size perforated forms that can be fed through most laser, ink jet, and dot matrix printers. The simplest alternative is to use the prestamped postcards available at any post office. Another alternative is to use laser forms such as Avery's Laser Index & Postcard form (#5389, available in most office supply stores), which costs around $20 for a pack of one hundred.

DO NOT JUST SEND OFF YOUR RESUME AND COVER LETTER AND WAIT FOR THE PHONE TO RING. IT WON'T.

Remember, a mailing campaign should be limited and targeted. The Reply Postcard works very poorly when accompanied by a "To Whom It May Concern" letter. Take the time to properly research your target companies, and direct your materials to the target prospect at each of the companies you contact. Then be sure to follow up with a phone call later. Sound like a lot of work? Not when you consider the payback. The initial investment per letter is more than a mass mailing, but the benefits are far greater. Mass mailings often generate zero results (and are far more expensive), while a targeted mailing and follow-up campaign can generate 10 to 15 percent or more in interview production. Do more with less. You are much more productive targeting twenty than blanketing two hundred.

For more details on how to gather information about the target companies and how to make contact with them, see the chapters ahead.

COVER LETTER CHECKLIST

Use this checklist to ensure that your cover letter is complete:

❑ One page only and limited to three targeted paragraphs

❑ Typewritten or word processor, with full spell check and proofing

❑ Written to someone specific, with the name and title spelled correctly

❑ Company name and address are correct and complete

❑ Quality bond paper, 8½ x 11 inches, ideally the same as your resume

❑ Three focused paragraphs (focused on the reader's needs, not yours)

❑ Closes with "Sincerely,"—anything else can be too chummy

❑ Signed with a blue or black pen

❑ Includes a P.S. for emphasis

❑ Place the resume behind the cover letter with no staples

❑ Send in 9 x 12 envelope, unfolded

❑ Type or neatly print address on envelope

❑ Seal the envelope (not just with the metal clasp)

❑ Conservative stamp on the envelope

❑ Final step: do not forget to follow up, or all the other steps will be in vain!

Chapter 5

BEST COLLEGE REFERENCES

If a man is called to be a streetsweeper,
he should sweep streets even as Michelangelo painted,
or Beethoven composed music, or Shakespeare wrote poetry.
He should sweep streets so well that all the hosts
of heaven and earth will pause to say,
here lived a great streetsweeper who did his job well.—
Martin Luther King

References are often ignored until late in the job search. "I'll get to it when they ask for them, but right now I have more important things to do." Yet, properly used, references can be an effective tool toward making your job search even more productive. Having them prepared in advance speeds up the final steps of the job search process; it can also give your job search a much needed jump start at the beginning.

THE VERY BEST SOURCES OF OUTSTANDING REFERENCES

Following is the preferred order of sources, in the eyes of your potential employer:

- ➤ Professional
- ➤ Extracurricular Advisors
- ➤ College Administrators
- ➤ College Professors
- ➤ Personal Professional Acquaintances

The one major exception to this is when your personal professional acquaintance is also connected with your potential employer (yes, it's called "pulling strings" and it's done all the time, so don't be ashamed).

Then it goes to the top of your list. Please leave off personal acquaintances (one candidate I interviewed listed his mother as a reference, saying "Who would know me better!") and religious acquaintances (five years as an altar boy is not typically considered a measure of employee loyalty).

THE VERY BEST WAY TO PRESENT YOUR REFERENCES

Ask each of your references to write a letter of recommendation. There are three reasons for this: (1) if they are not willing to be a reliable reference, they are unlikely to put forth the time necessary to write the letter of recommendation, (2) you will be able to use it as a ready-made reference to supply to potential employers, and (3) a letter of recommendation is a good way for you to prequalify those who will give the best reference. It is best to allow your references some latitude in developing the letter of recommendation, but for those who are clueless, ask them to follow this format:

> POSITIVE WORDS OF PRAISE FROM OTHERS SPEAK VOLUMES.

➤ How they know you and how long they have known you
➤ What they think of you (professionally and/or personally)
➤ Why they think you would make a great _____ (their recommendation)

This letter should always be typed on the letterhead of the company or institution. The following is a sample letter of recommendation:

Prospective Employer:

I have known Tracy Graduate through her work experience with our firm during the summer of 1997, when she served as an Auditor Intern in our New York office.

Tracy became immediately involved in the annual audit of Zephyr Megalithic, conducting much of the historical accounting research required for the audit. In addition to gathering the financial information, Tracy was instrumental in the development of the final certification report. Tracy also participated in several other smaller audits, including her instrumental role in the quarterly audit of Alpha Bank, where she developed several Excel macros to audit the inputs at the PC level. She later further developed these macros for use in future audits, which we have integrated into our Auditors Toolkit.

Tracy has shown the kind of initiative which is necessary to be successful over the long-term in the public accounting field. She has excellent forensic skills, yet remains focused on the overall needs of the client. I believe she will be a strong Auditor and has an excellent future in the public accounting field. She is a conscientious worker and has an excellent work ethic. We would gladly have hired Tracy upon graduation if she were open to the New York City area.

I recommend Tracy to you without reservation. If you have any further questions with regard to her background or qualifications, please do not hesitate to call me.

Sincerely,

Terry Thompson

Terry Thompson
Partner-in-Charge

HOW AND WHEN TO USE LETTERS OF RECOMMENDATION

When asked by potential employers for references, give them your one-page list, along with contact names, addresses, and phone numbers. But your list should also include the individual letters of recommendation that each reference has already given you. Many employers will actually forego formal reference checking when they have a letter of recommendation from a listed reference. Result? You have control of the reference check and it will shorten the hiring process.

THE TALKING REFERENCE TECHNIQUE

Instead of just supplying a standard reference sheet, add a "one-liner" from each reference, a quotation that summarizes a particular qualification or skill. It should be a one-line quote that gives personal insight into an element of your background that normally would not surface in the impersonal form of the standard resume/cover letter/references-type materials. You might be able to pull the quotation from a letter of reference or from a conversation with the person. If you are quoting verbal conversation, make sure you quote accurately and confirm the quote with the person—no paraphrasing allowed.

Example: "Tom is the brightest student I have ever known."

Example: "I am confident Julie will be an outstanding Accountant."

Example: "I could always count on Anne for our toughest projects."

THE LIVE REFERENCE TECHNIQUE

A unique yet effective spin on the standard reference is to actually record (either on audio tape or video tape) your references talking about you. It requires some time, effort, and a level of technical proficiency to put together, but when used in proper application (especially in the creative arts fields) it can supply a key differentiating factor in distinguishing you from your competition. A broadcast communications major used this technique and edited the references into a master tape of short clips, which was provided to interested potential employers. It not only delivered his references live, but also gave an indication of his professional editing capabilities.

Use caution when using this technique. Don't just do raw cuts with an available camcorder or tape recorder. Make sure you take the time to have it done in a professional manner. If you lack the necessary technical skills, you might be able to encourage a more proficient friend or classmate to take on the task. As a by-product, they can then use this experience as a project listing on their resume.

An additional caution: like any technique that varies from accepted standards, use only as appropriate. While it will almost always work in any of the communications and creative arts fields, it would likely be considered too extravagant for a stodgy accounting firm.

HOW TO MAKE SURE YOUR REFERENCES ARE THE VERY BEST

Your references will often be contacted by phone for further information. It has never failed to amaze me that people willingly supply references from individuals who end up giving negative references. Obviously, they were not aware that the references would be negative. But that is my point—you need to protect yourself in advance to ensure you have the very best references.

How? By checking your own references. Why? Because while many people are unwilling to tell you to your face what they really think about you, they may be very willing to "submarine" you when they get the chance.

How to do it: do not call them yourself. Rather, have a friend call for you. Have him explain that he is checking a reference on your background and would appreciate a candid opinion of your skills and abilities. If it does come up negative, the best thing to do is quietly drop that person from your list. If you confront a negative reference, you run the risk of that person seeking to further influence others. By quietly dropping that reference, you have done your job in containing this "closet enemy."

> YOUR REFERENCES SHOULD BE SPOTLESS. REFERENCE CHECKING IS OFTEN THE LAST STEP BEFORE THE OFFER IS MADE.

THE REFERENCE REFERRAL TECHNIQUE

Your professional and personal references can also provide you with an excellent opportunity to develop initial company referrals. After you have dispensed with the formality of asking these persons to serve as your references and provide you with letters of recommendation, ask your references which companies you should get in touch with. Ask for a recommendation of the top five employers in your field you should definitely contact. And ask if there are any personal contacts at the companies they could refer you to.

Not only are these people serving your indirect needs as references, they are also serving your more direct needs as referral sources in your new job search network.

Chapter 6

JOB SEARCH CENTRAL

*Far and away the best prize that life offers
is the chance to work hard at work worth doing.*
—Theodore Roosevelt

Job hunting is serious business. To be successful, you need to organize your job search like a business. Having a manila folder labeled "Jobs" buried under a pile of papers on your desk will not be adequate for long-term survival. You need to set up a control center for your job search, what we will refer to as *Job Search Central*.

SETTING UP YOUR JOB SEARCH CONTROL CENTER

Job Search Central is a physical location where you can organize and plan your job search. For many, Job Search Central is located at their desk in their dorm room or apartment. But don't fight for space within the midst of an otherwise unorganized life. Job search requires the utmost in organization to be fully effective.

First, plan out and organize the physical area itself. You need to set up a work space where you can quickly access your information, make phone calls, and plan out your search. Get a comfortable chair where you can truly do productive work for long periods of time. Make sure you have plenty of desktop space in which to work. And keep the work space clean and neat, not because Mom asked you to—do it because it will make you more efficient and productive. You might even consider placing some inspirational quotations or phrases on your wall to cheer you up and cheer you on when the going gets tough. Even the most effective job search will comprise a series of rejections before the ultimate acceptance. So make your work environment as positive and uplifting as possible.

Once your physical work space is set up, it's time to get organized. Excessive layers of wood pulp strata on top of the desk tend to suck in and obliterate new information, so beware. The "piling filing system" only serves to perpetuate disorganization. Do not make end-of-year the only time you sort through the paper mountain. Worse yet, disorganization unwittingly serves

> THE QUALITY OF YOUR LIFE AFTER COLLEGE MAY DEPEND UPON HOW ORGANIZED YOU ARE RIGHT NOW. IT'S TIME TO BEGIN PLANNING FOR LIFE BEYOND NEXT WEEKEND.

as an accomplice to procrastination because of the perpetual feeling that you "can never seem to get organized." And your disorganization can serve as a convenient excuse for not beginning your job search, perpetually putting it off. Master the mountain now, even if it means filing all paperwork in a vertical file marked "General" until it is later sorted. Always keep your work area open and accessible.

As part of a successful job search, you will be gathering and utilizing enormous amounts of information. It is not enough to just write down notes on slips of paper and pile them onto an open corner of the desk. Believe me, there is nothing worse than losing the phone number of the company that just called to set up an interview. Set up and label vertical files to organize information on each and every company you have an interest in. In this way, you can file away information you gather until it is needed and necessary. You may also want to set up files on job search topics you run across. Your copy costs will likely go up dramatically this semester. But do not just accumulate and file away worthless information. Always ask: "Will this help me in the future?" Then file it—or throw it away.

One of the most basic ways to track information is a simple "While You Were Out" pad and pen tacked down next to the phone. If you live alone, it gives you an automatic location for capturing information. If you live with others, it can be a lifesaver (or jobsaver) for capturing that critical phone call. It is amazing how often phone numbers are lost or taken down incorrectly, especially in the college environment. When I hear, "Just a minute, I have to find something to write on," I know that my name, company name, and phone number are being written on a gum wrapper, an empty twelve-pack box, or maybe worse. Make sure you have the message pads available and ask anyone/everyone who answers your phone to use them. If you are personally taking down the information, it is best to take it down directly in a pocket organizer, such as a Day-Timer or Franklin Planner (more on that coming up) so that it is captured and logged for future reference. As a fallback, make sure you have an organized way for yourself and others to capture the information. Remember "The Roommate Factor"—the probability of your roommate losing the phone number is directly proportional to the importance of the call. Have a central location—a bulletin board on the wall next to the phone—for posting the message.

TELEPHONE ETIQUETTE

Consider for a moment how your phone is answered. Professional courtesy is quite often not the standard for most college students. An abrupt "Yeah!" could be listed among the more courteous greetings. The more outrageous remarks will often buy you a major black mark in the professionalism category—even if it was your idiot roommate. A simple, "This is ____" is always a pleasant change for the average college dorm room. Make the change today, before the next company phone call. As difficult as it may seem, you should also encourage your roommate to do the same.

> **FIRST IMPRESSIONS DO COUNT. MAKE YOURS A GOOD ONE.**

One final note on phone etiquette: if you (or any of your roommates) persist in the use of creative phone answering lines ("Sam's Mortuary, you stab 'em, we slab 'em"), just remember that the click you hear on the other end of the line may be the sound of your dream job being passed forward to Contestant #2.

PROPER USE OF AN ANSWERING MACHINE

An integral part of Job Search Central is the effective use of an answering machine to take your calls when you are out. If you do not have an answering machine yet, purchase one immediately. If you already own one, you might consider updating your "Doctor Strangelove" or other "unique and unusual" greeting. Just imagine your future boss being greeted by your answering machine and then answer this question: will it enhance or detract from what they think of you? If it is the latter, change it. Otherwise, your future boss may end up being someone else's future boss.

I realize I should not even have to address this subject, but woefully, some 75+ percent of the college answering machines I reach have an inappropriate outgoing message. They often are references to social habits ("I'm unable to answer my phone because I'm either out partying or passed out on my bed"), references to study habits ("I'm blowing off my normal classes to pursue advanced studies in chemical inebriation"), or even sexist remarks ("guys leave your phone number, girls leave your measurements"). And there are many others, some not suitable to print. I have heard them all. Take note—when I hear one of these sophomoric messages, that is likely the end of your candidacy with our company. You will never even know that I called. I will probably just hang up and cross you off my list. Think about it the next time you hear the caller "click off" on your machine without leaving a message. That could have been your dream job gone bye-bye. It may have been fun for the first few years, but don't blow your job opportunities over a stupid message. Stop right now, put down this book, and change your message to one of the following:

> **THE TIME YOU INVEST IN PLANNING WILL PAY BACK SEVERAL TIMES OVER IN TIME AND PRODUCTIVITY.**

(If you live by yourself) "Hello. This is (phone number). I'm not available to take your call right now. Please leave your name, phone number, and the best time to reach you. I will get back to you as soon as possible."

(If you live with others) "Hello. We are not available to take your call right now. Please leave your name, phone number, the best time to reach you, and the name of the person you are trying to reach. We will get back to you as soon as possible."

THE FOUR D'S OF GETTING THINGS DONE IN YOUR JOB SEARCH

Job search requires proper management of your time and resources. Use the following four D's to manage your job search priorities:

1. **Drop** — this is the easy one. Yet often we are unable to let go of things that "we are supposed to do." Says who? Focus your job search on your objective. Drop those activities that are not truly important. And extend this prioritization to all aspects of your life to make more time for the truly important activities.

2. **Delegate** — you have been used to doing it all yourself. Now may be the time to tap into the help of others. We usually delegate only when we are swamped and have no choice. Then it's not really delegating, it's dumping. Make the choice to seek out the help of others. There will be plenty of people who will help, if you are willing to ask.

3. **Delay** — it's amazing how many "important" things go away when they are ignored. Not that I am advocating procrastination in your job search. Just focus on doing the right thing at the right time in the right way. Put aside the other tasks until they truly need attention (if at all).

4. **Do** — the critical step of accomplishing anything. All the planning in the world will accomplish nothing unless you actually do something with the plan. Organization is only a means to an end. In the end, you need to just do it.

Every minute (up to fifteen) invested in daily planning returns three to five minutes. And every minute (up to thirty) invested in weekly planning returns five to ten minutes. So plan out your job search and plan out your life for success.

THE JOB SEARCH TRACKING SYSTEM

As you go forward in your job search, you will find yourself accumulating a large amount of information. If you do not currently have a pocket Day-Timer or Franklin Planner, now is the time to get one. It is absolutely vital for planning your time and keeping track of all the contacts you will be making. If you do not have a pocket day-planner, call Day-Timers at 800-225-5005. Ask one of their order takers to send you their free (can't beat that price) Pocket Day-Timer Sample Kits. They will promptly send out to you a three-month supply of planners in a variety of styles and full instructions on how to use them profitably. This will give you enough time to get used to the system and decide which style you like best if you want to order more. But make sure you stick with a pocket-sized planner. The desk-sized planners lack the portability you will need for keeping information current and always available.

> YOU CANNOT ALWAYS CONTROL WHAT HAPPENS TO YOU, BUT YOU CAN ALWAYS CONTROL HOW YOU REACT TO WHAT HAPPENS TO YOU.

It's not rocket science, but applying the simple planning and organization principles of the Day-Timer system will greatly increase your efficiency and productivity. No more missed appointments. No more forgotten assignments. No more lost phone numbers. And a much greater emphasis on completing tasks and reaching a definable goal, day in and day out.

PERSONAL INFORMATION MANAGERS

For the computer literate, you might also look into using a PIM (Personal Information Manager) to automate the planning and tracking process. My personal suggestions would be Maximizer, ACT!, or Lotus Organizer. Don't make the mistake of scrimping to buy a second-rate or shareware software PIM—you will end up spending more time working with it (or working around it) than it is worth. These three packages all provide an easy-to-use interface, event planning/tracking, and the capabilities to both capture and manipulate information about the people you are contacting. But whether you work with the hard copy planner or automated PIM—or both (I religiously use a Day-Timer for daily event planning and ACT! for contact management)—they are only as effective as you make them. Dedicate time to using them properly.

Use your computer software only for "batch" events. Never get yourself stuck in a situation where you need to boot up to capture live information. Always be ready with pen in hand. Pocket organizers are portable, computers are not (they are still luggable). Computers are great as long-term storage devices, yet are still not practical for day-to-day living away from the desk and screen. Be prepared to record each and every bit of information, no matter how minor or insignificant it may sound, as it occurs. Do not get caught in the "I'll write it down later" trap, because often you will either forget or lose the information by then.

It's amazing how often you find yourself going back to a name or phone number you recorded weeks or even months ago. After your job search is complete, the information you have gathered will serve as the networking foundation for all future job searches. Capture the information and use it wisely.

YOUR JOB SEARCH TOOL KIT

During the course of your job search, you will need to rely on a tool kit of items to assist you. Following are recommended items for you to purchase or borrow for the duration of your search:

➤ **Dress** — both men and women need a conservative interview suit for future interviews, whether on campus or at a company-site. Keep it conservative and in with current fashion. The suit you wore to your high school graduation might have held over for the college years, but it is probably out of fashion by now. You do not need an entire wardrobe—one well-chosen suit can work with several shirt/blouse/tie/accessory combinations to produce a varied yet consistent look for you throughout your job search. If you need further information, refer to Appendix A—Guidelines for Successful Interview Dress.

➤ **Portfolio** — not the kind that artists carry around, but the 9"x12" leather-bound or vinyl-bound type, such as those made by Stratford. You can usually pick up a quality vinyl-bound portfolio for less than $10. You will use it for interviews and job fairs, both for carrying your resume and for taking notes.

➤ **Briefcase** — a briefcase will provide you with a mini-office from which to operate when you are at a job fair or a company-site interview. But before you go out to K-Mart to buy a $19 vinyl briefcase special, consider the value of buying a professional leather briefcase. Both Sam's Club and Office Depot carry leather briefcases for less than $40. Be aware also that the type of leather, although not greatly affecting the initial appearance, will have a large impact on the long-term appearance of your briefcase. Bonded leather is leather parts glued together, which is used in the cheapest—and lowest quality—leather briefcases. It would be much better to spend an extra $10 to $20 to buy either a split-leather (better) case or a top-grain leather (best) case. Buy quality. Remember, you will be using this case well beyond graduation. Invest now in quality that will last you far into the future. And there you have it—your complete buyer's guide to briefcases, included at no extra charge.

➤ **Pen** — whether at a job fair or in the course of your eventual interviews, the type of pen you use will send a message about who you are. Bic pen, poor college student. Cross pen, prepared job seeker. Even if you truly are a poor college student, spend the $10–$15 to purchase an entry level ball-point and keep it reserved for interviewing situations. Function is fine, but form is always more impressive in this category.

➤ **Pocket Organizer** — keep your Day-Timer or Franklin Planner with you at all times. You never know when you will need to capture information for later retrieval. At slow points in your day, use your organizer to plan out your activities for the remainder of the day and week. It can also provide a gentle reminder for completing that term paper you have been putting off.

Following are optional items you may choose to add to your tool kit, as available funds allow:

➤ **Computer** — as discussed previously, a computer can benefit you in organizing your job search effort, although it is certainly not a requirement. It can be used for tracking information, generating letters, faxing your resume, and surfing the Internet. But don't go out to buy a computer just for your job search. You will spend far more time setting it up than you will gain in productivity. If you already have one, use it. If not, wait until the first (or second) paycheck arrives.

➤ **Pager** — want to make sure you do not miss that all-important phone call? A pager is an inexpensive (usually no more than $10-$20/month) method to stay in constant touch. And it also serves as an excellent job search conversation starter. "Why are you wearing a pager?" "To stay in touch with people during the course of my job search." "Really? How is your job search going?" And so the conversation begins as your network expands.

➤ **Cellular Phone** — if the bucks are there and you want the ultimate in personal connectivity, you might consider investing in a cellular phone. Many providers are giving away phones for free or little cost, but the monthly service can add up quickly, so beware. Also note that you are often required to sign up for a year or more of service, which may not work for you if you are planning to relocate after graduation. However, you can usually find some decent hand-held phones in the used market and then sign up for a month-to-month contract (since you own the phone). Use it only for your job search and other critical calls. If you start giving away your number to others, you may end up working the first couple of years to pay off your cellular phone bill.

THE SALES MANAGER TECHNIQUE

You have probably heard the saying before—if you fail to plan, you plan to fail. Although I won't be giving you the long and boring goal-setting speech that you have probably heard at least a dozen times by now, I will make reference to those same basic principles. If you are to succeed in your job search, you need to have specific goals and an overall plan in place.

Start by drawing up a master plan for what you will be doing between now and graduation to find a job. Then break it down into one-week segments. Then break down each one-week segment into your daily planning. Then take the next step that will ensure your success—hire a "sales manager." Not a real sales manager. Just someone who is willing to work with you in helping you reach your career goals. Find a friend, roommate, career counselor, or parent willing to work

> PROCRASTINATION IS THE GREATEST ENEMY TO YOUR JOB SEARCH.

with you. Parents are usually the toughest—but also the best, since you likely share the common goal of you moving out of the house after college. Make a copy of your weekly plan, give it to your sales manager on Sunday night, then have them check your progress both Wednesday night and again the following Sunday. A new week, a new plan. A good sales manager is more than just a nag—a good sales manager should have your best interests in mind and seek to keep you motivated. Amazingly, you will find your parents to be quite good at this activity. If you are afraid of your parents assisting you (because you are afraid of failure?), you might consider reciprocating with a fellow student by serving as his or her sales manager. But be careful—if one of you lets down in your responsibilities, it's easy for both to fall back.

The key is that you have set out an actual written plan with attainable goals in place. Don't worry if your master plan has to be modified and updated along the way. That is part of the job search process. You will need to invest at least five hours of work per week in your job search to be truly effective and may find yourself spending as much as ten to fifteen hours per week when things get rolling. Spend the twenty to thirty minutes it takes to properly plan your week's activities at the beginning of each week so that you are operating at peak efficiency.

FREE QUICKSTART JOB SEARCH™ SOFTWARE

Making employer contact is a vital step in the job search process. To assist you in locating employers, I am making available to all readers of this book a free copy (well, not exactly free, since you still have to cover the minimal cost of shipping and handling) of my entire database of entry level employers. This database contains more than three thousand entry level employers throughout the United States, including company name, address, and contact information. Also included (when available) is an e-mail address of the contact and the company Website. The database is provided in ASCII DOS-delimited file format to allow you to import it into your database software of choice, such as ACT! or Access or even Excel. From there, you can sort it, merge it, and print it to your heart's content. Take note that this database is not actual database software. Instead, it is the database information that can be imported into any of the popular database, contact manager, or spreadsheet programs. Or you can simply use it with a standard word processor as a mail merge file. No matter how you choose to use it, the information could prove to be invaluable in your job search.

> TAKE ADVANTAGE OF EVERY RESOURCE THAT IS AVAILABLE TO YOU IN YOUR JOB SEARCH.

Quickstart Job Search is an easy and efficient way to broaden your job search exponentially. If you have not yet sent in the offer on the last page of the book, please take time to do so.

Chapter 7

YOUR CAREER DEVELOPMENT OFFICE

There are so many things you can learn about.
But you'll miss the best things if you keep your eyes shut.
—Dr. Seuss

Graduation week always produces an interesting parade of students through the campus Career Development office. Students who have avoided this office during the entirety of their college career suddenly show up, half hoping that a job offer will be handed to them to accompany their new diploma. When the job offer is not magically produced, they wander to the jobs posting board and grunt in dismay at not seeing the ideal job at the ideal company waiting for them to sign on the dotted line. And then they walk out, resigning themselves to the notion that grad school may not be a bad idea after all.

Your campus Career Development office is there to serve you and your needs. It is the only place in the world that will place your job search needs above all others. And usually it is free or at very little cost, included as part of your student fees or tuition costs. Far too many students wait to utilize the services until very late in the final year. Yet the resources contained in this office are plentiful for those who wisely invest the needed time in advance.

CAREER DEVELOPMENT OFFICE ORGANIZATION

To obtain optimal benefit, you need to understand your campus Career Development office organization. There are two distinct career functions that are provided on most college campuses: career planning and career placement. The former involves vocational counseling and testing to assist you in choosing a future career. The latter is designed to assist you in locating your job after graduation. As discussed earlier, you need to know what you want to do before you attempt to find it. Always complete the former step before you begin the latter.

Some colleges divide these two functions into separate offices, with career planning handled by a "Career Services" or "Career Planning" office. This can sometimes be part of Student Services or Counseling Services. The primary emphasis of career planning is to help you better understand your individual aptitudes, personality, interests, and values in relation to career options. This evaluation may be done through a series of standardized tests and computer-based programs, which are then analyzed by an experienced career counselor, who subjectively assists you in mapping the results against potential careers. Career planning is best accomplished as early as possible in your college career, although you should never skip the step simply because you "got started late" and now you need to start looking for a job. Take the time necessary to properly evaluate your background and explore all the opportunities that may be available to you. It will help you immensely in becoming more focused and targeted in your eventual job search. And in achieving greater happiness in your eventual career.

> YOUR CAMPUS CAREER DEVELOPMENT OFFICE IS THE ONLY PLACE ON EARTH WHERE YOUR JOB SEARCH IS THE NUMBER ONE PRIORITY OF OTHERS. YET RELATIVELY FEW TAKE ADVANTAGE OF THIS VALUABLE RESOURCE. MAKE SURE YOU ARE ONE OF THE RELATIVE FEW.

The career placement function is usually found on campus at the Career Development office (which can go by many different names, such as "Graduate Placement" or "Career Placement Center"). In some schools, the placement function is contained within a single office, sometimes even combined with Career Planning. At other schools, the placement function may be divided by undergraduate and graduate degrees, or may be divided by specific majors. Some schools also maintain an active alumni placement office, often as an adjunct to the Alumni Relations office. If this all sounds confusing, it's not intended to be. You simply need to locate the office designed specifically for you. And if you wander into the wrong one, they will surely be able to point you in the right direction.

BENEFITS OF THE CAREER DEVELOPMENT OFFICE

Whereas your job search is new to you, it's a way of life for the Career Development office. The Placement Counselors have ongoing experience in working with students of similar backgrounds and interests, and will already have established links with interested employers. Placement Counselors actively survey the job market, seeking out the best practices for you to employ in your job search. They are constantly in touch with companies in order to bring the broadest mix of potential employers to your campus for on-campus interviewing.

> THE CAREER DEVELOPMENT OFFICE IS THERE TO SERVE YOUR INDIVIDUAL NEEDS. THEY WILL DO EVERYTHING BUT GET YOU THE JOB— THAT'S YOUR JOB.

The Placement Counselor is there to assist you. While the Company Recruiter is looking for the best person for the position, the Placement Counselor is looking for the best position for the person. It's in your best interest to develop a personal and continuing relationship with your Placement Counselor.

SERVICES OF THE CAREER DEVELOPMENT OFFICE

The Career Development office is an excellent place to begin your job search. In addition to the assistance of the staff, you will have access to probably the most complete library of job information and employer information available on campus. Following are some of the resources that may be available to you in the Career Development office:

1. **Books** — on specific careers and industries
2. **Occupational Listings** — information about a variety of different occupations, including economic outlook and forecast for future demand and growth
3. **Directories** — listing employers who hire at the entry level, often categorized by job type, industry, and geography
4. **Employer Listings** — information on employers who are coming to campus in the coming semester, those who have come in the past, and other employers who have an interest in students from your school, although they may not be coming to campus

5. **Job Postings** — specific jobs may be posted in the office, either in advance of on-campus interviews or for employers who are not able to come to campus

6. **Employer Information** — individual files of information are kept for specific employers, including general information about the employer and specific information about positions available

7. **Computer Databases** — information about employers, including positions available, geographic locations, and contact information

8. **Subscriptions** — magazines specific to supporting the needs of college student job search

9. **Seminars** — a variety of seminars may be offered, on topics ranging from resume preparation to networking to interview preparation

10. **Counseling** — one-on-one counseling designed to assist you in succeeding in your job search

In addition, the Career Development office is usually the coordination point for on-campus interviewing activities. If you want to take part in on-campus interviewing (and you should), this is your starting point for both registering and researching.

In short, you will have access to a wealth of information which can be found nowhere else on campus. And you will have a real human being with your best interests in mind to guide you and support you in the job search process. Make sure you take advantage of this valuable service.

> THE SAME SERVICES AVAILABLE FOR FREE OR LITTLE COST FROM YOUR CAREER DEVELOPMENT OFFICE WOULD COST FROM $500 TO $3000 AT A PROFESSIONAL CAREER COUNSELING SERVICE.

SIGNING UP

Most campus Career Development offices require you to register with the office before taking advantage of the services provided. This may be as simple as a line item check-in, but more likely will involve filling out a registration form or data sheet. In addition to supplying basic information internally for the office, this form often doubles as an information sheet for employers, so take the time to fill it out neatly and completely. You may also be required to sign a release form giving your permission to release your credentials to employers.

Request a listing of all the services provided by the office. You may find that seminars and classes are provided to further educate you in the job search process. The office may also offer mock interviewing. They may sponsor speakers from employers visiting campus and speakers on subjects relating to job search.

Many Career Development offices are now using electronic resumes and some are using full electronic applicant portfolios for transmission to potential employers. This process cuts down on the paper flow while improving keyword searchability. When providing a resume to Career Development, whether in paper or electronic format, always attempt to follow the resume format covered in this book rather than the Career Development standard. If you follow their standard, you will end up looking like everyone else, with only minor content differences. Always attempt to be an original when possible.

> UNTIL YOU HAVE FOUND YOUR NEW JOB, MAKE THE DEVELOPMENT OFFICE YOUR SECOND HOME.

MAXIMIZING YOUR RELATIONSHIP

Ideally, you should make your initial visit to the Career Development office no later than the beginning of the first semester of your final year. Many of the best positions are already being offered (and filled) early in the year. But if that time has already passed, do not put off your initial visit any further. It will take time to effectively build a relationship and develop a personal program for meeting your specific needs.

Seek a professional yet personal relationship with your Placement Counselor. You will likely be given a set of tasks and activities to accomplish, including filling out forms and developing your job search materials. Complete these activities on time and you will earn the respect of the counselor, who will see that you are committed to succeeding in your job search. Your counselor, in turn, can provide you with job search information above and beyond what is being publicly posted. And when a potential employer calls campus to arrange for closed (restricted) interviews, your relationship with your counselor will increase the odds of inclusion on the list. Keep in close touch, but not too close. Most placement counselors are overworked and underpaid, so do not expect them to conduct your job search for you. They are simply the front-end contact to help you get started. You need to take personal responsibility for the eventual success of your job search. You will need to put forth the effort to make it happen.

As your search progresses, provide the courtesy of communicating all second interviews and eventual offers to your Placement Counselor. The counselor can likely provide you with some historical salary information, both for the employer and for your major and field. By providing information back to your counselor, not only will you gain a competitive edge in your job search, you will also be providing information for the next generation of graduates.

FINDING HIRING COMPANIES

Chapter 8

NETWORK INTELLIGENCE GATHERING

*Do something for somebody every day for
which you do not get paid.*—Albert Schweitzer

Networking is often considered a less than noble activity reserved for only the most desperate in their job search. Yet nothing could be (or should be) further from the truth. Networking is one of the most effective and efficient activities in finding your first position.

The reality of the job market is that most positions are never advertised, never recruited for, never made known outside of the organization. Yet they continue to be filled. How? By referral. By referral of someone internal or external. By the "who-do-you-know" method of job search. Networking.

> WE NETWORK EVERY DAY. WE JUST DON'T CALL IT NETWORKING.

Let's understand some of the dynamics behind networking by looking at a practical case example:

Entry level hiring within our company is usually planned a full eight to twelve months in advance of the actual hire date. The first persons made aware of our entry level hiring needs are our local management team. Planning for entry level hiring is part of our strategic planning process, and the first step toward potentially filling the positions are internal recommendations from our local management staff. The process goes to the next level when we announce the potential hiring needs to all of our local employees. Next level is a request to our area office. Then a request to corporate, each time seeking qualified candidates who may be "already in the pipeline." If we have not yet identified potential candidates for the positions, we will integrate the positions into our on-campus hiring process. And no, we will never advertise the positions. And college students who have tapped into our internal network often gain job offers before we even begin our on-campus interviewing.

The "who-do-you-know" network is alive and functioning quite well, thank you, in the employment marketplace.

Yet most college students do not consider themselves to be very well plugged in when it comes to networking. "After all, who do I know who can give me a job?" Probably no one. But networking is NOT about first-level contacts. The key to effective networking is what I call "The Ripple Effect." Simply stated, the Ripple Effect is similar to what happens when you toss a stone into a pond. The first ripple is the largest ripple, but it is the second and third ripples that further widen the affected surface area. The more stones that break the surface, the greater the amount of the pond that is filled with your ripples. Moral to the story: if you want to give yourself the opportunity to make a ripple in the employment world, you are going to have to toss a few stones into the pond. Otherwise you probably will not even break the surface.

In building your job search network, you will need to develop a list of potential network contacts. Don't worry about whether they are personally responsible for hiring. It's not who they are, it's who they know.

THE PURPOSE OF NETWORKING

There is more to networking than just "get a job." Networking is an activity that takes place every day of our lives, whether job-related or not. Did you talk to someone at breakfast about what might be on the upcoming exam? That's networking. Did you ask your professor which reference materials would be the best in preparing a term paper? That's networking. Did you ask friends if they knew of anyone driving home for the weekend? That's networking.

Networking is already far more active in your life than you might have originally thought. The key to making it effective in your job search is to provide clear focus and direction. Following are several objectives to keep in mind when speaking with others about your job search:

1. To make others aware of your job search and your career focus.
2. To open up additional lines of communication in the job market.
3. To increase your knowledge about a particular career field or industry.
4. To find out more about potential employers.

5. To discover hidden job opportunities.

6. To open up the possibility of creating a job where none currently exists.

To achieve your networking objectives, you need to consider each contact with another human being as a potential opportunity to further expand your network. You will come in contact with other people each and every day. How you integrate that contact into your job search network will greatly determine your potential for overall success in your job search. And there are scores, if not hundreds of people out there who are ready and willing to help.

THE LAW OF 250

The Law of 250 states that every person knows at least 250 other people. For example, if you were to make a list of people to invite to your wedding, you would likely be able to come up with about 250 people. These people might not appear to be outstanding first-level job networking contacts, but many will be able to refer you to others who are.

Expanding the concept of the Law of 250 further, each one of your contacts knows an additional 250 people. Yes, there may be some overlap in the 250, especially with a family member or close friend. But the exponential multiplying factor of the additional contacts is what makes networking so potentially valuable in your job search.

Use the Law of 250 as inspiration to contact one more person to enter into your personal network. Although you may not find your next job within your 250, it is very likely that it may exist within someone else's 250.

> NETWORKING CAN BE DIFFICULT TO START, BUT ALMOST IMPOSSIBLE TO STOP ONCE YOU HAVE BUILT MOMENTUM.

THE STRENGTH OF WEAK TIES

A corollary to the Law of 250 is the strength of weak ties. As we stated earlier, if one of your 250 is also a family member or close friend, there will likely be some overlap. You may have fifty, one hundred, or even one hundred fifty contacts in common. So actually it is those who are the weakest ties who have the greatest potential for you. Your weekend tennis partner may share no first-level contacts within your 250, potentially opening you up to a totally new group of people.

It is typically not your first-level contact who may be your eventual Hiring Manager. Actually, you will usually find your hiring contact two, three, or even four levels deep.

This is not to discount the importance of the first-level contacts—they are the starting point and will determine your eventual success or failure in networking. But don't be surprised if one day you get a call from a person completely unknown to you—a "friend of a friend of a friend" referring you to a particular company. Cultivate all your contacts and watch them grow!

WHOM TO CONTACT IN NETWORKING

In short, you should contact everyone you know (your 250) and everyone you do not know. I realize that seems rather open-ended, so let's start with some specifics.

First, contact your relatives. Not just your immediate family—branch out into the family tree. And not just those who are "well-connected in business." Aunt Mabel may play bridge with someone who knows someone who is a Hiring Manager in your field. Remember, it's not necessarily who you know, but who they know.

> EVERYONE KNOWS SOMEONE.

Next, contact friends. Old and new, high school and college, neighbors and social acquaintances. They might even be a friend of a friend or relative, such as someone who plays tennis or golf with your parents. Spread the word. Some of the best contacts in this group are your college friends who graduated last year. They are already through the job search process and probably have lots of contacts (and free advice).

Next, contact every known entity within your college. Professors, advisors, administrators, counselors, coaches (they are often amazingly well connected!), and anyone else who has ties to your school. Beware that some in this group (especially some of the "academic purist" or "research first" professors) are not nearly as well connected with the real world as they would like you to think, but the guilt factor—their not wanting to admit this little secret—often pushes them to come up with some creative ideas. And be sure to reach beyond your circle of known alums to all alumni (recent or past) who are working for target companies, within your target geography, or within your chosen profession. Spend an afternoon at the campus Alumni Affairs office. They are usually more than willing to help.

Also contact past and present employers, coworkers, professional associations, and social contacts through your church, synagogue, club, or other organizations. Make it your goal to reach out to your entire list of 250 and then some.

THE ADVICE REQUEST TECHNIQUE

"But what do I say?" The actual process of networking can seem somewhat mysterious, yet it really isn't. You are simply making contact with individuals who may be able to assist in your job search. The best method for making contact with others is to ask for advice. You are not asking for an interview, you are asking for advice. By making advice requests, you can tap into a vast network of people who can assist you in your job search.

The Advice Request Technique is the door opener to asking questions of your network contacts. You can preface your question with: "May I ask your advice about something?" Then ask away. Most people are more than willing to pass along their advice to you. It plays well on the vanity factor and opens the lines of communication for you to ask further questions.

THE TEN-SECOND SOUND BITE TECHNIQUE

In networking with others, always be prepared to present a short sound bite of information about who you are and what you are looking for. Even though Aunt Mabel has known you from birth, she probably does not have a clue as to what type of work you are seeking after graduation.

Remember your career mission statement and resume objective? These two statements will form the basis of your ten-second sound bite. It will be a compound "I have" and "I'm looking for" statement. Following are some examples:

> "I have experience and a degree in accounting and I'm looking for a position in the public accounting field in the Chicago area."

> "I have experience in Delphi programming and a degree in Computer Science. I'm looking for a position with a computer consulting firm."

> "I have experience in newspaper reporting and a degree in Journalism. I'm looking for a position in the newspaper or journalism field in Boston."

Keep it short and sweet. If more detail is required, your contact will ask. The intent of the ten-second sound bite is to give them a tangible statement they will be able to remember. Just as a politician is always seeking a memorable sound bite (remember the famous "Read my lips—no new taxes" sound bite?), you should also seek a sound bite that is specific and memorable.

THE THIRTY-SECOND ELEVATOR PITCH TECHNIQUE

Occasionally, the explanation of who you are and what you are looking for requires greater detail. Perhaps you are speaking with someone who is unfamiliar with your background. It may require that you provide more detail than the ten-second sound bite. However, it should still be a tightly structured answer.

Imagine getting onto an elevator in an office building after a job interview. As the doors almost close, a person walks onto the elevator. As you both prepare for the silent journey downward, the person turns to you and says, "I noticed you were interviewing with Jane Brown today at our company. What's your background?" The timer has started. You now have thirty seconds or less before the elevator reaches the bottom floor to succinctly state your background. Can you do it?

> MOST PEOPLE ARE HAPPY TO HELP YOU IN YOUR JOB SEARCH. ALL YOU NEED TO DO IS ASK. BUT YOU DO HAVE TO ASK.

The Thirty-Second Elevator Pitch is something you should practice and perfect. It is the basic introduction of who you are and what you are looking for. It will form the basis of your introductory message when networking, your opening statement in telephone contacts with employers, and the foundation of your "Tell me about yourself" answer in interviewing.

Don't just assume you will have a great answer when the time comes. As you reach out to network with others, you will be required to cut to the chase quickly. Most contacts are not looking for your life history. They are looking for your bottom line. Develop a level of comfort in your personal presentation of who you are and what you are looking for.

HOW TO TURN CONTACTS INTO NETWORK CONTACTS

There is no special magic in converting personal contacts into network contacts. Just give them a call (or visit in person), let them know that you are currently searching for a job as a _____, ask them if they will help by being part of your personal network, and ask if you can send a copy of your resume to them for their advice and input. After they receive the resume, call them back to ask for their advice regarding your resume and any recommendations they may have with regard to potential employer contacts. Then utilize some of the following techniques to strengthen and expand your network of contacts.

THE TOP FIVE TECHNIQUE

Ask your network contacts the following question: "Who are the top five companies that you recommend I contact?" Most people are able to give a "Top Five" list quite easily. After they give you the names, ask them if they have any personal contacts at any of those companies. Keep in mind that over time you will begin to hear some of the same company names (especially if they are well-known industry leaders) being repeated. But keep asking for the names of the personal contacts at each—you can never have enough. After they give you the contact names, selectively consider (depending on your comfort level with the contact) asking if they will contact the company on your behalf. Sometimes your network contact can do some of the work for you! When they make the referrals, be certain that you follow through in a professional manner since they are putting their personal/professional reputation on the line for you. Attaching their name with your name puts a heavy responsibility on you to meet or exceed all expectations.

> EVERYONE KNOWS AT LEAST FIVE COMPANIES YOU SHOULD CONTACT. EVEN AUNT MABEL.

JUST SAY THE MAGIC WORD

This is an unusual revelation, I must admit. But just saying the magic word "NETWORK" when you talk to potential network contacts takes the conversation (and the productivity of the contact) to a much higher level. I realize it seems rather trivial, so let me explain why this happens.

When you are speaking with potential network contacts, no matter how you state your case it sounds one-sided (your-sided) and of no benefit to them. But the moment you mention the magic word—"I would like to include you in my network of contacts"—you have brought it to a new level. Just watch the reaction. All of a sudden, they perk up and become quite attentive to your needs. Why does this happen? Because we have all been trained to network with everyone and everything; yet as a professional society, we often do not recognize networking unless the actual word is used.

I know that sounds belittling to the average intellect in the professional marketplace, but it is reality. "Oh, you want to network with me!" is the typical response—we fail to understand the request until the actual word is used. Summary: when you want to network with someone, always make sure you lead with that magic word.

THE ONE-A-DAY TECHNIQUE

Talking about (or reading about) networking is not networking. Networking is picking up the phone and making the call. It involves getting the phone time (or face time) to make a contact and make a request. You need to be networking consistently in your job search. An initial flurry of calls is not sufficient to keep your network alive and moving forward.

NETWORKING IS NOT A ONE-TIME ACTIVITY. IT IS AN ONGOING PROCESS WHICH MUST BE CULTIVATED OVER TIME.

Set a personal goal to make at least (remember, this is a minimum) one networking contact per day. And voice mail does not count. You need to make at least one live connection per day. Every day. It's really not as difficult as it may seem. Once you begin your networking, you will find that there are contacts whom you should be calling on a weekly basis. As your network expands, you will find additional contacts being added to your list almost daily.

Remember, networking is where many of the best jobs are found. The competition is low. The odds are high. Networking is by far your best opportunity for finding your new job. Keep up the momentum by making a minimum of one network connection per day.

THE LAW OF SEVEN

The Law of Seven is a selling strategy which states that the sale is not truly lost until at least seven sales attempts have been made. Or the converse, which states that the sale sometimes will not be made until at least seven exposures to the product are completed. The Law of Seven is followed faithfully by media advertisers who continually pummel us over and over with the same ad to ensure that we have reached the saturation point of product recognition.

The same principle applies to networking. It is not enough to contact people once, then cross your fingers. Networking is more than making one call or writing one letter. You should regularly give your network contacts updated information on your job search and at the same time find out if they are aware of anything new. If you are actively pursuing employment, it's best to contact them once every two weeks. If you are passively seeking employment, once every one or two months is sufficient. And what if they remain "cold" after seven contacts? Remember that seven is merely the minimum for making full impact. Do not stop making contact unless you are asked to do so. Some of the very best contacts may be the most difficult to fully develop a networking relationship with. Use personal discretion in making contact (one voice mail per week is max unless there is a critical timing need), yet make sure you do your part to keep in touch.

Let your contacts know when their help resulted in positive action. We all appreciate positive feedback, and when you express yours, it helps encourage even greater success in the future.

THE LAW OF NETWORK GRAVITY

The Law of Network Gravity states: It is always easier to be bumped down in the organization than it is to be bumped up.

What this means is that if you have been referred to the President of the company, but you realize your potential Hiring Manager is the Accounting Manager, you should still contact the President. It may seem intimidating at first, but if you have a referral to rest upon, it usually goes quite smoothly. Let the President know who referred you, the purpose of your call, and ask if they could refer you to the proper person within the company.

That's when the magic starts. Why? Because now you have a referral within the company who is in the reporting order of the Hiring Manager. This is golden.

Let's take the example of seeking an accounting position. The President, not likely to have the name of the Hiring Manager, might refer you to the Chief Financial Officer. Onward and downward to the next level below. When you call this person, make sure you state that Mr./Ms. President asked you to call them. Just watch how quickly your call is accepted. The CFO will take the call and will probably refer you to the Controller, who in turn will refer you to the Accounting Manager. At each level, you continue to "layer on" the name dropping from all the previous levels. By the time you get "bumped down" to the Hiring Manager, you can now state that you are calling based on the recommendation of the President, CFO, and Controller. Wow! Watch the results! Interestingly, they usually do not ask why they recommended you talk with them. So it could even go as far as the Hiring Manager wondering if you are in some way related to the President or have some other "insider" connection. Now you have become an insider! Congratulations—make the most of it!

On the other hand, if you were referred below the Hiring Manager, you not only lose your "referral bonus," you also greatly reduce the chances that you will ever reach the actual Hiring Manager. This is most often where the "you will have to contact Personnel" response comes in. So don't be intimidated if you are given a high-level contact. Instead, treat it as a wonderful gift and spend it wisely.

THE CHAINING TECHNIQUE

If your network contacts are only one layer deep, you are missing an excellent opportunity to expand your network exponentially. How? By using the same method as successful multilevel marketing—don't just sell your product, sell others on selling your product. Simply put, instead of just updating your contacts as to your situation, ask them to pass on the information to anyone else they feel could help you. You continue to chain from one contact to another as your network continues to expand.

> IT'S NOT ABOUT WHO YOU KNOW. IT'S WHO THEY KNOW.

As you regularly keep in touch with your contacts, ask them if there are other people you should be contacting. When they inform you of these others, give them a call directly. This will include second-, third-, fourth-level contacts and beyond as direct first-line contacts. When you contact next-level contacts, send them five copies of your resume and ask them to pass your resume along to those who may be able to help you further in your job search. Let them know that you will be getting back in touch with them after a week or two, then contact them to gather in the names of the people they have passed your resume along to. Start the process over again with each new person and you will have a nearly continuously expanding network of potential contacts. Following this simple chaining technique will grow your network far beyond your immediate circle of contacts.

THE BIRD DOG TECHNIQUE

Similar to the Chaining Technique, the Bird Dog Technique is especially well suited for those network contacts who are unable to help you at the first level, yet are willing to put in an extra effort on your behalf. Aunt Mabel would probably be a good example. Ask these network contacts to reach out and do some work for you. It may include pulling the want ads in your local newspaper. Or contacting the local chamber of commerce. Or doing some library research. Or even some basic phone calls. This technique is especially important if distance is a factor in your job search. If you have a local "bird dog" who can sniff out and track down opportunities for you on your behalf, you will have gained a valuable scout in your job search battle plan.

> "PLEASE" GOES A LONG WAY IN A JOB SEARCH.

Bird dogs are most likely to be friends and family members, since it requires asking a personal favor for them to fill this role. Explain what your specific needs are in the early stages of your job search and what they should keep their eyes and ears open for, then ask for their continued assistance as your job search develops. They will usually be more than happy to help (assuming you have been a good friend/neighbor/nephew/etc.), and it will give them an opportunity to provide you with valuable assistance in your job search. But a note of caution: do not use this technique as a crutch to get others to do your work for you. This technique is to be used as an extension to reach into a marketplace that you cannot reach due to personal constraints. Don't abuse the privilege.

THE NETWORKING BUSINESS CARD TECHNIQUE

One of the difficulties in making introductions at the entry level is that you lack the standard "business card introduction" that most businesspeople rely upon. However, there is a valid alternative for the entry level job seeker—the Networking Business Card.

Before attending job fairs or business association meetings, you may want to develop your own personal Networking Business Card. You will have ready information to hand out to any contact at any time when making an introduction. Networking Business Cards are different from standard business cards in that they provide information about you independent of a particular employer. They are ideally suited for the entry level.

A Networking Business Card gives you a distinct competitive edge in the entry level job market. Why? Because virtually none of the other grads have a business card yet. Why would they? We usually receive our first business card along with our first professional job. But as you will see, the Networking Business Card can be vitally important in your search for that first job.

Have your information printed in the standard business card size (3½" wide by 2" high), but with the following "kicker" format:

Your name
Description of your target career interest
Home street address
City, state, zip
Phone number or fax phone—if you have one

The "kicker" is the second line, which can provide descriptive information, such as "Unix Systems Specialist," or specific job search information such as "Seeking Retail Management Position," or other "Seeking..."

information. This line replaces the standard title line on most business cards, and stands out in the eyes of the receiver.

> BUSINESS CARDS PROVIDE YOU WITH AN ASSUMED LEVEL OF RANK AND STATUS IN THE WORLD OF WORK.

You can develop this card format using a business card template with most of the major word processors (Word, WordPerfect, WordPro) and a laser printer. You can also have them printed for you at Kinko's (they can set it up for you) or other print shop. Or you can also order business cards directly from Artistic Greetings of Elmira, NY, which offers a low-cost business card (they refer to them as "Calling Cards") for the price of $9.95 for 200 (or $14.95 for 400) cards (plus $1.50 S&H) for a six-line card (I like their classic #3923 style) with a limit of 28 letters and spaces per line. You may contact them at: Artistic Greetings, Inc., One Artistic Plaza, Elmira, NY 14925.

THE MINI-RESUME CARD TECHNIQUE

The Mini-Resume Card is similar to the Networking Business Card in that it is contained within a standard business card size using the same format on the front (name, "kicker," home address, city, state, zip, and phone numbers). But the back side of the card becomes a "mini-resume" in that it provides a summary of the high points of your resume. It is comparable to the Summary section of the resume. Don't feel you have to be comprehensive-this is just a "hook" to get a potential employer interested.

Networking Business Cards and Mini-Resume Cards are an outstanding technique that will get you noticed, and they have an additional advantage in that they are often filed differently from other job search materials. While resumes often get locked away in the "applicant vault" and may never again see the light of day, business cards are often placed in Rolodexes or business card folders, or are even entered into contact databases. Their uniqueness is part of their appeal. Once you have them, you will wonder how you ever marketed yourself without them!

YOUR VERY BEST PERSONAL CONTACTS

Ironically, your very best network contacts are sitting there with you every day, in class, at lunch, even in the library. Your best network contacts are other students who are also in your major and seeking jobs in your field. If they are truly active in their job search, they will have access to additional first-line contacts that can greatly benefit you. The relationship should be one of give and take, so that you are also providing them with networking contact information.

Be sure to ask who they are contacting and what kinds of results they are getting. Find out if there are any companies on their list that you have missed. There can often be a great synergy among students who have worked together for the past several years. They may be seeking another geographical area and are happy to pass on their leads in the areas you are interested in. You may be seeking jobs in a particular industry and are happy to pass on leads in the other industries to them. Some students have even organized informal job search groups to provide net-

> YOUR COMPETITION CAN ALSO BE YOUR GREATEST ALLY.

working support on campus. If there isn't a job networking group (either formal or informal) organized on your campus, put a bulletin board up on your wall, offer a beer to all those who stop in with "Hot Tips for Job Seekers," and watch your board (and your social life) fill to the max. Your Job Search Central may indeed become Job Search Central for many others.

YOUR SECOND-BEST PERSONAL CONTACTS

The next best network contacts are also close to home—all your friends who graduated last semester or last year. These are college grads who have (hopefully) just completed their successful job search. Unless they burned or buried their notes when the job offer came through, they probably have scores of potential contacts whom they worked long and hard to dig up. Think of it as using last year's chemistry final to prep for this year's final. They have all the "class notes" that will get you off to a quick start. In addition, they are

> JOB SEARCH IS A GREAT EXCUSE TO CALL UP ALL YOUR FRIENDS WHO GRADUATED LAST YEAR.

often well placed in the field and can give you insider support like no one else.

While it can be difficult to locate your old friends after graduation, you can probably locate them through the Alumni Office. If that fails, try to locate them through their old home address (Mom and/or Dad). Or send them a letter first class to their old campus address. If it is within one year and they gave the post office their forwarding address, your letter will reach them by mail forwarding, or it might be returned to you undelivered with their new address stamped on the outside of the envelope.

THE APPLE ON THE DESK TECHNIQUE

As previously stated, many professors are poorly connected with the work world outside campus. However, there are two types of professors who have impressive external contacts, some of which you may not be aware of at all. But you should be.

Remember the apple on the desk routine that some kids went through back in second grade? Well, that technique of endearing oneself to the teacher may have lost some of its luster in the collegiate world, but its value has not diminished. There are several professors right there on your campus who are able to help you tremendously in your job search if you are willing to reach out to them.

The first type of professor network contact is the Company Connection professor. This professor usually is a department head or teaches some of the required courses for final year students. The professor may teach the capstone class for the major or may be involved in career advisement within the major. The key is that companies (such as ours) will target this professor as their campus connection, the one who will steer them to the "prize students" and, as appropriate, steer the prize students to them (us). Companies such as Keane, Andersen, and others spend a great deal of time and energy cultivating this relationship. It may be with more than one professor on larger campuses, but at some campuses all students are required to go through a particular professor's capstone class. And that professor usually has an excellent feel for who will be the outstanding hires from this year's graduating class.

The other type of professor who can assist greatly in your job search is the Company Consultant professor who spends time consulting with outside companies. Ever notice how vacant the campus becomes during summer? Where do you think most professors go? Off to terrorize nine-year-olds as a counselor at some backwoods summer camp? Unlikely. Most are either doing further academic work or are consulting with businesses. Those who are consulting are likely to be very well connected. And they are often willing and able to help those students who seek out their assistance in job search.

So if you thought that your profs were just a sideline aggravation on your way to your future goal of work, you may want to reconsider your teacher-student relationships. You are being evaluated from the moment you set foot on that campus. All of your contacts can be potentially helpful or potentially damaging. Treat all people with common courtesy and respect. And it does not hurt to put an apple on the desk (figuratively) of the professors who teach the final year classes. Most professors develop a personal relationship with less than 10 percent of their students. Please include yourself in that

10 percent with all of your professors, especially those who are well connected. Developing this personal relationship is as simple as stopping by their office during open office hours. Attempt to learn more about the subject than that which is offered up in class. Attempt to internalize the classroom information so that you can better understand its practical work world application. And attempt to develop a rela-

> YES, PROFESSORS CAN HELP YOU IN YOUR JOB SEARCH. BUT YOU MUST MAKE THE FIRST MOVE.

tionship with your professor above and beyond the lecturer/notetaker passive model many students accept as the norm—not just as a selfish ambition for using the professor in your job search, but because you sincerely want to learn more about the subject and the profession.

This contact alone could pay off enormous dividends in your job search. Yet that is merely a by-product of your taking the time to develop a personal relationship with your professor. If you do so, you will greatly benefit. But it is up to you to make the first move. Your professors will not come looking for you. You must go looking for them.

YOUR VERY BEST PROFESSIONAL CONTACTS

They are out there. They are well placed in industry. They have never met you before. Yet they are ready and willing to help you find your first job.

Who are they? Alumni—probably the most underutilized contacts a college grad can have, yet also the most valuable. Why alumni? Because they meet all of the key criteria for becoming a top-notch network contact. They are often working in professional-level positions with employers you would have an interest in (especially if they graduated in the same degree program). They have knowledge about your background since they graduated from the same college (some things never change). And they are willing to help you in your job search. A recent survey showed that more than 90 percent of active alums are willing to help new grads from their alma mater.

So the key is to find active alums. Where? The Alumni Office. Your Career Development office might also have a listing of alumni who are willing to work with new grads, but don't limit yourself to that listing. Most Alumni Offices have the basic search capabilities to locate alums far above the abbreviated listing that may exist in the Career Development office. Make sure you take the time to use this valuable resource.

> ALUMNI HAVE A BOND WITH YOU THAT CAN HELP YOU TO SUCCEED IN FINDING A GREAT JOB.

First, search for alums who are working in your chosen field. Next, search for alums who are working at any specific companies you have targeted, regardless of position. Next, search for alums that are in your targeted geographical area. You might get some grumbling from the administrative person in the Alumni Office responsible for doing these searches, but push until you get all the information you need. If you are not getting any results, remind this person that you will be an alum in just a few months and that you would have a lot more interest in becoming a contributing alum if you were actually making some money. If the person still fails to get the point and remains unwilling to help, ask to speak with the Director of Alumni Affairs, who will almost always see to it that you get the information you need.

What to do with these names once you get them? Contact each and every one by phone and then follow up by letter. Set up face-to-face meetings whenever possible. Bring these alums into your circle of contacts and make it personal! If there are local chapters of the Alumni Association in the city or area you are targeting, find out when their meetings are and ask if you can attend. This is networking paradise! Help them to get to know you (the only "unknown" in the entire equation) so that they can help you more effectively. Believe me, you will be amazed at the positive results.

PROFESSIONAL CONTACTS IN YOUR OWN BACKYARD

During the course of your college career, you have undoubtedly been exposed to a variety of professionals who have come to campus for one reason or another. Most common are the professionals who guest lecture in classes. Or the professionals who give presentations to clubs. Or the professionals who give lectures before the student body.

Did you take good notes? Do you know their names, what company they are with, and where they are located? If so, now is the time to track them down! If not, trace back to the original contact who arranged their campus visit and ask for contact information. Then call them up to inform them of your job search. Let them know that you remembered them and the information they provided when they were on campus. Let them know that you are now ready to enter the field. Ask them for their list of the top five companies you should contact. Be sure to include them as part of your personal network by sending them a copy of your resume and asking for their critique. By keeping in close contact with these industry movers and shakers, you will have an "in" that very few others have tapped into.

THE NETWORKING BY ASSOCIATION TECHNIQUE

Association networking is a popular way to establish truly valuable network contacts among professionals, yet very few entry level candidates make use of this available resource. If there is an association for your chosen profession, find out if you can join as a student member in the local chapter (not the student chapter) in the city you are most interested in living in after graduation. The membership dues are often reduced for student members, and most associations strongly encourage student participation. Note: don't just join the student chapter on campus. Make sure you are a member of the local association chapter.

After you have joined, you will usually be given a membership directory. If not, call and ask for one. This membership directory can be worth its weight in gold to you since it is the "who's who" of your field for that local area. As a start, call the Membership Director (or Coordinator or Chairperson) and ask for recommendations of people within the association whom you can speak to about seeking entry level jobs in the local area. You will usually be given the name of a well-connected member who is willing to refer you to others or who may even be willing to help you personally. You now have an outstanding contact who can serve as a starting point for further contacts.

> THAT PERSON WHO SPOKE ON CAMPUS MAY BE YOUR DIRECT CONNECTION TO YOUR FUTURE EMPLOYER.

When you speak with this contact person, make it clear that you are a student member of the association and are seeking help in locating entry level employment. Most association members feel a professional obligation toward helping others get started in the field. You often will be given the names of companies and other individuals to contact. Or the person may offer to contact them on your behalf. Either way, you now have a "warm call" instead of a "cold call" into prime hiring companies in your target geographical area.

If you are nearby or plan a trip to the area, make it a point to attend one of the association's meetings. Most meet on a monthly or bimonthly basis. These meetings are a networking contact dream! Walking, talking, living, breathing contacts. All in your field. All in one room. And all willing to help you in your job search. Remember to have plenty of Networking Business Cards in your pocket—you will need them. But use them only at or near the end of a conversation. If you just walk around handing them out, you will likely get the quick boot—figuratively, or possibly even literally. When you do give out your card, don't be shy in asking for one of theirs.

When you are at this type of gathering, carry a small notepad so you can record the information from your many conversations. While it is acceptable to record specific information being supplied during a conversation (such as when a contact gives you a phone number to call), remember to follow this simple etiquette rule: if you want to write notes about the person you are talking with, do it later; if you want to write notes about another person (such as the name, title, and company of a recommended contact), you may do so during the conversation. It is still important to take notes on each person you speak with for later reference. Just make mental notes, and then retreat to a corner or pop out to the restroom to "download" when you reach your point of information overload. An excellent place to record information is directly on the person's business card, if you are offered one—if not, remember to ask for one. If you forgot to get that all-important business card, be sure to make good notes in your notepad, including the person's title and company name. Trust nothing to memory.

> IF THERE IS AN ASSOCIATION FOR YOUR CHOSEN PROFESSION, JOIN IT. IF THERE ARE TWO, JOIN THEM BOTH. IF THERE ARE THREE, JOIN ALL THREE. BE A JOINER.

If you are prone to forgetting a person's name, get in the habit of asking people to repeat their names to you and ask for a spelling if it is an uncommon or unusual name. Asking the person to repeat their name is a very common name memory technique which also serves as a compliment to the person, since you are telling them that you consider their name important enough to remember. It is an excellent way to make a positive first impression.

Follow up on all contacts made at such meetings with a phone call or letter. Again, it will broaden your network exponentially since nearly all the people you meet are connected to others who are able to help.

Don't forget your association membership directory. It can provide you with a series of warm calls in tracking down potential employers. Be sure to mention you are a student member of the association—it's an instant icebreaker!

THE NETWORKER'S NETWORKING TECHNIQUE

There are certain people who have jobs that are dependent upon networking for survival. These include stockbrokers, bankers, real estate agents, insurance agents, even barbers—all are dependent upon personal networks for their livelihood. If you have a personal relationship with someone in one of these or some other sales-oriented profession, ask if they will tap into their personal network to assist you in your job search.

Our company recently hired an individual from out of town who had originally contacted a real estate agent our company works with on relocations. The real estate agent was aware of our hiring needs and referred the person to our office. The networking link between candidate and employer had come from a third party. Yet the real estate agent will also benefit, since the new employee is now her dedicated lifetime customer and part of her network of contacts for future business.

Is the networking concept starting to sink in? In practice, it can be extremely powerful. The business world is like a large web, with many interconnecting parts. You may not always know where each part connects in, but you do know that there are many more connections from there. Your job is to tap in to the initial connections.

TAPPING IN TO THE POLITICAL NETWORK

Want to have some fun with networking? Contact the state senator, state representative, or U.S. representative for your chosen geographical area. Now here are people who are truly well connected! If they know that a potential voter is going to be in their area, they will usually "oblige you ever so kindly" by giving you several business leads to tap into. If you happen to be active in a Young Republicans or Young Democrats group, that is an additional plus in your favor (assuming you are in the "right" camp). If you actually did volunteer campaign work for a politician, now is the time to cash in your chips. Yet no matter what your political affiliation, you will always be a valuable political connection to the politician.

> SOME PEOPLE NETWORK FOR A LIVING. TAP INTO THE POWER OF THEIR NETWORK.

Politicians are not likely to be continuous contacts, but if you use the following line with them, it is almost guaranteed to generate strong, one-time results:

"As I was making calls to others and asking for referrals to hiring companies, it suddenly dawned on me—you, Mr./Ms. Politician, are probably the most knowledgeable person in our entire district on the subject of jobs. I would certainly appreciate any recommendations regarding employers that might have work in the _____ area."

Guaranteed results! What politician would admit they are not the most knowledgeable person when it comes to jobs in their district? In addition, you may end up with referrals at some of the highest levels within the company (often CEO/President/VP level), which always works well when making your initial contact (see "The Law of Network Gravity" mentioned earlier).

Also, be sure to mention the name of the politician who referred you when you make the contact. Many of these businesspeople owe "political favors" to the politicians and are more willing to help you when the politician's name is dropped.

Even if you do not get through to the actual politicians directly, you will likely find someone on their staff who can assist you. Many modern politicians have assumed the role of ultimate consumer advocates and have staffs ready to assist you in every facet of life. Do not be intimidated by the fact that most politicians will be caught off guard by this approach—it is rather unique and you may be the very first person to make such a request of them. Remember, their life is totally devoted to serving their loyal constituents, right? Your tax dollars at work!

USING EMPLOYMENT AGENCIES SUCCESSFULLY

While employment agencies tend to be fairly well connected, they are often difficult to work with at the entry level. Before you even consider working with an employment agency, you need to understand the different types and how to approach each one.

➤ **Executive/Retained Search and/or Executive Recruiters**
These firms are paid by their company clients either by retainer or on a per assignment basis. They work primarily at the line management level and above, which is usually $80,000 plus. They tend to be a rather elitist group that proudly turns away all candidate inquiries with the "Don't call us . . . " line. The reality is that they make careful note of everyone they come in contact with since they are "networkers extraordinaire."
How to approach — realizing there is absolutely nothing they can do for you professionally, many firms are nonetheless willing to give out free advice in the form of company referrals. Just ask who their "Top Five" would be for you to contact, and then ask if they can give you the names of contacts at each of these companies. It's a short

phone call, but can be very productive, as this group is usually the best connected in the field.

➤ **Employment Agencies - Contingency Employer-Paid**
These firms work in fields all the way from clerical to technical to line management and sometimes above. There can often be as many as ten different contingency firms working on the same assignment, and only one will get paid—by the employer that hires the employee—so there is a tendency toward very aggressive tactics. Although they are well connected, most are not willing to work with you professionally until you have at least one year of experience. Why? Simply put, companies do not have to pay a fee to find an entry level candidate—they are free, immediately available, in abundance, and easily located. It sounds like a meat market, but you really do not have any value for most employment agencies until you have at least one year (or more) of experience beyond college.
How to approach — contact those companies that work in your field, especially those that specialize in your field. Attempt to set up an interview, even if you are told they will not be able to help you. Often they will either give you company referrals or refer you directly to their clients as a free service. Emphasize to them that in just one year you will have real work experience and if they can help you get in the door, you will be eternally grateful. Again, ask for their "Top Five" and who to contact at each company.

➤ **Employment Agencies - Contingency Applicant-Paid**
These firms are often restricted or outlawed altogether, depending on the state. They work primarily at lower levels, including the entry level. They are paid a fee by you if they successfully place you in a job. The fee is usually a percentage of the first year's salary, anywhere from 10 to 25 percent. The fee can often be as much as $5000 or more. Yes, that is a lot of money, so it is common for them to offer you time payment plans and other methods of "creative financing."
How to approach — don't. Unless you are willing to pay thousands of dollars to someone else for what you can do yourself, you are best advised to steer clear.

➤ **Employment Consultants - Fee-Based Applicant-Paid**
The recent waves of unemployment that are hitting the country have brought more and more of these firms out of the woodwork. They offer services ranging from career counseling to testing to resume writing to job search assistance to anything else they think they can get paid for. The cost usually ranges from $250 to more than $5,000. There is no guarantee of the end result. They are just playing on your lack of security in trying to find a job.
How to approach — don't. It is a waste of your time and money. Most of the services they offer in career planning are available for

free or very little cost right there on your own campus. As for the job search skills they claim they can teach you, keep in mind that you are currently holding a book that goes far beyond their cookie cutter strategies. Just studying the strategies in this book will take you further than anything they can dangle in front of you. Besides, I am not trying to get my fingers into your wallet—they are. I must admit, though, that there is one thing that these "counselors" are quite good at—finding new reasons for you to give them more money. Save your bucks.

➤ **Temporary Help Agencies**
These firms are vastly different from the "Kelly Girl" days of decades past. Today they work in many technical and professional fields. And they are often very willing to work with someone with little or no experience. They usually charge their client a markup of anywhere from 40 to 100 percent of what they pay the employee. Some of the technical contracting firms mark up as much as 150 percent. The assignments can vary from one day to one year or more. Quite often a temporary assignment can blossom into longer-term assignments or possibly even offers for permanent employment by the client.

How to approach — unless you want to put in some part-time hours while you are still attending school (which is an excellent way to gather valuable experience), wait until two weeks before graduation to contact these agencies. Most of their assignments turn over in less than forty-eight hours, so early contact would do little good. They are not very interested in giving out client information since they would like to work with you after graduation. If you reach graduation without a job, this is an excellent alternative to unemployment. Most will allow you to continue your search for permanent employment, including some measure of flexibility in scheduling any interviews you might have.

Chapter 9

EMPLOYER RESEARCH STRATEGIES

What is success?
I think it is a mixture of having a flair for the thing that you are doing;
knowing that it is not enough,
that you have got to have hard work and a certain sense of purpose.
—Margaret Thatcher

And you thought your library days were over! In reality, if you are good at mining the mountains of information to find the nuggets of gold, it will pay off handsomely in your job search and in your future career! Consider the fact that your future career may lie with a company you have never heard of before. You will find that company through your research.

Utilizing your research skills can provide you with a nearly continuous flow of information that others do not have access to. Yet it is not enough just to find the information. You need to put it to work for you. For example, right now you are reading an insider book that very few other college grads have access to. Are you using all of the information in this book to its fullest degree? Don't just read this book and think to yourself, "That's interesting. I bet that would work." It will not work until you put it into action!

> IT IS LIKELY THAT YOU HAVE NOT YET HEARD THE NAME OF YOUR FUTURE EMPLOYER.

One critical aspect of job search preparation that can truly set you apart is employer research. Employer research is what brings you together and keeps you together with those who have the power and authority to offer you your first position.

Employer research serves a dual purpose. First, you need to identify and target specific hiring companies in your job search. Second, you need to gather detailed information about each target employer in order to be adequately prepared for making direct contact. While the research guides provide the basic information that will give you a broad overview, it is the detailed information that will set you apart from the crowd.

Sadly, most college students know little if anything about the employer they are contacting or even interviewing with. The quickest show-stopper can come when I ask (whether on the phone or in person), "What do you know about our company?" If you have not even taken the time to do this basic research, why should I commit a segment of my busy day to speaking with you? Unfortunately, few are able to respond with even the basics. Strike one. Fewer still are able to articulate any information specific to our company. Strike two.

But it doesn't have to be that way. Employer information, even detailed information, is usually available for the price of some simple digging. It's out there waiting for you to discover it and bring it to the surface. The end of the interview is not the time or place to gather employer information. If you are serious about your job search, do your best to acquire detailed employer information before you make contact with the company or its representatives. It is those who are well informed from the start who consistently are given the opportunity for company-site interviews and eventual job offers.

Job search is a two-way street. Don't just go begging for any job. Doing detailed research on each potential employer will assist you in better understanding which companies you may have an interest in working for. And it will give you the ammunition you need to be successful in securing a job offer from the employer of your choice.

The source locations where employer information can be found include (in order of ease of access): your campus Career Development office, campus library, public library, and direct company contact.

THE VERY BEST HARD COPY RESEARCH GUIDES

Following are some of the best hard copy (print) research guides, listed along with their strengths and limitations. Remember that with hard copy sources, the timeliness of information is critical. Information can often be dated even at the time of printing, so keep in mind the importance of utilizing the most current version of the particular resource. Also, some resources are geared toward target audiences and segments, so utilize those that apply to your specific situation and needs.

➤ **Job Opportunities in _____**
   Petersen's Guides, P.O. Box 2123, Princeton, NJ 08543
   800-338-3282

Petersen's has three different versions of this popular guide: one for business, one for engineering and technology, and one for health care. They include detailed information supplied by actual employers (and therefore subject to the employers' bias), including address information, phone numbers, a general company profile, estimated entry level hires for the coming year, which majors they typically hire, and a contact person (usually Human Resources, since they are the ones supplying the information to Petersen's). Companies are listed alphabetically, with industry and location indexes located in the back of the guide. Excellent information, although the limited number of companies keeps it from being a truly comprehensive listing. This is a great guide if the company you are looking for is in there. If not, you will have to dig elsewhere. It is also excellent as a starting point for deciding which companies you may want to initially pursue. If your vocational objective falls into one of the three broad categories listed above, this is a great place to start your research. It is usually available through your Career Development office or campus library.

➤ **Professional's Job Finder**
Non-Profits & Education Job Finder
Government Job Finder
International Job Finder
Planning/Communications, 7215
Oak Ave., River Forest, IL 60305
708-366-5200
Not sure where to start in your networking? These books are pure networking nirvana, with instant access to your target market. They include listings of job hotlines, job matching services, specialty and trade publications, on-line job services, computerized job and resume databases, salary surveys, and directories of all types. If you can't find it here, you are not really looking.

➤ **The National Job Bank**
Adams Media Corporation, 260 Center St., Holbrook, MA 02343
800-872-5627
Includes information on more than twenty thousand employers, including address, main phone number, and name and title of the contact person (although usually in Human Resources). Very detailed listing of product line and typical positions at each location. Sorted alphabetically within each state with a separate industry cross-index in the back of the book. The publisher also prints several "city" editions which are updated yearly. You will probably find these to be more valuable than the national edition if you are targeting any one of the covered areas, since the information is more comprehensive. Current city editions include Atlanta, Austin/San Antonio, Boston, Carolina, Chicago, Cincinnati, Cleveland, Dallas/Fort Worth, Denver,

Detroit, Florida, Houston, Indianapolis, Las Vegas, Los Angeles, Minneapolis/St. Paul, Missouri, New Mexico, Northern New England, Metropolitan New York, Upstate New York, Greater Philadelphia, Phoenix, Pittsburgh, Portland, Salt Lake City, San Francisco Bay Area, Seattle, Tennessee, Virginia, Metropolitan Washington, D.C., and Wisconsin.

➤ **Job Seeker's Guide to Private and Public Companies**
Gale Research, Inc., Book Tower, Detroit, MI 48266
313-961-2242
Comes in four volumes: West, Midwest, Northeast, South/Mid-Atlantic/Great Plains. Contains basic address information, phone number, fax number, number of employees, years in business, type of company, business description, annual sales, and Human Resources contact. This resource is fine for locating the basic information on the company, but not much beyond the basics. The format is geared toward the general job market, not the entry level market specifically.

➤ **The Corporate Yellow Book**
Leadership Directories, 104 Fifth Ave., New York, NY 10011
212-627-4140
Provides an excellent listing of the management of the largest eleven hundred companies in the United States, often down to specific department managers. A good basic source of major players—just make sure the edition you are working with is current since the key players are often in constant rotation.

➤ **The Career Guide: Dun's Employment Opportunities Directory**
Dun & Bradstreet, 99 Church St., New York, NY 10014
Provides an alphabetical listing of employers along with a list of educational and experience backgrounds typically hired. Also includes an index of employers by industry, geography, and job disciplines hired.

➤ **Directory of American Firms Operating in Foreign Countries**
Uniworld Business Publications, 50 East 42nd St., New York, NY 10017
If you are thinking of working overseas, make sure you gain access to this directory. Plain and simple, your odds of finding employment are much higher with an American firm that has overseas operations than with foreign companies. This guide is your starting point. Information is sorted by country and includes multiple listings of those companies that operate in multiple foreign countries. Most listings are rather brief, but provide you with the basic information you need to get started, including both foreign and domestic addresses. Do not even consider an international search without this guide.

➤ **Encyclopedia of Associations**
Gale Research, Inc., Book Tower, Detroit, MI 48266
313-961-2242
If you are trying to find an association or organization in your chosen occupation or industry, this is the book to use. Includes more than fourteen thousand national and international organizations of all sizes and types. Useful in establishing contact with associations that may benefit you in your job search.

➤ **How to Find Information about Companies**
Washington Researchers Publishing, 2612 P St. NW,
Washington, DC 20007
202-333-3533
If you get stumped with any of the above reference guides, this one will lead you down paths hitherto unexplored. This is the company research guide, giving you information on ways to get information when all else fails. It takes extra time to work with, but if you really need to know, you need to know this book.

If you are seeking only general company information, two additional directories—*Standard and Poor's Register of Corporations* and *Dun & Bradstreet's Million Dollar Directory*—have the basic address information, financial information, and top corporate officers, but little else. However, there is information on companies located here that you might not find elsewhere.

If you cannot find one of the above directories at your campus library on the checkout shelves, make sure you look in the Reference section. These are large, expensive directories that are usually not available for checkout. Expect to plunk down several bucks at the copy machine to gather information for later use back at Job Search Central. If your library does not carry the guide, ask if a copy can be located through interlibrary loan.

> "WHAT DO YOU KNOW ABOUT OUR COMPANY?" SHOULD BE THE EASIEST QUESTION FOR YOU TO ANSWER. IT SHOWS ME WHETHER OR NOT YOU HAVE DONE YOUR HOMEWORK.

THE VERY BEST CD-ROM RESEARCH GUIDES
The availability of electronic research guides has grown substantially in the past several years. These electronic resources are often underutilized by most college students, often due to lack of awareness. Look through the following list and

check into the availability of the resources through your Career Development office or campus library:

➤ **Career Search on CD-ROM**
Career Search, 21 Highland Ave., Needham, MA 02194
617-449-0312
Although a relatively new product, Career Search is the most compre-hensive and targeted database search product on the market today. It contains over two hundred thousand companies—large, medium, and small—with over four thousand industry selections. In addition, it is designed specifically for entry level jobs. The information is complete, accurate, and fairly up to date. The only real drawback is the high price tag, which limits the number of Career Development offices and libraries that utilize it at this time. Check with your Career Develop-ment office or campus library to see if they have it. If not, call Career Search to find out if there is another college nearby that has it—you might be able to access that copy.

➤ **D&B Marketplace on CD-ROM**
Dun & Bradstreet, 460 Totten Pond Road, Waltham, MA 02154
617-672-9200
D&B Marketplace has over ten million companies that can be searched by a variety of criteria, including type of business, Stan-dard Industrial Classification (SIC) codes, geographical area, and number of employees. Each record contains the business name, year started, address, city, state, ZIP+4, county, metro area, phone numbers, type of business, business ranking, number of em-ployees, and key executives. The information is primarily gener-ated through the Dun & Bradstreet listings. This CD is usually a popular item in libraries with large CD-ROM collections.

➤ **Business Periodicals Index (BPI)**
H.W. Wilson Company, 950 University Ave., Bronx, NY 10452
800-367-6770 or in NY 800-462-6060
BPI is available on-line, on CD-ROM, and in hard copy format. It serves as an index of articles in other publications, much like the *Reader's Guide To Periodical Literature*. Although it is much more comprehensive than most on-line services (with combined information from over three hundred periodicals), you still need to dig up the actual periodical for the full article, whereas many on-line services save you that step with the information available directly. It also includes basic company infor-mation above and beyond its listings of available articles.

➤ **Internet-based Employer Information**
The internet (and specifically the Web) has greatly increased public access to employer information, with many companies ded-icatimg entire sections of their corporate Website to job related in-formation. For the inside scoop on accessing this information,

please see "The Search Engine Research Technique" in the Internet Job Search Strategies Chapter.

THE WORLD'S LARGEST LIST OF POTENTIAL EMPLOYERS

The Yellow Pages. It may not seem very scientific, but if you are targeting a specific geography and a specific industry, product, or service, the Yellow Pages may serve you well as a potential resource. But don't be swayed by the size of the ads. Often, some of the very best companies do very little advertising. The most important point is the listing. Beyond that, you will have to do further digging to fill in the details.

THE VERY BEST SOURCE OF EMPLOYER INFORMATION

There is one source of employer information that is usually easily obtainable and unsurpassed in value: the annual report. Why? Because the annual report contains that marvelous insider report known as the "Letter to the Shareholders" written by the President or CEO. This letter catalogues not only the history of the past year, but even more important, the company vision for the future. Therein is contained all the insider information on what is important to the company; the insider information on what managers are focused on for the coming year; the current buzzword in the company; and all of the insider "hot buttons" that you can push in getting the interview and getting the job.

In addition to the Letter to the Shareholders, you will also find information on principal lines of business, financial statements, principal suppliers/customers (often showcased), target markets, challenges/ difficulties, and the internal view of competitive advantage, past, present, and future. Truly insider information.

You may rightly ask: "Why do you call it insider information? This information is available to the public, right?" Right. But most people look at an annual report only if they are interested in stock ownership of the company, not if they are interested in the company as a potential employer. When the

> READ THE ANNUAL REPORT COVER TO COVER BEFORE YOUR FIRST INTERVIEW. YOU WILL HAVE A WEALTH OF INFORMATION TO DRAW FROM DURING THE INTERVIEW PROCESS.

information is used in the job search, it becomes insider information because you now know what is known only by people who are company insiders.

How to get one? Call the company's corporate office and ask for its Shareholder Services Department. Tell the appropriate person within that department that you are interested in the company and would appreciate a copy of the most recent annual report.

Key fact: your competition is not reading the annual report. Make sure you do. It will give you a distinct competitive edge.

THE SECOND-BEST SOURCE OF EMPLOYER INFORMATION

This resource is also valuable, yet can be more difficult to come by. Reason? Usually your only source for it is the Human Resources Department, and they tend to keep a rather firm lock on information. This source of information goes by a variety of names, but typically it is titled "Employment Opportunities with . . . " or something similar. Often this information is geared directly toward the entry level job market and lists the entry level jobs and corresponding departments (or business units).

Ironically, most students do not receive this valuable information until after their first interview with the company. Take the time to get the information ahead of time. Your campus Career Development office may have this information in its library, in which case all you need to do is make some copies. But if the information is not there (these materials have a tendency to sprout legs—make sure you make copies only if there are no extras), call the company directly, ask for the Human Resources Department, and use the following script with the very first person who answers (usually a secretary or receptionist in the department):

> "Hello, my name is _____. I am planning to interview with your company in the near future and would appreciate it if you could send me some information about your company so that I am better prepared for that interview. Can you help me?"

Unless you reached "Fraulein Frieda, Guardian of the Gate," the person will usually send you the information. Once they have agreed to supplying you with the basic information, feel free to ask for additional information. If you do happen to get shut down by Fraulein Frieda, read the information in the Getting Inside Hiring Companies chapter on how to get past her (or any other Guardian of the Gate).

THE THIRD-BEST SOURCE OF EMPLOYER INFORMATION

Although the above-noted documents can provide you with very detailed information, they are usually available only from larger companies. Yet nearly every organization has a third type of information that can assist you in your job search: marketing information. This is one type that is not usually available through public access, so it will require a direct call to the company. Ask for the Marketing Department, then ask if they would please send out some general marketing information about their company and its product line. Marketing people are usually more than happy to assist anyone who wants to know more about their company.

> DON'T WAIT UNTIL THE FIRST INTERVIEW TO FIND OUT ABOUT THE COMPANY. IF YOU DO, THERE MIGHT NOT BE A SECOND.

Why product information? Because most entry level interviewees are woefully ignorant of what a company actually "does for a living." For example, can you tell me what Dow Chemical produces? I know, "Dow helps you do great things." But what is their product line? Scrubbing bubbles? Is that it? When you take a look, the depth and breadth may surprise you.

Remember, the Marketing Department is the one department "authorized to blab" about the company. The information you are given from this department can often be quite comprehensive and available through no other source. If you find a friend within the Marketing Department, even one who will talk with you for just a few minutes about the company, you have found a true jewel.

An excellent question to ask a marketing person is:

"What gives your company its competitive edge in the marketplace?"

Most marketing people are well prepared for the question—they answer it every day, either directly or indirectly, with their customers. Let them know that you are potentially a "future customer" of the Marketing Department by virtue of your prospect for the interview. Let them know that if you do eventually get the job, you will do your best to support their department and their product line.

Astute marketers will understand that any customer, external or internal (even those who may be nothing more than "potentially future internal"), is a valuable resource to be cultivated. They will usually be more than happy to assist.

YOUR FRIENDLY NEIGHBORHOOD STOCKBROKER

If you are looking for an excellent source of "insider information" on companies, look no further than your friendly neighborhood stockbroker. I say "insider" because it is information that is not normally accessed by those who are seeking entry level positions.

You can handle this contact in one of three ways. First, if you are already an active investor (even if it is just a small amount), you likely already have full access to a qualified broker—they are your contact to lean on for information. If you are not personally associated with a stockbroker (few college students are), you might be able to leverage the relationship of your parents or your rich aunt or uncle. Otherwise, contact a broker and say exactly what you are doing—researching companies to find a potential future employer—but be sure to give the broker a hook for the future: "If you give me access to your knowledge and resources in helping me earn money, I will work with you once that money starts coming in." Almost any broker will see the promise of a potential future professional (who will soon have money) at their door and will be happy to work with you.

Note that you should contact a broker at a full-service firm (such as Merrill Lynch, Shearson Lehman, etc.) rather than a discount firm, since they have superior research departments and full access to company information. Also, it is usually best to contact a broker who is fully established in the business. The younger, more inexperienced brokers are often less willing to deal with someone who cannot produce money for them today. The best choice is to work with a recommendation from family or friends, especially if it is someone with a large account. If rich old Aunt Sally referred you, the broker has a commitment not only to you as a future customer, but also to Aunt Sally.

What do you ask for? Make sure you are specific—if you have a specific company you are researching, fine. If not, wait until you do. After asking for the specific company information, also ask the broker for their top five recommendations. If the company you are seeking information on is not publicly traded (such as Arthur Andersen), the research may be more difficult to obtain via the standard sources. Lest you receive only the financial numbers, always ask for general company information.

Don't be afraid to ask about recommendations (or lack thereof) for a specific company. If XYZ Company is very close to bankruptcy, it would be nice to know about it now rather than later. Although not a perfect corollary, the companies that perform best in the market are usually the best managed, and are also usually the best to work for. Not always the case, but fairly consistent. Poorly managed companies are highly likely to have poorly performing stocks.

When researching companies, remember that while many large companies are deluged with resumes and job inquiries, it is actually the medium-sized and smaller companies that are providing long-term job creation in this country. The traditional wisdom of working in the "security" of the big corporation no longer rings true. Often, the only security you will find will be generated by your personal accumulation of experience over time. The availability of opportunities for gaining that experience will generally be greater with small companies than with large ones.

Most smaller companies are much more accessible and penetrable than their larger counterparts. And many of these companies are able to make hiring decisions based on the quality of the individual, rather than on whether or not they have an opening in their entry level training program at that particular time.

So the next time you hear about a company you have never heard of before, consider it an opportunity to enter the fast-paced world of small company growth.

HOW TO USE THE NEWS TO YOUR ADVANTAGE

You are probably already scanning the newspapers and industry trade publications for information on people in your industry (if you are not, you should be). So the next time you see someone's "name in lights" you may want to clip the article, make a copy for your own files, then send the original newsprint to the person. Ironically, the higher up these executives are, the less likely they are to be aware of stories where their name appeared in print. Even if they are aware of the story, most will appreciate having an extra copy. And this is an excellent time to enclose one of your Networking Business Cards.

> PEOPLE LOVE TO SEE THEIR NAME IN PRINT. THEY LOVE IT EVEN MORE WHEN OTHERS SEE IT.

RESPONDING TO CLASSIFIED ADVERTISING

Why even bother with employment advertising? After all, isn't it just a waste of time? Yes, it can be, if used improperly. If all you do is scan for entry level jobs in your field, you will likely end up wasting your time. You are looking for the proverbial needle in the haystack. Even if you do find it, so have hundreds of others.

But employment ads go far beyond the occasional entry level listing that your eyes might happen to fall upon. Think about it. Where else can you find a full listing of companies that are actively hiring along with descriptions of the organization and what they think are their strongest benefits for potential employees? Nowhere else but the classifieds.

But don't expect to find an abundance of entry level positions advertised. That is not our purpose in scanning the classifieds. Our purpose is to locate hiring companies, possibly Hiring Managers, then work toward finding a potential entry level position within the organization.

First, you need to locate the right resource. If you have a specific geographical area (or areas) targeted, you should be subscribing to the major Sunday paper(s) for that area as your resource. In addition, if there is a national newspaper targeting your job type or industry (such as *Computerworld* for information systems, *EE Times* for electrical engineering, *The Wall Street Journal* for finance and accounting), make sure to include it on your subscription list. Yes, I said subscription list. With Sunday newspapers, make sure you tell them to include the classifieds since some papers will mail only the news sections if you are outside of their local area. In either case, ask for a student discount and a short subscription period (such as two to three months—you can always renew).

When scanning the ads, look first for entry level jobs in your field. It is unlikely you will ever find even one, but you might as well look. And if you see it, be there bright and early Monday morning (I don't care what the ad says about "mail your resume" and other such screens). Next, look for entry level jobs in other fields. Although they are hiring in a different field, they are hiring at the entry level. Next, look for experience-required jobs in your field, no matter how high the level is. These ads are often the most valuable to entry level candidates since they often list who the new hire will report to and what the responsibilities will be. It gives you plenty of ammunition for approaching the company. Last, use the ads for other positions as a research tool; they will give you further information about companies in the area. Always read the company description. Find something interesting? Find companies appropriate to your background? Include them in your list of companies to contact.

> THE WANT ADS WILL HAVE FEW ENTRY LEVEL JOBS, BUT A WEALTH OF JOB INFORMATION.

THE OLD IS NEW TECHNIQUE

When reviewing newspaper ads, often the best ad is an old ad. An ad that is two, three, or even four months old may provide your best opportunity for positive exposure. Remember, companies often run ads to replace employees who have left the company. Employees who have left were no longer entry level when they left (even if they began as entry level). They were experienced employees, so the company wants to replace them with other experienced workers. That is why you rarely (if ever) see ads for entry level positions.

So if after two or three months the company is still unsuccessful in replacing the person with an experienced person in the field, it may be time for the company to reconsider how it will fill the position. Entry level may be under consideration for the very first time in the process. Since virtually no one is still looking at the old ads, your competition is next to nil.

> OLD CLASSIFIED ADS ARE AN EXCELLENT SOURCE OF EMPLOYER INFORMATION.

Do not write the company to say that you are responding to the ad from last September. But do target your resume and cover letter toward summarizing your qualifications for filling the particular job. State that you "heard through the grapevine" that there might be a need for a _____ and that you will soon be available.

THE BEST RESPONSE TO A CLASSIFIED AD

The best is the Baby on the Doorstep Technique. Show up on their doorstep. For further details, see the Guerrilla Insider Techniques chapter later in this book. The ad said no phone calls, so you decided to communicate in person. What have you got to lose?

THE NEXT-BEST RESPONSE TO A CLASSIFIED AD

If your qualifications closely match those listed in a classified ad, consider sending your resume with a cover letter designed in a two-vertical-column format, with your qualifications summarized in the left column and the ad content (either retyped within your letter—preferred—or a paste-up of the actual ad) in the right column. Forget about other details for now and concentrate on what is in the ad. Remember that the person receiving a response to a classified ad is usually just a "gatekeeper" who screens out resumes based on the key requirements they have been given. If you show that you have those basic requirements, you are much more likely to get a positive response.

MONDAY IS MAGIC

If you are going to contact employers that have just run classified ads over the weekend, Monday is magic. All weekend they have been thinking about the position (I'm not kidding!) and how to fill it. If you are the solution, let them know right away. Even if they just ran an ad on Sunday, be ready to be their quick solution. Mailed resumes will not start arriving until at least Tuesday or Wednesday, so personal visits or well-placed phone calls will have virtually no competition. Employers that run ads usually have a position that needs to be filled now! And most employers that run ads would love to avoid the "resume onslaught" that awaits them later in the week.

THE LAST LISTED TECHNIQUE

If there are two or more contact names in the ad to choose from, always choose the last person as your choice for responding. We are creatures of habit, and we almost always choose the first name listed. While the first name listed may be inundated with mail and phone calls, second or third listed persons usually get few if any calls. So why do companies list more than one person? Vanity. There are two (or three or four) persons in the department and they all want their name in the paper. But usually only the first one is contacted. So if you choose the last name listed, you will be reaching a far more receptive in-basket and telephone than the one listed first.

HOW TO TURN BLIND BOX ADS INTO AN OUTSTANDING CONTACT

Believe it or not, classified ads with a "blind" post office box (POB), in which the ad does not give a company name, can be the very best ads to respond to. But don't mail your resume like the ad requests. Contact the company directly. Yes, I said directly. There is a very legal and very honest way to find out who the company is that owns the POB, and it will put you miles ahead of the competition. The next time you see an ad that has a POB, call that post office branch and say:

> "Can you please give me the name of the company that uses post office box ___?"

Fifty percent of the time you will get the answer just by asking this simple question; if not, continue with:

> "This company is soliciting directly from the public by a newspaper ad." Again, at least fifty percent will give you the information at this point; if not, continue with:

> "According to the Freedom of Information Act, the post office is required to give out the information on any company that uses a post

office box to solicit from the public. Can you please give me the name of the company and their address?"

Nearly all will give you the information at this point.

In reality, the Freedom of Information Act requires that you make a written or in-person request, so if the postal worker wants to be a stickler, you might be required to either mail in your request or supply it in person. But here is another secret. Most POB ads are placed with branch post offices, so call the main post office for your city first and ask: "Does the Freedom of Information Act require post offices to reveal the identity of companies that solicit from the public?" The correct answer should be "Yes." Then if the branch balks about giving you the information over the phone, just say: "The main post office downtown has already told me that the Freedom of Information Act requires that the information be given out." Watch how quickly they jump. And for the "toe-the-line" group (less than 2 percent) that will not give you the information over the phone, mail for the information or stop by personally. Stick with it and you will get 100 percent results.

Then contact the company directly. When you reach the Hiring Manager, simply state,

"I understand you're currently seeking to hire a _____. I believe I'm the person you're looking for."

Go on to state your background and abilities. Don't be surprised if the person is surprised that you are aware of the opening—even to the point of embarrassment! Many companies place POB ads thinking they are totally anonymous—in fact, many companies place the ads to replace existing employees. So if the question "How did you find out about the position?" comes up (it will), just say,

> **BLIND BOX ADS ARE OFTEN THE BEST AD LEADS TO TRACK DOWN AND RESPOND TO.**

"One of my network contacts informed me that your company was interested in hiring someone in this area." You don't need to reveal that this particular "network contact" works at the post office. The Hiring Manager will usually be fascinated that you are aware of their need. This is a great contact, since there is virtually no competition. Make the most of it!

P.S. If the ad is a blind newspaper box (i.e., replies must be sent to an address in care of the newspaper), it is generally impenetrable. Results with these ads are usually quite thin.

Chapter 10

INTERNET JOB SEARCH STRATEGIES

The voyage of discovery is not in looking for new landscapes,
but in looking with new eyes. —Anonymous

While the Internet has earned a well-deserved "Hype of the Decade" title for all its media coverage, job search has become established as one of the truly viable activities taking place on the Net. While most colleges have been wired into the Net for more than two decades, the rest of the world has only recently become aware of its existence. It is only in the past few years that the Net has come into widespread commercial usage. This spells good news for you, since most college students have more experience with the Net and have free (or nearly free) access to all that the Net has to offer. If you truly want to find a level playing field for your job search, the Internet is your stadium.

Note: this chapter is not meant to serve as an "Introduction to the Internet" or to provide you with information on how to gain initial access. It is assumed that you have full Internet access or can find access through a friend who is familiar with the technology required to make full use of this chapter. If you lack the knowledge, work with others who already have it. Doing so will give you a jump start on what could otherwise be a frustrating learning process. And keep in mind that Internet knowledge is an important competitive advantage that you can provide for a potential employer.

Also note that, while the information in this chapter is current as of print publication, much of it is probably already being changed and updated. To keep this information current, this entire chapter is available to you via the College Grad Job Hunter WebSite. The URL (Web address) for this chapter is:

http://www.collegegrad.com/jobs/internet.html

In addition to keeping the information in the chapter updated, all of the information contained in this chapter is hot-linked to the specific sites. So you can read the information about the sites as you directly connect via the hot links. Surf on over!

Keep in mind that the purpose of this chapter is to point you to only the best of the best. The Internet certainly has innumerable nooks and crannies where computer geeks can hide loads of useless information. If you searched long enough and hard enough, you could probably find a job in Podunk, Iowa, listed in some obscure Usenet discussion area. But the truly productive and efficient areas are few, yet rich in resources waiting to be mined. They include:

WEBSITES

➤ *College Grad Job Hunter* (http://www.collegegrad.com) — our Website is the only site in this listing that is designed as a hub site. You are given the opportunity to hub to any and all of the listed sites in this chapter through a variety of hot links, plus additional job search information you won't find anywhere else on the Web. There is also a job search forum, recent articles from my *Job Hunter* syndicated column, and job postings from some of the nation's largest employers. Plus information on resumes, cover letters, networking, interviewing, offer negotiation, and more. It's designed to provide one-stop job search shopping for college students and recent grads. Make it your first visit and bookmark it as your hub to all the best that the Web has to offer. And if your college Website does not yet have a link to our site, I would greatly appreciate it if you would put in a request for a link. We're here to help.

➤ *Online Career Center* (http://www.occ.com) — OCC was one of the first career sites on the Web and continues to provide excellent links to jobs and employers through their simple, no-frills interface. You can keyword search all job postings (about fifty thousand), or view them by industry, city/state, or alphabetically by employer. OCC also provides a job seeker agent, which allows you to enter a profile on the type of position you are seeking. When an employer posts a job meeting your criteria, you will be directly informed via e-mail. You can also post your resume for free and make it available to all who are interested (remember-entry level is not a time to be shy or overly confidential). Send your resume in either text format (ASCII format with lines no more than 65 characters each, with a hard carriage return at the end of each line) or HTML (Web) format to **occ-resumes@occ.com** with the subject line giving your one-line tease about your background/summary/skills, and the text of your resume in the body of the message. Remember that your subject line is the first information that an employer will see, so make sure that it is enticing—but you must keep the subject line to 45 characters or less, so be specific. Your resume will stay active in the OCC database for six months, although you can update it (and therefore restart the six-month clock) at any time. Note that each e-mail account is permitted only one resume at any given time, so if your roommate uploads via your account, your resume is history. For those of you that lack Internet access altogether, you can mail your typed resume (cover letter optional, maximum three pages total, along with a subject line) and the $15 mail processing fee to:

Online Resume Service
1713 Hemlock Lane
Plainfield, IN 46168

➤ *E.span* (**http://www.espan.com**) — E.span provides a fully searchable jobs database (of approximately twelve thousand jobs) where you can search based on keywords, company name, location, education level required, and years of experience. In addition, E.span offers CareerMail, another spin on the job seeker agent: you enter your personal profile (including your educational level, years of experience, search phrase, search state, and job level). E.span will then keep you posted via e-mail on all new job opportunities added to the database that match your profile. You can conduct an initial search against the jobs database, then have E.span keep you informed via e-mail as new positions are posted. Participating employers are given basically the same function in reverse: they can conduct a search against the resume database, then post a job which will "troll" for new resumes as they are submitted. In addition to the Web, E.span can be found on CompuServe (where it can be accessed free as part of the basic services included in their monthly flat fee program), America Online, and GEnie. Most of the on-line databases are updated on a once- or twice-per-week basis, while the Website is updated continually. You can also upload your resume for free directly to the E.span ResumePro Database, where it can be viewed by interested employers. E-mail your resume in text (ASCII) format in the body of the message to **resume@espan.com** and use the subject line as the title for your resume. You will be given a passcode by return e-mail which will allow you to view, edit, and delete your resume so that you can keep it current.

➤ *CareerMosaic* (**http://www.careermosaic.com**) — Career Mosaic is a very well designed Website brought to you by Bernard Hodes Advertising, one of the leading employment advertising agencies in the United States. Their J.O.B.S. (Jobs Offered By Search) database allows you to search by job title, description, company, city, state, zip code, and country. In addition, CareerMosaic's Usenet Search allows you to search the multitude of national, regional, and local Usenet newsgroups for job opportunity postings. Their front-end search engine, which allows for a combination of geographical and keyword search, is the most intuitive front-end for Usenet search on the Web. Their International Gateway provides access to jobs in Canada, the United

Kingdom, Japan, Hong Kong, and France. Their on-line ResumeCM form allows you to cut-and-paste your ASCII resume for upload to their database. CareerMosaic also serves as home to some of the very best employer jobs pages on the Web, so be sure to check out their Employers listing.

➤ *Monster Board* (**http://www.monster.com**) — what do monsters have to do with job search? Maybe it's a play on the nightmarish view we tend to have of job search, but it does make for an interesting motif at this site, which is scattered with a variety of graphics-run-amok. Monster Board uses this very cool interface to connect you with their fifty thousand plus jobs database, searchable by location, discipline, and keyword. Monster Board also offers a Personal Job Search Agent, although it forces you to log in to the site to find out if there are any matches (while other sites update you via e-mail). You can also submit your resume to the Resume City section or use the Resume Builder to create an HTML resume for you. Definitely worth the visit.

➤ *JOBTRAK* (**http://www.jobtrak.com**) — JOBTRAK is an excellent source of job listings for college students and new alumni. Many college and university Career Development offices use JOBTRAK as a replacement for their internal job posting board, with JOB-TRAK taking over the building and maintaining. While the overall number of jobs posted here is impressive, access to each job is restricted based on the school you attend, so no one has access to all of the jobs. Since access is limited, you will typically need to log in through your university Website or get the password from the Career Development office. If your school is not currently listed with JOBTRAK, you will not be able to gain access to the job postings.

➤ *JobWeb* (**http://www.jobweb.org**) — JobWeb is sponsored by the National Association of Colleges and Employers (NACE) and provides a variety of job and employer listings for entry level. Click on "Jobs" and you will be taken to a keyword search front-end that allows you to search by keyword and geography. Or simply view the entire database of jobs and employers. Complete with contact information, it's like having NACE's *Job Choices* research guides on-line.

➤ *CareerPath* (**http://www.careerpath.com**) — CareerPath allows you to search help wanted ads from more than thirty major newspapers, including: *Atlanta Journal-Constitution, Baltimore Sun, Boston Globe, Chicago Tribune, Cincinnati Enquirer/Post, Columbus Dispatch,*

Denver Rocky Mountain News, Des Moines Register, Detroit News and Free Press, Hartford Courant, Houston Chronicle, L.A. County Press-Telegram, Los Angeles Times, Miami Herald, Minneapolis-St. Paul Pioneer Press, New York Times, Orlando Sentinel, Philadelphia Inquirer, Pittsburgh Tribune-Review, Sacramento Bee, San Jose Mercury News, Seattle Times, South Florida Sun-Sentinel, and Washington Post. Includes search capability by newspaper, job category, and keywords. Note that if there is a particular geography that you are interested in that is not covered by CareerPath, you may want to check if the major newspaper in the area has a Website. If they do, you may be able to search want ads directly at their site.

BEFORE YOU SEND AN E-MAIL

If you are going to compete in the world of cyberspace, take note: students often unknowingly advertise their entry level job seeker status via their e-mail address. The ".edu" extension hanging off the end of an e-mail screams out entry level.

There are now e-mail aliasing services available which allow you to keep your current e-mail account, but use a different e-mail address for correspondence. The aliasing service forwards your e-mail directly to your current account. An additional plus with this type of service is the ability to move to a new service provider (which will likely happen upon graduation) while keeping the same e-mail address.

One of the best (and least expensive) e-mail aliasing providers is *iName* **(www.iname.com),** which offers complete aliasing for only $14.95 for a full year, with a sixty-day free trial. You can choose from hundreds of domain extensions (all with .com or other commercial extensions), including generic names such as username@mail.com or custom names such as username@engineer.com or username@journalist.com (all of which where you specify the username). It's a great way to get a commercial e-mail address without the additional expense

> THE INTERNET LEVELS THE JOB SEARCH PLAYING FIELD—IF YOU KNOW HOW TO PLAY THE GAME.

of signing up with an ISP. And all of your e-mail will still be delivered to the same in-box as before. You simply make a change in your e-mail initialization for your new e-mail reply-to address.

INTERNET RESUMES

Internet resumes are a different breed from the typical paper resume. Most paper resumes are verb oriented. But Internet resumes need to accomplish a different purpose, since they function best in searchable format. And employers do not search for verbs, they search for nouns. Nouns are the keywords or "buzzwords" that employers look for in pre-qualifying potential candidates.

In preparing your resume for posting on the Net, be sure to examine your resume from the perspective of searchability. Even if the resume is not initially keyword searched, it may find its way into an employer or general resume database beyond its initial posting location. In constructing your Net resume, consider the view from the other side of the desk and what you would look for in searching for a candidate such as yourself. If the proper keywords are not already included, revamp your resume to a specialized format that includes a separate KEYWORD section.

If you initially formatted your resume with a word processor, make sure you save it in text (ASCII) format. Then double-check all formatting (especially if you used columns) to ensure a clean look upon printing. Your resume is then ready for posting.

> INTERNET RESUMES ARE NOUN ORIENTED, NOT VERB ORIENTED.

The default standard for posting your resume is ASCII text format, which generally allows for greater searchability. However, with the greater usage of the Web, HTML (hypertext markup language) format is also growing in acceptance. The benefit of HTML is the flexibility with regard to graphics and overall presentation format. You can create a Website all your own, complete with your fully formatted resume. And many e-mail packages (such as Netscape Communicator) are now HTML enabled, allowing for full formatting within the body of the message.

To understand Net postings, note that there is more to posting your resume than just placing it on a Usenet Newsgroup and then sitting back to wait for the phone calls (or e-mails) inviting you to interview. Although most "passive postings" such as this take little time to generate, they are also less likely to produce positive results. The best results are achieved through both passive and active posting.

Passive posting includes posting to all of the "usual" sites, such as (in order of importance) the misc.jobs.resumes Usenet Newsgroup, Online Career Center, E.span, CareerMosaic, and Monster Board. Make sure you post directly from the e-mail address you are most active with, since many employers will respond directly to that address. The key with such passive postings is the use of an informative subject line. You will need to state your objective clearly and succinctly in 80 characters or less. Forget your English grammar class and simply force as many keywords into the subject line as possible. And unless you want to guarantee that your resume will not be read, do not put the words "Entry Level" in the subject line. Very few employers are searching the Net looking specifically for entry level.

> LIKE OTHER AREAS OF JOB SEARCH, INTERNET JOB SEARCH SUCCESS DEPENDS ON BEING ACTIVE, NOT PASSIVE.

When posting your resume passively, you will have no idea who has viewed your resume, when, where, how, or why. You are passively waiting for them to contact you. For all you know, your resume was never viewed by anyone; or if it was, it may have been printed, reviewed, and entered into a database, while still producing no direct contact. An alternative is to e-mail your resume to targeted employers.

Active posting involves surfing individual employer postings or job postings and responding directly with an e-mail resume. This is actually a much more productive method, since it is more direct and personal. And you can add comments that relate to a specific employer and a contact point for later follow-up.

When sending your resume via e-mail, use one of these three formats:

1. **Microsoft Word** — the standard industry word processor; if they do not have it, they will usually have a utility to convert from this format. Usually best to save in Word 6.0/95 format.

2. **Text** — this format is most appropriate for a resume you know will be scanned into a database, since there are no embedded characters.

3. **HTML** — for posting on the Web, or if you are certain the recipient has an HTML-enabled mail program, such as Netscape Communicator.

When sending your resume as an attached file, MIME format works best. The most consistent standard for sending your resume via e-mail is to embed your text resume into the body of the message and attach your resume using MIME in Word (.doc) format.

By sending your resume via e-mail, you always have a point of reference. Since you are the one who initially matched your background with the employer and the employer's requirements, it is up to you to take the contact to the next level. Because of your initial contact you will always have an avenue to follow and a reference point to return to. Do not expect that merely sending an e-mail will generate a job offer. Or an interview. Like any employer contact, it often requires multiple contacts before you get past square one.

Resume posting on the Internet is ideally suited for those who are seeking more technical professions, such as computers or engineering. But remember that the supply side in these areas is very crowded with experienced candidates. So if your background is nontechnical, you will actually be more of a standout on the Net. And don't ever be shy about publicly proclaiming your availability. Discretion will come later in your career. For now, the more people who are aware of your availability, the better.

THE EXTREME RESUME DROP TECHNIQUE

Ready to perform the paper mail equivalent of blindly sending your resume to every company with a pulse? Then the Extreme Resume Drop is for you! Although you already know my feelings about mass mailing your resume (i.e., usually ineffective for the amount of time expended), this technique is so quick and simple that it truly is effective in reaching a large number of companies inexpensively and efficiently. So fire away!

The concept is simple. Companies that are hiring have e-mail addresses. Collect them all together, blast out your resume to the whole list, then sit back, cross your fingers, and hope something happens.

MainQuad offers the Extreme Resume Drop at their site, located at:

http://www.mainquad.com/resumedrop.html

Connect to their site and you will be given a quick and easy way to drop your resume to over two hundred different companies via e-mail. Yes, you are sending your resume blindly. No, this is not the end-all for job search. Yes, it is worth a free drop. Cross your fingers, drop off your resume, forget about it and get on to other areas of your search. But do not forget to check your e-mail daily for responses.

THE SEARCH ENGINE RESEARCH TECHNIQUE

One of the most effective components on the Web is the proliferation of search engines that are tracking the multitude of sites. By using these search engines in your job search, not only do you increase your power to research companies you are already aware of, you can also find companies (and jobs) that you did not know existed.

First, use the search engines as a research tool to gather more information about a potential employer you have already identified. My recommendation is to begin with the *Yahoo!* site, located at:

http://www.yahoo.com

Yahoo! is my first search engine choice because all the listings at their site are submitted (versus robot detected), and therefore the search results are fewer and more select than the listings produced by search engines using robots to scour every known crevice on the Web. Why is this better? Because it quickly cuts through the chaff to the key page(s) you are seeking. This is often where you will find the home page for the company you are searching for and any associated pages put up by suppliers or customers. Use the front-end search engine to search by company name. And click through to the listed site(s) for further information. Keep in mind that many companies maintain an up-to-date listing of jobs at their site, so this provides you with an excellent tool for finding out about current opportunities. Many companies also maintain an entry level jobs page to give further information about their entry level training program.

After you have gleaned the information you are seeking at the company site, back up to *Yahoo!* to expand your search. First, click on the category line under which the company name appears. This will expand out to a full listing of other companies in similar industries or touting a similar product line. Minimally, it will provide you with a great deal of competitive information. Maximally, it may direct you to the up-and-comer in the industry, a company you may not have been aware of otherwise.

> SEARCH ENGINES CAN GUIDE YOU TO INFO ON COMPANIES THAT FEW OTHERS ARE AWARE OF. BOTH THE GOOD AND THE BAD.

Next, back up again to the *Yahoo!* search results page and click through to Alta Vista **(www.altavista.digital.com)** at the bottom of the page. This will greatly expand your listings based on your original search keywords. The Alta Vista site (maintained by Digital Equipment Corp.) is generally regarded as the best and cleanest of the robot sites. You will now have access to those companies that have the keyword(s) submitted within either the title or the short description, as well as any page anywhere on the Web that uses the keyword(s). The results can sometimes be rather daunting (for example, you probably do not want to search Alta Vista for "IBM"), but the results will generate sites that are both employer sponsored and generic. You will often find a wealth of information about the company, and commentary (both good and bad) about their reputation, product line, position within the industry, and so forth.

Using this technique will deliver information to you about both target employers and new employers, further expanding the scope and quality of your job search.

THE SEARCH ENGINE KEYWORD TECHNIQUE

After you have completed your employer name searches, return to the Alta Vista site and perform a keyword search, just as you would at any job posting site. Why? Because this search will tap into all of the companies that maintain pages containing those keywords. Many of these pages will be job postings.

Keep in mind that you will likely come up with scores of personal resume pages in the results of your search. Don't be discouraged by the number of others out there. In fact, use it as your inspiration to create your own HTML resume. Remember, there are plenty of Hiring Managers (myself included) who are doing the same keyword search from the other side of the desk. I sift past the company sites to get to the personal resume sites.

DEVELOPING YOUR PERSONAL HTML RESUME

Want to cut-and-paste your way to an HTML resume you can call your own? Then visit the Resumix site, where their HTML resume generator will do all of that nasty HTML markup for you. You can find Resumix at:

http://www.resumix.com

You will have to stick with the Resumix format, but with some creativity you should be able to produce quality output. You can then save your resume in HTML format (view document source, then cut-and-paste to Notepad or any other ASCII text editor) and place it at new sites as needed. Your HTML resume will likely take 10K or less in storage space, so it will prove to be very portable for you.

THE HTML RESUME POSTING TECHNIQUE

The key to posting your HTML resume on-line is to make certain that it will be found. It is not enough to create your resume and post it at your university's Web server, then wait for visitors. You will not be found.

I have a friend who made his HTML resume available through his local Internet Service Provider and added a counter on the page to tell him how many times it had been viewed. He was quite excited to learn that it had been viewed over twenty times, until he realized that those twenty times all came from the same address—his own. Lesson learned—to be found, you must be findable.

The key to being found is being linked to another site or search engine. When a search engine robot (such as those used by Alta Vista, Open Text, and Webcrawler) visits a site, it indexes all linked pages at the site. It is not enough to be located at the site; you must be linked from somewhere else within the site. Then the search engine will automatically index all the words found on your page, which will come up in keyword searches at their site. If your university allows links to student resumes (check with your Career Development office), this is your best connection. Otherwise, check with the developers of other externally accessible pages to request a link.

Then take it one step further. Publicize your page. Just as a company would publicize its home page, you should do the same for your resume home page.

The best (and quickest) way to publicize your page is through The PostMaster submission service, located at:

http://www.netcreations.com/postmaster

Postmaster will provide you with a single form to fill out and distribute the information to all the top search engines, including Yahoo!, Alta Vista, Open Text, Webcrawler, and twenty more. Don't bother with the paid service (designed for companies with open checkbooks). Instead, choose their free demo, which will submit your site to two dozen top search engines. It takes about thirty minutes to complete the form, but it's time well spent.

Caution: if your personal home page is filled with mindless trivia about rock bands, inebriation, and stupid HTML links, with your resume included as a side note, do not submit it to Postmaster. Keep a clean resume URL without the associated trivia. And do not link to your personal page from your resume unless you really, truly want a potential employer to see that side of you. Probably not.

USENET NEWSGROUPS

The Usenet Newsgroups have had an Internet presence much longer than the Web and continue to provide a forum for focused discussion and postings. Several of the newsgroups are job and career related. You can even use DejaNews (accessible through *Yahoo!*) as a Web front-end to extend your search capabilities. Following are the best sites to utilize in your job search:

➤ *biz.jobs.offered* — the best Usenet Newsgroups are also the most popular and contain mountains of data to sift through. The **biz** newsgroup includes both the common ("Managerial Trainee Position Offered"—translated, "Swing Shift Manager Position at McDonald's") and the uncommon ("Warp Space Engineer Needed"). It excels in the uncommon, so make sure you are using a top-notch browser to cut through the myriad of diverse listings.

➤ *misc.jobs.offered* — while there is some overlap with **biz** (mainly in the "Make a Million Dollars Stuffing Envelopes" category), it is still worthwhile to do some surfing here. Technically, the **biz** groups are designed more toward business interests, so **misc** tends to be a catchall of some of the more obscure job openings. But **misc** has been around the longest, so some continue to post here first. If you have a good browser and the time, check out both.

➤ *misc.jobs.offered.entry* — after you are finished cutting through all the "experience required" ads in the previous two newsgroups, come join a newsgroup whose sole purpose is to serve you, the entry level job hunter. Sure, there aren't nearly as many postings, but remember—these postings are all geared directly toward your job market. Take time to not only browse, but to also read through (and download or print) those that you have an interest in. You will need to make direct contact with the company, by e-mail, fax, or phone.

➤ *misc.jobs.resumes* —this is the place to load up your resume with your own Usenet posting. Remember to make sure your subject/title line is succinct and your resume is in text format and keyword searchable. It should be noted that your resume will either be purged or filtered by most browsers within less than one week, so diligence is the key to keeping your resume visible in this very popular newsgroup.

➤ *geo.jobs newsgroups* — no, that's not an Internet newsgroup location. The geo.jobs tag is short for geographical jobs newsgroups, of which there are quite a few, covering a diverse area nationally and internationally. They are great for those who are geographically focused on a particular city, state, or country. Following is an incomplete listing of what is available (no Net listing is ever fully complete).

CITIES

Atlanta, GA (atl.jobs)
Austin, TX austin.jobs)
Baltimore, MD (balt.jobs)
Chicago, IL (chi.jobs)
Cleveland, OH (cle.jobs)
Columbus, OH (cmh.jobs)
Dallas-Fort Worth, TX (dfw.jobs)
Houston, TX
    (houston.jobs.offered)
Huntsville, AL (hsv.jobs)
Ithaca, NY (ithaca.jobs)
Los Vegas, NV (vegas.jobs)
Los Angeles, CA (la.jobs)
Long Island, NY (li.jobs)

Milwaukee, WI (milw.jobs)
New York, NY (nyc.jobs)
Pittsburgh, PA (pgh.jobs.offered)
Philadelphia, PA (phl.jobs.offered)
St. Louis, MO (stl.jobs)
San Diego, CA (sdnet.jobs)
San Francisco Bay Area
    (ba.jobs.offered)
Seattle, WA
    (seattle.jobs.offered)

STATES

Arizona (az.jobs)
Florida (fl.jobs)
Illinois (il.jobs.offered)
Indiana (in.jobs)
Michigan (mi.jobs)
New England (ne.jobs)
New Jersey (nj.jobs)
New Mexico (nm.jobs)
North Carolina (triangle.jobs)
Ohio (oh.jobs)
Pennsylvania (pa.jobs.offered)
Texas (tx.jobs)
Washington, DC (dc.jobs)

INTERNATIONAL

Australia (aus.jobs)
Bermuda (bermuda.jobs.offered)
Canada (can.jobs)
Denmark (dk.jobs)
Europe (euro.jobs)
France (fr.jobs.offres)
Germany (de.markt.jobs)
Israel (israel.jobs.offered)
Ontario (ont.jobs)
Ottawa (ott.jobs)
Toronto (tor.jobs)
United Kingdom (uk.jobs)
South Africa (za.ads.jobs)

ON-LINE SERVICES

Whereas the Internet provides the broadest array of job search databases and tools, many of the commercial on-line services also provide their own proprietary job search tools. Each on-line service offers varying levels of Internet access, as well as its own brand of personal service geared toward job search. Most of the services are free or for a limited fee during the first thirty days, which gives you plenty of time to decide if that is where you want to surf and then stay on their turf. All you need is a credit card in order to dial the 800 number provided and receive a log-on ID and/or intro packet. The following is a summary of the services currently offered and the best areas to access.

➤ **America Online (AOL) — 800-827-6364**
AOL is now the largest on-line service in the world, and for good reason—it was the first with a slick graphical interface and continues to lead the pack in ease of use. This, combined with an aggressive marketing campaign for new users (I have probably received fifteen to twenty free AOL sign-up disks either sent in the mail or attached to almost any and every magazine having to do with computers), has made them the front runner with more than two million subscribers. The E-Span access (keyword JOBS) has a simple keyword search front-end that lacks the sophistication of the Website. AOL also has Help Wanted-USA (keyword JOBS), which sports a similar keyword front-end to E.span, yet fewer jobs listed. The AOL classified employment ads (keyword CLASSIFIED) is a posting forum that has eleven different job categories and about three thousand listed jobs. There are eleven corresponding categories where you can post your resume.

➤ **CompuServe —800-848-8199**
As stated previously, CompuServe offers access to the E.span databases (GO ESPAN) as part of the basic service price. While AOL and GEnie do not charge directly for the service, you end up getting charged for extra hours if you go over their minimum. If you truly want to take your time browsing through the E.span information and lack direct Web access, CompuServe is the place to get it done. It has recently lowered the basic monthly fee to under $10, so it is well worth the money and time to gain access here. CompuServe has a well-deserved reputation for being the business on-line service. The true strength of CompuServe is in the multitude of business forums on nearly every subject (and occupation) imaginable. For more information on how to tap into this forum fest, see the SIG Posting Technique below. The job posting classifieds (GO JOBS) is a poorly designed and hardly used classified posting area. Since it costs per line, per week, few companies actually post here.

In addition to the career-specific information you can find with the on-line services, each of them has volumes and volumes (electronically speaking) of reference materials on companies, technologies, and market trends. You can use these services as an adjunct to your search by filling in further details about hiring companies you have located.

THE SIG POSTING TECHNIQUE

Then again, who says you have to look for jobs where the on-line services want you to look for jobs? The best place to look for work is often directly where most of the on-line service action is—in the SIG (Special Interest Group) or Forum areas. These are the specialized bulletin boards that cater to every goofy whim dreamed up by the providers (and users) of these services. While there are some very unique SIGs, there are also some that will tie in directly with your future career. The most obvious career-related SIGs are for those of us who work in computer-related fields. If that is your field, you can find a host of specialized SIGs (down to your favorite programming language and database). For the rest of the world, it is still fairly easy to find a SIG that has subscribers in your chosen career. When you find that SIG, spend some time reading the messages (especially if they have an FAQ—Frequently Asked Questions—section), and then consider submitting your own humble posting, similar to the following:

(subject)   **Assistance Request—Seeking Job In _____ In The _____ Area.**

(body)   Soon-to-be-college grad is seeking to make his/her mark in the _____ world. All I need is a little help from you to find the job of my dreams. I know it's out there, but I haven't located it yet. Will you help me? If you have any information, please contact me at (phone number) or (mailing address) or (e-mail address). I will be eternally grateful. Thanks!

It is not the most eloquent impassioned plea, but it usually gains some attention from the helpful souls who continuously wander the on-lines searching for ways to further benefit humanity. You may be their next cause for virtual adoption.

Obviously, you will want to customize it to your situation and use your own wording (otherwise all of the readers of this book will end up with duplicate ads). Then make sure you diligently log on at least twice a week, since most will reply via e-mail. You will get suggestions, leads, contact names, and possibly even find your eventual dream job. Remember also to read "down the thread" from your initial message since many people will just post to your message (for all to read). While there are rules for any SIG, as long as you are requesting help within that focus group you should not have problems from the SysOp.

THE SIG E-MAIL TECHNIQUE

> SIGS AND FORUMS ARE THE NET BASTION FOR THE SUBJECT MATTER EXPERTS AND EXPERT-WANNA-BE'S. BOTH ARE WILLING TO HELP YOU IN YOUR JOB SEARCH.

Another innovative way to reach those in your career focus group is to spend some time surfing the SIG board postings, making note of each posting and the underlying threads. If you are using an on-line information manager (such as WinCIM) that allows you to capture the e-mail addresses of those doing the posting, log the addresses of those who appear to be authorities in your career area. If you do not have an automated way to log the addresses, you may end up having to write them down by hand. Depending on the SIG, you might find anywhere from ten to over one hundred addresses of major and minor authorities in your field. When your collection is of sufficient size, send an e-mail letter to this group similar to the above posting. Amazingly, this type of direct e-mail can often generate over 20 percent response or higher (while traditional snail mail techniques average 2 to 3 percent at best). You might only get a "Have you contacted _____ yet?" response, but it can be another lead on your way to your new job!

THE RESUME DATABASE TECHNIQUE

Several companies now provide electronic resume databases nationwide, with two in particular geared toward entry level candidates. They gather information from students such as yourself, then enter it into databases from which companies can conduct searches for candidates nationwide.

Check with your Career Development office for applications or send off directly to the following companies to request their candidate application:

Connexion
Petersen's Guides
P.O. Box 2123
Princeton, NJ 08543-2123

NAPA Computerized Job Matching Service
National Alumni Placement Association
P.O. Box 974
Sausalito, CA 94965

A variety of resume database services are also available for the general job search market. The advantage for a college grad in using these services is that they are more broadly accessed by employers. The disadvantages: you can become lost in the sea of experienced professionals, and there may be a cost involved (ranging anywhere from free to $50 to participate). But if you are truly seeking to leave no stone unturned, the following five services are among the best:

NCS Jobline (free)
National Career Search
2897 Mapleton Ave., Suite 1A
Boulder, CO 80301
303-440-5110

Electronic Job Matching (free)
1915 N. Dale Mabry Highway, Suite 307
Tampa, FL 33607
800-749-4100

Job Bank USA
1420 Spring Hill Road, Suite 480
McLean, VA 22102
800-296-1872

National Resume Network
30 Maplewood Ave., Suite 205
Portsmouth, NH 03801-9940
800-758-9918

National Career Services
66 Witherspoon St., Suite 1400
Princeton, NJ 08542
800-321-0458

Please note that your value will be recognized only if there is something quantifiable in your background that would bring you up in a database search. This is no place for plain vanilla grads to throw in their names—they will end up being buried. So before you start filling out yet another form, consider whether you are "searchable" or, better yet, "findable." Remember, when a company is doing a search, it has to use parameters that pare down hundreds of thousands to produce search results of one hundred or less. So companies restrict their searches by several criteria. Following are some of the criteria that would make you noticeable:

➤ Minority, disabled, or female candidate
➤ High GPA (3.4 or above)

> ➤ Name school (you know who you are)
> ➤ Relevant work experience
> ➤ High-demand major or field
> ➤ Very specific targeted job type
> ➤ Very specific targeted industry
> ➤ Very specific targeted geographical area

If you have at least one of the above attributes, it is very worthwhile to take the twenty to thirty minutes to fill out each different form required for entry. As of this printing, Connexion is available as a free service, while NAPA has a nominal charge of $2. NCS Jobline is free, Electronic Job Matching is free, Job Bank USA is $30, National Resume Network is $35, and National Career Services is $49. You might be able to get information on Connexion and NAPA directly through your Career Development office. If not, contact the provider directly to request an enrollment form. Also, NAPA offers a free resume referral service. Mail your resume to:

NAPA Resume Referral Service
National Alumni Placement Association
P.O. Box 974
Sausalito, CA 94965

These database listings are gifts—plant the seed, then go on to other things. If the seed takes root, you will have made a very efficient connection. If not, all you have lost is a seed.

ON-LINE DATABASE SEARCHING

In addition to the aforementioned on-line services available, you can also utilize on-line services to conduct extensive database searching. The leading on-line service for this type of searching is Dow Jones News/Retrieval (DJNR - Dow Jones and Company, P.O. Box 300, Princeton, NJ 08543-0300, 800-522-3567). DJNR is an on-line database available through Tymnet, Telenet, Sprintnet, or Internet links. If you are looking for information on just about any business of note, DJNR is likely to have it. There are over thirty-five different databases within this on-line service. You can search by company name to pull business articles compiled from over twenty different sources, including *The Wall Street Journal* (Dow Jones' flagship publication), *Barron's*, AP press wires, *Forbes*, *Fortune*, and others. The time lag from publication to availability on-line is often as quick as ninety seconds. This is true, up-to-the-minute reporting. In addition, you can go back through several years in searching for articles. Check with your local library or campus computer lab for connection to the service. Or contact your friendly neighborhood stockbroker, who either has direct access to the service or can steer you to someone who does. Or call DJNR and get on-line directly.

OFF-LINE DATABASE SEARCHING

Don't have direct access to the on-line world? You can still reach into the depths of the electronic databases using your telephone. Nexis Express, part of the Lexis/Nexis service from Mead Data Central, will provide you with a full and complete listing of a very broad range of U.S. and international companies. The catch? The fee can be rather steep for extensive searching ($6 per minute for the time spent on-line, plus a printing, express mailing, and/or faxing charge). While the price is prohibitive for broad searches, this service is ideal for gathering otherwise elusive information on a specific company you are already set to interview with. A basic search will usu-

> TO BE FOUND, YOU MUST MAKE YOURSELF FINDABLE.

ally produce a full corporate dossier, including company history, product line(s), sales, income, stock performance, top executives, subsidiaries, locations, and more. You will be fully armed above and beyond the top 1 percent. Ready to impress? Nexis Express is ready and willing to fill your order. You can reach Nexis at 800-843-6476.

Chapter 11

JOB FAIR SUCCESS

In the middle of difficulty lies opportunity.
—Albert Einstein

Job fairs are becoming a common means of entry level recruiting. For the corporate recruiter, they offer an opportunity to reach interviewing terminal velocity—the highest possible number of prospects in the shortest possible amount of time. For many students, job fairs provide a "freebie" opportunity to meet with hiring companies.

However, unless you do your homework, you will end up wasting your time at a job fair. Job fairs are the meat markets of the entry level job market, with employers sizing up candidates quickly, based on appearances and first impressions. Job fairs have a set of rules and protocols all their own. But if you understand how to effectively work within the system, you can easily double or triple your productivity and effectiveness.

Usually a full 50 percent or more of the attendees at job fairs are "window shoppers" who are just browsing to see what is available. While this approach may seem valid, take note that job fairs are not a "get-acquainted session" for you to meet prospective employers. They are multiple interview sessions where the plain vanilla candidates are stepped on and over by

> JOB FAIRS—JOB SEARCH NIRVANA? ONLY IF YOU ARE PREPARED.

those who are targeted and prepared. Yes, even the two- to three-minute greeting and exchange of sound bites is considered a real interview. You are being evaluated, whether it is for thirty seconds or thirty minutes. You always need to be at your very best. If you are to succeed at the job fair of the '90s, you have to take a very aggressive yet structured approach.

UNDERSTANDING THE DIFFERENT TYPES OF JOB FAIRS

Understanding what type of job fair you are attending is crucial to your planning, since each type has distinct differences in approach, setup, and general level of success for entry level candidates.

➤ **Campus-Sponsored Job Fairs**

The campus-sponsored job fair is by far the most popular for college students. For many, this is *the* job fair. Larger campuses will often have several different job fairs, each one geared toward a specific discipline. They are usually sponsored by the Career Development office on campus, although some may be sponsored by a particular academic department, club, or group. The campus-sponsored job fair is ideal for most college students since it is convenient, the lines are generally shorter than at commercial job fairs, and companies are predisposed to and familiar with your college. Many companies attend the job fair in advance of their on-campus recruiting activities, while some use this as their only campus visit. Often the more astute companies will bring along a recent grad, possibly even from your school, to talk with prospective grads. Another trend in recent years has been for smaller colleges to combine together to create consortium job fairs.

> ATTEND CAREER FAIRS AND JOB FAIRS EARLY IN YOUR COLLEGE CAREER SO THAT YOU ARE FAMILIAR WITH THE PROCESS LATER WHEN IT COUNTS.

➤ **Campus-Sponsored Career Days**

As a sideline to the campus job fairs, many campuses now have an event they call "Career Day" in the fall semester, and a "Job Fair" in the spring semester. The big difference is that most companies who come for Career Day are not actively recruiting. They come for the exposure to students ahead of on-campus interviews or the spring job fair. It serves as more of an information-sharing activity than a recruiting activity. In short, it's a good time to meet companies in advance and gather up all their slick glossies on what they think makes them the best company in the world to work for. But remember, actively hiring or not, it is still an interview.

➤ **Commercial Entry Level Job Fairs**

These job fairs are run by independent companies and hosted in centralized locations throughout the country. They are highly advertised events that draw large numbers of students from a geographical radius of three hundred miles or more. These job fairs are a good deal for companies that are hiring at the entry level since they tend to attract large quantities of anxious students. Unfortunately, the lines tend to be long (sometimes as long as two to three hours to meet just a single employer) and the competition is intense. It is only a wise use of your time if there are specific companies in attendance that you have an interest in. Otherwise, you are just window shopping, which buys you little in end results. Your competition runs the gamut from grads without a clue as to what they want to do all the way to scores of overqualified and unemployed MBAs.

> **Commercial Professional Job Fairs**
These general professional job fairs are geared to a wide range of professional occupations, from accounting to programming to engineering to sales. Be aware that you are running with a new herd at this one. You have to be prepared

> CAMPUS JOB FAIRS WILL ALWAYS BE THE MOST PRODUCTIVE, SINCE THE EMPLOYERS ALREADY HAVE AN INTEREST IN YOUR COLLEGE.

to compete directly with those who have practical work experience in the field. Get ready to hear a lot of no's, but the occasional company that does have a need at the entry level could make it worthwhile. Your main objective should be to gather information for later direct follow-up with the companies. Do not expect anyone to call you back based only on your dropping off a resume.

> **Commercial Specialty Job Fairs**
These professional job fairs are geared toward a specific specialty group, such as "Computer Job Fair" or "Technical/Engineering Job Fair." If you are in one of the specialty groups, this is an excellent resource for finding hiring companies. Again, you are competing against literally hundreds of better qualified candidates, so your purpose should be to gather information about hiring companies for later direct contact.

> **Community Job Fairs**
These are free-for-all job fairs offering everything from Swing Shift Manager at McDonald's to professional and management positions. There are often over one hundred companies involved. If you choose to attend, make sure you are very targeted and very direct.

THE PEOPLE BEHIND THE TABLES

The recruiters you will be meeting with at a job fair are seldom the actual Hiring Managers. They are usually Personnel/Human Resources recruiters who make their living as professional screeners. Their job is to weed out the undesirables so that Hiring Managers can spend "quality time" with the candidates they are truly interested in.

You need to have a different focus for Human Resources recruiters than you would for Hiring Managers. They are looking to screen you out, not qualify you in. Your objective should be to show that not only do you have all the necessary basic requirements, you are also an appropriate candidate for their work environment. Consider *their* focus. Whenever they make a recommendation for further action, they are putting their basic "stamp of approval" on the person. The last thing they want is for the Hiring Manager to come back to them and say, "Why did you give your okay on that person?" They want assurance that company resources will not be wasted in taking the next step with you. Ideally, they should be able to visualize you as someone who could eventually become "part of the team."

> CONSIDER THE OTHER SIDE OF THE DESK AT THE JOB FAIR: ONE HUNDRED PLUS NEW FACES IN SIX TO EIGHT HOURS. WHO WOULD YOU REMEMBER?

Although recruiter styles vary, you can usually get a good feel for a recruiter at a job fair by two very observable features:

1. **Do they stand in front of the table at their booth? Or behind?**
   Those who stand in front are likely to be approachable and want more qualitative information about your background. Those who stand (or sit) behind the table are likely to be more quantitative and analytical, and may even have a checklist—written or otherwise—of items that you must satisfy in order to go on to the next level.

2. **Do they smile and act comfortable with their role? Or not?**
   Those who smile are more likely to interview in a more conversational style. Those who do not smile are likely to be more structured and analytical in the questioning approach.

Is the above always the case? Obviously not. These are general observations I have made over the years from going to a myriad of job fairs and sizing up the competition. You will find about an 80 percent positive correlation (meaning that I'm wrong a solid 20 percent of the time) in the observations above. Another observation is that fully 90 percent of government recruiters sit behind the table with no smile. Definitely weird. It's like they are all cast from the same mold or something. Must be government regulation at its strangest.

YOUR JOB FAIR PORTFOLIO

Following are some of the things you will need to bring with you to the job fair:

> ➤ **Resume** — yes, you are required to bring one. And it better be an outstanding one because at the end of the day it is often difficult

for recruiters to sort out the bad from the good. Bring at least one copy of your resume for each company you plan to speak with, plus several extra copies. This is a good time to use colored paper (colored, yet conservative). If you have multiple job objectives, bring multiple resumes. And do not bring a cover letter—you are the cover letter to your resume.

➤ **Letters of Recommendation** — make copies of your top three letters of recommendation multiplied by the number of companies you plan to meet with. Make sure all of the companies you are interested in get copies of your letters of recommendation. It will force them to file you differently from the rest of their stack of resumes.

➤ **Portfolio** — your 9"x12" leather-bound or vinyl-bound portfolio will be used to store your resume and letters of recommendation, and for taking notes after talking with each company.

➤ **Briefcase** — the amount of information you pick up at a job fair can sometimes be rather daunting. A briefcase gives you a mini-office from which to operate, including storage for extra copies of your resume and letters of recommendation. It also provides a much more professional look than the plastic bag most job fair attendees walk around with, loaded with their information cache of the day.

> PREPARATION WILL SET YOU APART FROM THE CROWD AT A JOB FAIR.

➤ **Dress** — image is crucial at a job fair—even more important than at a normal interview since decisions are made much more quickly. This is not the time to model the latest in campus fashions. Make sure you wear a classic business suit. Keep it conservative so that their focus is on you, not your clothes. If you need further information, refer to Appendix A - Guidelines for Successful Interview Dress.

THE MAJOR JOB FAIR ERROR NEARLY EVERY COLLEGE STUDENT MAKES

They get in line. If there is one reality of life that college provides excellent training for, it is standing in lines. Whether it's waiting in line at registration at the beginning of the year, waiting in line outside the bookstore for your textbooks, waiting in line for lunch, or just waiting in line outside your professor's office with the other three students who flunked the midterm, college is very good for developing the "there-is-a-line-let's-go-stand-in-it" mentality.

Behold the line, stand you in it? No! There is a better way.

THE WALKABOUT TECHNIQUE

Instead of just getting into the first line you see, you should use the Walkabout Technique. There are two steps:

1. **Walkabout the job fair.**
   When you first arrive at the job fair, walkabout the entire room to get a feel for the layout and where each employer is located. Most rooms are laid out in a "maze format" which requires walking through the corridors to see what is on the other side. Make note of those companies that are conducting secondary interviews either at their booth or in another location. If there is a separate area devoted to secondary interviews, ask one of the job fair workers which employers are conducting second interviews in that area. Survey the area as a military general would in planning an attack strategy. Know specifically whom you want to talk to and in what specific order. But be ready to change your plan if long lines suddenly appear in your planned corridor of attack.

2. **Walkabout the employer.**
   Instead of just getting in line, approach the company booth from the side and quietly pick up some of the slick glossies that are prominently displayed on the table. Then take a few steps back. The reason for this is twofold: first, you now have in your hands some extremely valuable pre-interview reading material; second, and most important, you have an opportunity to get a free preview of the company and recruiter. How? By staying put 4 to 6 feet away and *listening*. You will be far enough away to be unobtrusive, yet still within earshot of the conversation taking place. Listen to what the recruiter asks. Be prepared to answer the same questions yourself. Listen to the responses. Did the recruiter respond positively or negatively? Listen to two or three different interviews to compare different responses. If there is more than one recruiter for the company, note the different styles of each and choose the line behind the one who is the closest fit to your own personality range.

> IMAGE IS EVERYTHING AT A JOB FAIR.

If you have done your homework properly, you should be able to determine what the company's needs are and what they are specifically looking for in filling those needs. Ask yourself two questions: (1) "Is this something I'm interested in?" and (2) "Am I able to show that I am qualified for the position(s) they are offering?" If your answer to either question is "No," then don't waste your time by standing in line. Very few sights in life are sadder than the look on the face of the engineering student who spends over an hour in line to meet with Xerox, only to find out that Xerox is only interested in hiring sales reps.

If you have an interest in what the company has to offer and you can meet its basic needs, it is time to get in line yourself. This is the time to really soak up the information in the company materials you have already picked up from the table. Remember, most people do not get this information until after they have met with the company, so you have a great advantage at the start. And you are not forced to stare blindly off into space as do 90+ percent of job seekers while standing in line (therefore reaching the same level of mental alertness achieved by a five-year-old mesmerized before the TV screen). You will be, on the other hand, mentally alert and focused on what is important to the company and its recruiters, and what your role can be in furthering the company's goals. In short, you will be ready above and beyond all your competition.

Congrats—you have just taken a simple step that will put you a giant step ahead of your peers. Why? Because you have already learned "from the inside" what they are looking for and have preread all of their company propaganda. You are fully prepared while your competition is wandering aimlessly about, staring blankly into space. When your turn arrives, step up with confidence, introduce yourself, and state succinctly your specific career mission statement and how it fits in with their needs as an employer. You will truly stand apart from the crowd.

> **PREPARE YOURSELF FULLY FOR EVERY EMPLOYER YOU MEET AT THE JOB FAIR. YOU MAY NOT GET A SECOND CHANCE.**

If you have never done the Walkabout Technique before, it can seem rather intimidating at first. After all, you are doing something that no one else is doing. Although you usually do not have to ask permission to pick up the company materials that are displayed, occasionally recruiters will tell you that the information is only for candidates they have already met with (translated: those they have determined they have an interest in). Simply respond, "I'm planning to wait in line and would like to learn more about your company during the wait." Dare they refuse?

The Walkabout Technique might feel uncomfortable at first because our "natural" (or is it unnatural?) tendency is to get in the line, not to go immediately to the front and then stand off to the side. Maybe we are afraid that we will be perceived as attempting to cut in line, ready to dart to the front when no one else is looking. Well, as Mom told you, don't worry about what other people think. Worry about what the company recruiters think. They are the only ones you are there to impress. And the Walkabout Technique is just one more way to improve your odds of impressing them. You not only have all the company materials in advance, you also know what questions will be asked. You will be fully prepared, instead of groping in the dark.

THE LINEAGE MILEAGE TECHNIQUE

First priority in lines is always to read the company material. But what then? Time to stare off into space? No. Long lines hold yet another opportunity for you to take advantage of in your job search. More networking.

> USE YOUR TIME PRODUCTIVELY. EVEN WAITING TIME CAN BE PRODUCTIVE TIME.

Simply turn to those in front or in back of you and ask them the standard job fair question: "What are you looking for here today?" Ask them about other companies they may have spoken with at the job fair—the good, the bad, and the ugly. Avoid the ugly. And ask them about their job search in general. Any particularly promising companies?

Remember that we all like to talk about ourselves. Now is not the time for you to spout on about your success (or lack thereof) on your most recent job search excursion. You are there to listen and gather information. You will learn infinitely more by listening to others than by listening to yourself.

Take copious mental notes. And remember that your network has just grown in size by one.

THE THREE TYPES OF JOB FAIR INTERVIEWS

It's important to understand the basic types of interviews that take place at a job fair since your approach should be different with each. As you watch and listen from the side, you will be able to determine which type of interview is being conducted and to modify your approach accordingly. Following are the three basic types:

1. **Screening Interview**
   By far the most common type of job fair interview. This interview usually lasts no more than two to three minutes and is usually conducted by companies whose main interest is gathering resumes and initial impressions before making decisions as to whether they will move to the next step. You will be asked questions about your major, your GPA, your experience, and what type of position you are looking

for. Your strategy should be to quickly point them to the key areas in your background that reflect their needs. What needs? The needs they enumerated six candidates ago when you were standing off to the side as another candidate naively walked up and asked, "So what is your company looking for?" You need to fill the company's list of requirements or you will never see the light of day at the next level. Ask for a business card and inquire as to the next step.

2. **Mini-Interview**

   This interview usually lasts five to ten minutes and is conducted at the employer's booth. Be prepared to give a full introduction of your background and quickly position yourself as someone who is a good fit in relation to that company's needs. The recruiter will usually want you to elaborate on the information contained in your resume, so it is crucial that you be prepared to comment on each and every item on it. Be prepared to give a full explanation of what might be only a single-line bullet item on the resume. Often there will be final questions related to some of the qualitative issues that resumes do not reflect. Make sure all your answers position you as the candidate who meets the company's needs. Ask for a business card and inquire as to the next step.

3. **Full Interview**

   The full interview usually takes place behind a curtain or screen at the employer's booth, or may be in another part of the hall altogether. Most employers use the full interview only as a secondary interview. In other words, you have to be invited to the interview based on the previous screening interview or mini-interview. Be prepared for twenty minutes or more, but probably no longer than thirty minutes, since most companies have a tight schedule to keep. Consider this interview the same as you would any full-length interview. Be aware that you may actually be interviewed by technical or line managers. You will be asked a great number of qualitative, open-ended questions and will be expected to provide elaboration of your answers. Make sure you are prepared for the interview by reading Section 3, Interviewing Success later in this book. At the end of the interview, if you are truly interested, let the interviewer know and ask what the next step will be. Assume that he or she is also interested.

Unless you are certain the company is conducting secondary interviews, do not consider it a negative if all you went through was the screening or mini-interview. I realize that it can be rather depressing to spend two quick minutes with a recruiter after a thirty-minute wait, but that is the reality of the meat market mentality of job fairs. Just make sure you know what the next step is and follow up. This is not the time to cross your fingers and hope—take charge and make things happen.

THE MOST COMMON INTRODUCTION QUESTION AT A JOB FAIR

"What are you looking for here at the job fair?" "A job" is not an acceptable answer. You should be ready with a clear and succinct description of exactly what you are looking for. If you have done your homework properly, what you are looking for should match quite nicely with what they are looking for. Your comeback after you have explained your career desires? "And what are you looking for here at the job fair?" The perfect setup for establishing common interests.

HOW TO GAIN INSTANT RAPPORT IN THE JOB FAIR INTERVIEW

Use the Personality Matching Technique found in the Mastering the Interview chapter later in this book. If you use this simple technique, you will not only gain instant rapport, you will also greatly increase your odds of being called back for secondary interviews.

In fact, to be truly outstanding at interviewing, you will need to read and understand all the information contained in Section 3, Interviewing Success. Do it before you attend any job fairs or interviews.

THE KEY TO THE TREASURE ROOM TECHNIQUE

At the end of your job fair interview, no matter how short or how long, ask the recruiter for the key to the treasure room: "What is the key to successfully moving on to the next step in the hiring process?" Rather bold, but they often will tell. Very specifically. Take careful note of what is said and make sure you follow through. It is the formula for success.

MAKING THE MOST OF THE TIME ALLOTTED

Unless it is a small or limited job fair, you will want to plan to spend the entire day there. You should always spend time in advance researching the companies that will be attending, not only to decide which you have an interest in, but also so that you are fully prepared for those you meet with. The very best time to attend is early in the morning and then again late in the day. Even at some of the commercial job fairs (which are notorious for long, long lines), by arriving early you can usually beat the lines and meet with the most popular companies first. During the "prime time mid-day crunch," you can usually expect long lines and lack of quality time with the recruiters. To estimate how long your wait will be, simply sample the average amount of time the recruiter is taking with each person, extrapolate over the number in line and you have your answer. At a recent job fair, the recruiter was taking five minutes with each candidate and there were forty people in line. How's your math? That's over a three-hour wait.

> ## BE READY FOR THEIR RAPID-FIRE QUESTIONS WITH YOUR RAPID-FIRE RESPONSES.

A good strategy to follow is to meet with the most popular employers early in the day, before the lines develop, and then talk with the "second-tier" companies during the main part of the day. Then before you leave, make one more contact with the companies you have an ongoing interest in. With proper planning and strategic timing, you can usually avoid the long lines and make your time more productive.

HOW TO GAIN FAVOR WITH BUSY JOB FAIR RECRUITERS

Bring them lunch. Or even a soda. Or even just a glass of water. Most recruiters have very little time to get away from their booth. There is a line a mile long and it is not getting any shorter. If you notice that they are in need of something, you can either ask them if they want you to get it or just get it for them. They will be eternally grateful, and it may be what sets you apart from the crowd at the end of the day.

HOW TO QUICKLY BYPASS LONG INTERVIEW LINES

You can only use this technique once during the day (or twice if you have a large gastric capacity), but it is a very effective way to bypass what might otherwise be a two- or three-hour wait. Ask the recruiter to lunch—your treat. Sitting with you, listening to your background, is all that you ask in return. Many will appreciate the opportunity to get away, even if it is just for thirty minutes. Set up reservations for lunch at a nearby (or, better yet, on-site) sit-down restaurant. Then approach the recruiter from the side of the booth and mention that you have a table for two reserved for lunch. If you are turned down, try it with other recruiters you are interested in until it does work. Usually you will have at least a 25 percent hit rate, so you probably will not have to ask more than three or four different recruiters before you get an acceptance. Then use that time productively by talking rather than eating. You will put the recruiter in a different environment than he or she is experiencing

> READ THE EMPLOYER MATERIALS WHILE YOU WAIT. IF YOU FINISH THEM, READ THEM AGAIN. KNOW THE INFORMATION AS IF IT WERE YOUR OWN.

with the rest of the "herd" and will gain a high probability of remembrance based on your willingness to meet their needs first. Try it!

THE MOST POPULAR JOBS AT JOB FAIRS

If you want to sell for a living, job fairs are job search nirvana. Retail sales. Insurance sales. Financial services sales. Manufacturing sales. If you want sales, you will definitely find it here. For the rest of you, job fairs will drive you crazy. Why so many sales jobs? Because most people who are in sales are not in sales by design. People don't typically go to college with the intent of becoming an insurance salesperson. At the same time, these companies rely on an efficient sales force to generate a profit. Most of them like to "grow their own," so entry level is often ideal. These companies are out there beating the bushes at the job fairs. Quite often you will see a "top-tier" company on the list of companies recruiting at the job fair, yet arrive to find they are only looking for marketing reps (i.e., sales reps).

But here is the key: even if companies are actively recruiting only for sales, if the line is not too long (and you have the time), approach them to inquire about whom to contact for a position in your field within the company. They might offer to take your resume and get back to you (in which case you will likely never hear from them again), but your objective should be a name and phone number for follow-up. Then call them directly to find out the name and title of the primary contact within the company who is responsible for hiring in your line of work.

Don't let the "Sales Reps Only Need Apply" sign turn you away from a company you are truly interested in!

THE LASTING IMPRESSION TECHNIQUE

Before you leave the job fair, return to the booth of any company you have an interest in. Wait for a break in the action, then step up to the recruiter and thank them again for their time. Let them

> MOST RECRUITERS DREAD HAVING TO GO TO A JOB FAIR. DO YOUR BEST TO MAKE LIFE EASIER FOR THEM.

know that you will be in touch and that you look forward to speaking with them again.

This lasting impression will help the recruiter to remember your name and face when you do make contact again. After all, there will be a stack of one hundred to two hundred resumes for the recruiter to filter through after the job fair is over. This is a guarantee that you will be remembered.

THE ABSOLUTELY CRITICAL LAST STEP OF THE JOB FAIR

As it is in any other part of the job search, the critical last step is follow-up! Yet, sadly, very few students ever follow-up. Make sure you are the one who stands out in the crowd. First, call the office number on the business card of the person you met with. They will obviously be out of the office, but they likely will be checking messages that evening. So ask to be put through to voice mail, where you will leave a personal "thank you." Then send a "thank you" card by mail to confirm your ongoing interest. What to say? Keep it short and sweet. But make sure you include the following topics:

➤ "Thanks for taking time to meet with me today . . . "

➤ "Here is why I feel I would be an outstanding employee for your company . . . "

➤ "I would appreciate the opportunity to speak with you further . . . "

➤ "I will call you next week to arrange a time when we can meet and further discuss how my skills can benefit your organization . . . "

Then make sure you do in fact call when you said you would. Again, very few follow through to this step, so you will be head and shoulders above the crowd at this point, and very likely the one they choose to go on to the next step.

No job offers will be made at the job fair. But if you perform at your very best and follow through on all the steps, you may be on your way toward the final step at the company location.

ATTENDING JOB FAIRS AT OTHER COLLEGES

Hey, who said you could only attend the job fair at your college? If you check into it, most colleges are willing to allow attendees from outside their college. In fact, most never even check to see if you are a student—you just walk right in. For safety's sake, it is always best to check with the sponsoring organization, which is usually the Career Development office

> THERE ARE JOB FAIRS TAKING PLACE NEARLY EVERY DAY AT COLLEGES THROUGHOUT THE UNITED STATES. TAP INTO THIS VAST RESOURCE.

for the college. If you are from a different geographical region and seeking to relocate to that particular area, most colleges are more than happy to accommodate your special request to attend. So if there is a job fair at another college, make sure you put it on your schedule. Don't limit yourself to your college alone—take advantage of all available resources.

For more information on how to take advantage of all the resources available through other colleges, see the Other Alma Mater Technique in the Guerrilla Insider Techniques chapter later in this book.

THE JOB FAIR NO-SHOW TECHNIQUE

If there is a job fair you would like to attend but are unable to do so, there is still a way to get noticed. Send your resume to the sponsoring organization twice, at least a week apart. The first one should arrive at least a week before the job fair and the second just after the date of the job fair. The reason? They will be accumulating resumes from those unable to attend in a stack or file. Then after the job fair, the resumes will be distributed to attending companies. When the company representative scans through the stack of two hundred to five hundred resumes, yours will be both at the beginning and at the end. And when it is seen the second time, the light will go on. "I know I have seen that person's resume before." You will get a long second look, which may be enough to make an impact.

Your resume should be specific and targeted. The two key areas on a job fair resume are the Objective section and the first job listed under the Experience section. Make sure yours are direct and to the point.

Chapter 12

SETTING UP ON-CAMPUS INTERVIEWS

Experience is not what happens to a man.
It is what a man does with what happens to him.
—Aldous Huxley

On-campus interviews are a gift. They will be by far the easiest interviews for you to find. Many students approach on-campus interviewing with little advance thought or preparation. As often happens, when something is given away for free, it has little perceived value. Be careful, however, that you spend this "free" resource wisely. On-campus interviewing is a once-in-a-lifetime activity. You will never again in your job search be granted the opportunity to simply "sign up" for interviews. Planning allows you to maximize this opportunity.

HOW TO CHOOSE THE VERY BEST EMPLOYERS TO INTERVIEW ON CAMPUS

Choose your interviews wisely. Year after year, students flock to the "household name" employers that come to campus (Exxon, IBM, General Motors, etc.), while some of the best employers go almost unnoticed, unable to fill their available interview slots. Why? Because they are not well known. And few students take the time to do the research and find out about these companies. Often there are pleasant surprises when looking into many of the smaller companies, which are usually more growth oriented and offer better opportunities for career advancement.

Think about it this way. If you were deciding whether to invest money in a company's stock, wouldn't you take the time to fully research the company, find out its product marketing, potential growth rate, and competitive position in the marketplace? Of course you would. So why would you settle for anything less when deciding in which company to invest your energies for the all-important beginning of your career?

Ironically, many college students end up going to work for companies they would not invest their own money in. Think about it. If you would not consider investing even $500 in the stock of the company, why would you consider investing your *life* in that very same company?

THE PERSONAL INVESTMENT DECISION TECHNIQUE

Use the Personal Investment Decision Technique as your litmus test for determining which are the very best companies to interview with on campus (and off). If you would not consider investing in the company from a financial standpoint, they probably should not be at the head of your list of companies to interview with. Conversely, those companies that are good investments will likely be good employers. Smaller companies may be less noticeable—with far less competition for available jobs.

Please note that this technique does not automatically count out all market giants due to sheer size and already established market domination. Merck, Microsoft, and Arthur Andersen are good examples of market leaders who are still at the top of anyone's list of great companies to work for. The key is not size, but whether or not you would be comfortable making a financial investment in the company.

Want some "insider information" in making these decisions? Hook up with a full-service stockbroker. Tell them you are interested in making an investment and that you would appreciate any information they may have on companies x, y, and z. Most are happy to oblige. The annual report is usually the stockholder's prime source of information. Even though it is obviously biased toward the company (after all, they wrote it), it is how they sell themselves as a good investment. You can also use some of the research resources listed in the Employer Research Strategies chapter before you decide whether to interview with the company.

In using this technique, it is important to keep in mind that, as in financial investments, there is always an unknown element involved. There may be some open questions, but do not wait until you have gathered "perfect information" before making your decision. Gather the information that is available, then make your choices. Do not get caught in the trap of trying to find the "perfect" company. It does not exist. And even if it did, it would not be perfect anymore after you went to work there, right? Instead, seek out a company that is fully committed to growth and excellence, in both the company and its employees.

Again, if you would not favorably consider making a financial investment in the company, then do not consider investing your heart and soul.

HOW TO BEAT THE LOTTERY

Apologies to the gamblers in our audience, but in this particular case we are talking about the interviewing lottery that takes place at most college campuses throughout the country. As the number of companies coming to campuses stagnates or declines, the demand for available interview slots increases so much that demand far outpaces supply. Most colleges have answered this demand/supply problem with some form of lottery (or bid) system.

For those of you fortunate enough not to be subjected to a lottery/bid system, feel free to skip the following sections. Or read along and thank your lucky stars that you don't have to go to such extremes to make the system work for you.

Although it may seem like there is no way around "the system"—which can often put an artificial barrier between you and potential employers—there most definitely are ways to work within the system. Following are some of the best techniques for beating the lottery.

THE BEST BID TECHNIQUE

What is the best bid? The best bid, obviously, is the lowest successful bid. Often the difference between the highest bidder and the lowest successful bidder is quite large, yet each person is perceived exactly the same by the recruiter. Therefore, why bid all five hundred of your allocated points when a low bid of five points will get you the interview? How can you determine what to bid? Several ways.

First, and most important, check the bidding from past years for the companies you are interested in. Then immediately contact the high-bid companies to try to secure an interview independent of the on-campus interviewing system. If you are able to secure the interview (see previous chapters for techniques) you will have saved a multitude of points that you can allocate elsewhere. Even if you are unsuccessful in

> ## THE HIGH BID SCORES NO POINTS IN THE ACTUAL INTERVIEW.

securing the external interview, the historical information you have gathered will give you the data you need to put in an effective bid. A good rule of thumb is to bid 20 to 40 percent above the previous year's low bid. Second, and also very effective, is to find out if there is any way to determine the status of bids to date. Most colleges use a sealed bid process, but many (amazingly) do not. Third, take a survey among your friends in the same major and extrapolate the results.

Another technique is to categorize those companies you have a passing interest in and bid just one point for each. Many lesser-known companies lack a full interview schedule when they come on campus, and for the paltry sum of just one point, you are given the opportunity to meet with them. Quite often it is these "second-tier" companies that offer the most interesting opportunities. Keep in mind that you might find yourself interviewing with the Microsoft or Merck of the next century.

THE EFFICIENT MARKET TECHNIQUE

This technique applies only to schools where lottery or bid points can be sold or reassigned from one student to another (most schools no longer allow this, but if yours does, make sure you use this technique). The solution is simple—make friends early with those who will be going on to grad school. Then buy up their supply of points as early as you possibly can (beginning of the fall semester is best), well ahead of the "feeding frenzy" (and subsequent drought of available points) that occurs in the middle of the spring semester. Don't worry about the cost—it will be well worth it, for two reasons. First, if you have not landed a job by spring, you will be glad to have the extra points already purchased at "pre-season" prices. Second (and even better), if you have landed a job, you can sell your points to the highest bidder. I heard from one college grad who made several hundred dollars by accepting a job before winter break. She held onto her points and finally sold them after the spring break rush. She used some of the money toward a down payment on a car. What a great added incentive for securing your job early!

THE IMPASSIONED PLEA TECHNIQUE

One of the worst things that can happen with a lottery or bid system is that you can fall short of making the cut for an interview with a company you really wanted to meet with. So what now? Roll over and die? No! Just because "the system" cut you out does not mean you have forever missed your opportunity to meet with this employer. Do some basic research and find out the name of the recruiter who is coming to campus—most Career Development offices will freely give you the information (if they have it). In other cases you may have to track down the information yourself by calling the company directly. Once you have located the person, call the company and leave a message for the recruiter. Have them label the message "Urgent." If you do not get a call by the day before the recruiter's arrival on campus, call the company, get the name of the hotel/motel where the recruiter is staying during the campus visit, and call there.

When you reach the recruiter, make your impassioned plea—you truly wanted to meet for an interview, but you were artificially (make sure you use that word!) excluded from the scheduled interviews by the lottery system. Ask if you can meet with the recruiter either early or late; during lunch, dinner, or breakfast; whenever! Even if you have to pay for the meal (usually you won't—most recruiters will offer to pay since they are on an expense account), it will be one of the best $10 or $20 investments you will make in your job search. Why? Because you will automatically stand out in the recruiter's mind as the person who was diligent enough to make things happen. One final note: if you do meet for a meal, order light—you need to keep your mouth unoccupied and available for speaking. Let the interviewer eat while you describe why you are the best thing to come along since sliced bread. Pass the toast.

INCREASING YOUR HIT RATE WITH INVITATIONAL INTERVIEWS

The current trend at many schools is the invitational, or "closed" interview. Resumes of all interested students are forwarded to the employer, who then selects those who will be interviewed.

The key to mastering the invitational interview game is to make each and every submitted resume specific to that employer. This is no time for the "generic resume," the one that speaks to everyone. This is the time to take the extra half hour to write your resume specifically for that employer. You might think that thirty minutes is a great deal of time to commit to gaining just one interview. It is not. Consider the amount of time it would take you after graduation to hunt down all necessary leads in order to garner your own live interview. Thirty minutes now is cheap insurance.

Ask the Career Development office at the beginning of the semester which companies will be holding closed interviews. Then ask for as much information as possible about each of these employers and the position requirements, including any minimum requirements for inclusion (such as GPA or major). Also ask when the screened resume packet will be mailed to the employer. Prepare your resume to emphasize those aspects of your background that meet or exceed the requirements. Remember, you should not lie or exaggerate about personal features that do not exist, but emphasize the positives in your background in relation to the specific employer. Then submit your personalized resume to the Career Development office for inclusion in the employer's resume packet.

> SPEAK TO MY NEEDS IN YOUR RESUME AND YOU WILL GET THE INVITATION.

While it may be "standard" for the Career Development office to send out the on-file generic resumes, requests to use a customized resume will usually be honored. Make sure your generic resume is on file for short-notice responses, but customize whenever possible.

As a final touch, you may want to consider adding "with _____" to the end of your Objective section, giving the name of the company as the final qualifier on your objective. If they know you are serious about them specifically, you are much more likely to get a positive response.

TIMING IS EVERYTHING

Always request the last or second-to-last interview slot of the day. In addition to being easier to work into your schedule, these time slots carry the significant weight of being the most memorable time slots for the interviewer. If you want to be remembered, schedule your interview as late in the day as possible.

NEXT STEPS

Once you have your on-campus interview scheduled, be sure to prepare properly for the interview by knowing everything you possibly can about the employer. Nothing turns me off quicker than a student who has no idea what my company does. And nothing will more quickly impress me than a student who has fully researched my company. Do your homework. Read Section 3, Interviewing Success and especially the On-Campus Interviewing Success chapter.

Also, keep in mind that you should not depend exclusively on interviewing on campus to guarantee you after-graduation employment. There are far more employers than just those that are visiting your campus. Many of the best employers may not be visiting any campuses. So make sure to take note of the chapters on how to reach out to these "other" employers.

Chapter 13

GETTING INSIDE HIRING COMPANIES

One man with courage makes a majority.
—Andrew Jackson

If a company is not interviewing on campus, it doesn't exist. This is obviously not true. Yet this is the unconscious job search approach of many college students who take their five or ten or twenty on-campus interviews, cross their fingers, and hope something happens. And in doing so, the entire job search universe has been restricted to only those companies that come to campus.

There are far more companies out there than those that are visiting your campus. To fully maximize your job search, consider all companies as potential employers. Reaching out beyond the campus bounds requires more effort on your part, yet the payback is considerable. In addition to increasing your overall odds of finding employment, you are also increasing your odds of finding the right job with the right employer.

Signing up for on-campus interviews is relatively simple, but it requires a great deal of effort to penetrate the armor of a company that is not interviewing on campus, especially if you have no internal leads or contacts. Keep in mind the reward in pursuing off-campus employers. You have the opportunity to target specific employers in specific industries in specific geographies. Simply put, it is proactive job search by design, rather than a reactive job search by default.

Getting through to a key contact should not be a blind shot in the dark. This is an exercise in quality contact, not quantity. It doesn't matter how many arrows you shoot if none of them hits the mark. After all of your preparation to date, make sure you drive home your point by aiming for the right target.

AIMING FOR THE RIGHT TARGET

Who your main contact within the company is will depend greatly on the size/structure of the company and your career focus. For those companies with large, well-established entry level hiring programs, there may be one or more persons focused solely on hiring you, the college student. This function is covered by a "College Recruiter" or "College Relations Representative" who is usually part of the Personnel or Human Resources Department. This is the person responsible for on-campus recruiting. This is the person whose job it is to screen out and disqualify. To pare down the long list into the short list.

The College Recruiter's criteria may be limiting—even to the point of counting you out before you even get in the door. Your main objective in making any contact should be to secure an in-person interview. And you cannot accomplish this if you are screened out. Why would you be screened? Most common is the school you attend. "It is not on our list." Or your GPA. "Too low for our standards." Or your major. "We are not hiring any of those this year." Or timing. "We have done all our entry level hiring for this year." Rather cold, but it's the reality of the typical College Recruiter. You may get nothing more than "what is on the board" of current entry level needs to be filled. But do not consider it the end of the line. The true bottom-line decision-maker is the Hiring Manager, or the line manager in the hiring department. Establish the College Recruiter as your target contact only as it serves your needs. Once it becomes a dead end or point of no further progress, you should be willing to immediately move on to the Hiring Manager as your target contact.

> IT'S EASY TO IDENTIFY AREAS WHERE YOU FALL SHORT OF THE DEFINED STANDARD. YOUR JOB IS TO FIND THE AREAS IN WHICH YOU EXCEL.

While it is almost always more difficult to locate and contact the Hiring Manager than to simply make contact with someone in Personnel, in the long run it pays to put forth the extra effort. Contacting Personnel is what everyone does. So if you join the party you merely join the competition in targeting a department whose primary task is to screen you out—your odds for success will likely be quite low. But direct contact with the Hiring Manager is golden. You are actually talking to a person who can hire you.

Hiring Managers determine hiring needs. Hiring Managers have the most latitude in determining what background will adequately fill the company's needs. And it is Hiring Managers who have the actual authority to hire.

Make the Hiring Manager your ultimate target contact. And do not give up easily.

THE TWO-STEP TARGETED CONTACT PROCESS

You should follow a two-step process in making contact. In the first step, do all of your research and information gathering, including identifying your target contact at a particular company. The second step is the actual direct contact with your target contact.

In the first step, you will often need to call the company to gather the needed information such as the name and title of the target contact. Even if the receptionist or other contact person offers to immediately connect you with your target contact, you should refuse: "Thank you, but this is the only information I need at this time." Speaking to your target contact should always be a separate step. It may seem rather futile to waste a phone call just to find out who your target contact is, so let me explain the reason for using this two-step method.

Think about what happens on the other end of the line. You have made an inquiry as to the name of the Hiring Manager,

> ### IF YOU ARE NOT PREPARED FOR THE SCREEN, YOU WILL BE SCREENED.

your target contact. As the person on the other end of the phone, I might give you the information on the person, then offer to put you through to that person's phone. You say that would be fine. Now I ask (if I have not already) who you are and what the call is about. "May I tell him what it is regarding?" *And you have just been screened.* Not just for this call, but for all future calls. I tell the manager that there is someone on the phone asking about titles and names and that the person is looking for entry level employment. The manager tells me to take a message. I do. And your chances of ever getting through to the Hiring Manager are greatly diminished.

Why is it so different doing it in two steps? Because when you use a second, separate step in calling your target contact, you can ask for the person by name, which puts your call on a different level from the information-gathering call. You have a great deal more leverage in getting through to the person and past the Guardian of the Gate who might have otherwise screened you out. So use the two-step target contact process. This entire chapter is devoted to step #1. Next chapter is step #2. An entire chapter just for finding and getting through to your target contact? Yes, since this is the pivotal activity that drives the next step. Sometimes it will be easy and sometimes not. This chapter gives you several tools for handling a wide variety of circumstances in gathering this information to help ensure your success in reaching the next step.

HOW TO FIND YOUR TARGET CONTACT

Before you can expect to locate your target contact, you will need to have a target title to focus on. This can be an industry-accepted title (such as "Controller" for accounting), or you can simply ask for the head of that particular department. For example, if you are an Accounting major seeking a position in corporate accounting, you could either ask for the name of the Accounting Manager or ask, "Who is the manager of your Accounting Department?"

Once you have established the target title, you need to find out the specific name and exact title of your target contact at your target company. If you have already received this information either via your research or through a contact referral, you are ready to go on to the next step.

Your starting point for researching the name of this contact should always be at the Career Development office on campus. If the desired information is not available there and your other research sources also fail your needs, you will need to make direct contact with the company.

THE MAILING LIST UPDATE TECHNIQUE

An excellent way to establish both the name and title of the Hiring Manager is the Mailing List Update Technique. Simply call the company switchboard and say:

> "Hi, I am updating my mailing list. Are you still at 123 North Main Street? And your zip code is still 54321? And what is the name of the manager of your _____ department? Could you please spell it? And what is her title? And does she have a direct extension? Thank you for your time."

If the switchboard operator asks, "Who is calling?" just give your name and nothing else. If the operator asks, "What is this in reference to?" or "What is this information for?" you should respond, "I am updating my mailing list for sending correspondence to this person and I would like to make sure the name and spelling are correct."

About 50 percent of the time this simple approach will get you all the basic information you need. But you will also find some professional screeners out there who will make their best effort to keep you from stealing the company secrets. So if the Mailing List Update Technique doesn't work for you, read on.

MORE WAYS TO FIND OUT WHO YOUR TARGET CONTACT IS

If you can't get the information you need directly through the switchboard, try the following additional methods:

1. When dialing the company, ask to be put through to the department, then ask the first person who answers. Department workers usually do not screen as heavily and may be more willing to provide the information.

2. Ask for the Personnel/Human Resources Department. But watch out! They are usually quite good at screening and may try to direct you straight to them if they know you are seeking employment. If so, give a polite "thank you" and try another method.

3. If you hit an automated-front-end-no-human-voice-hit-a-button system, usually you will have an option such as "0" to get to the operator. If not, feel free to wander through the system until you are able to reach a human voice, possibly someone in Customer Service. "Oh, I'm sorry, I was trying to get through to the switchboard and got lost in your telephone system. Can you please tell me the name of the manager of the _____ department ?" You get the idea. Keep trying until you find a responsive human. There is bound to be at least one in every company.

   If you have gotten this far and still don't have the basic information you are seeking, you are likely up against a screener who is attempting to keep you out. But never fear! We still have at least ten more ways to get through.

HOW TO GET PAST FRAULEIN FRIEDA, GUARDIAN OF THE GATE

Every company has its "Guardian of the Gate"—a person who rises to the level of mythological beast when you are trying to get through on the other end of the phone. As hard as we may try to get inside, this person keeps cutting us off. "Who is calling?" "What is this regarding?" "I'm sorry, but we don't have any openings at this time." "Just send your information to Personnel and they will call you if there are any openings." Whew! The Fraulein Friedas of the world can be a true pain when you are trying to get to the Hiring Manager. Do not give up easily. Here are ten nifty ways to get past Fraulein Frieda:

THE 7:30/12:30/5:30 RULE TECHNIQUE

The best way to get past the Guardian of the Gate is to avoid her altogether. The 7:30/12:30/5:30 Rule states that if you call early in the morning, during lunch, or late in the afternoon you will likely get someone who is not nearly as good at screening as the person who normally screens the calls. You can often gather all the information you need, since this person is not a true Guardian of the Gate.

Remember that extension number you asked for? Many companies now have automated call forwarding which allows you to enter a person's extension during the off hours. That extension number can usually put you through directly to the manager's office.

This is also an excellent approach in reaching a Hiring Manager who has been hitherto inaccessible. Why? Because if you are in management, you likely start early, work through lunch, or work late (or all three). Many managers end up answering their own phone at those times. For all they know, it's their spouse calling to ask them to pick up something on the way home.

P.S. If you are calling a different time zone, make sure to adjust your timing accordingly.

> ### After hours is the best time to reach a busy manager.

P.P.S. This is also a great way to reach a Vice President or even the President of the company. Keep The 7:30/12:30/5:30 Rule handy for future reference—you may need it in your career when you find yourself reaching higher within a company.

THE EVERYONE-LOVES-TO-HEAR-THEIR-OWN-NAME TECHNIQUE

If, per chance, the Guardian of the Gate uses her own name in answering the phone, reply,

"Oh, hello, _____, this is _____. May I speak with _____?"

The sound of her own name is disarming, and she will often send you through to your target contact.

THE AD INFINITUM CALL-WAITING TECHNIQUE

If you are told that your target contact is on the phone, simply reply, "Oh, that's fine. Will you please put me through as soon as that call is completed?"

If the Guardian of the Gate says it may be awhile or that she already has other calls waiting, reply,

> "Oh, that's okay—I don't mind holding. I'll be working on some papers while I'm on hold."

THE SPELLED NAME TECHNIQUE

If you are making a second attempt to get past a Guardian of the Gate who previously asked for your name, as soon as you recognize her voice, beat her to the punch by saying,

> "Hello, this is _____. That's _____ (spell your last name). Could you please put me through to _____?"

It's rather strange, but sometimes by spelling your name it disarms the Guardian of the Gate. She has to stop what she is doing and write down your name. And since you have called before, your name will likely be vaguely familiar, although she may not be sure when and where she heard it before. This is one time when having an unusual last name can truly work in your favor! Usually this will gain at least a check with the boss, and sometimes even fully unlock the gate. Try it!

THE IMPORTANCE-OF-THIS-CALL TECHNIQUE

The classic screening line from the Guardian of the Gate is:

> "May I ask what this call is regarding?"

If you are calling based on a referral, you can reply:

> "_____ asked me to call _____."

or

"This is a personal call." (if the referral is personal, not professional)

Otherwise, the best overall reply is:

"I was informed that I needed to get in touch with _____ directly."

The reply may sound nebulous at best—but amazingly, it often works. A truly astute Guardian of the Gate, however, will follow with:

"Regarding what?"

To which you reply:

"I was advised to only discuss this matter directly with _____."

How true! Who advised you to do this? I did. Here and throughout this book. You have read it, so consider yourself advised. Stick to your guns, even during that uncomfortable long pause that you may be forced to endure. Sure, it all sounds like a game and in a way, that is exactly what it is. Whoever has the most marbles in the end wins. You have just been loaded up with some tiger eyes, so take care to shoot them straight and fast.

THE UNANSWERABLE QUESTION TECHNIQUE

Another way to get past the "May I say what your call is regarding?" screen is to ask a technical question that Frieda will not be able to answer. If you have done your homework, you should have access to the industry buzzwords that can make this a very valid inquiry, one the Guardian of the Gate would not know the answer to.

The best way to do this is to ask a question that would further qualify your potential interest in the company. An example question for a Computer Science grad seeking to reach the Telecommunications Manager about networking positions might be:

"I needed to ask _____ whether your company is currently using either Token Ring or Ethernet LANs. Can you help me?"

Probably not. Once you get through to the Telecom Manager, you should still ask that question, then follow with how your background can potentially benefit them. For example:

"I recently received my Novell CNE certification and have been working with Ethernet and Token Ring configurations for the last two years. Is this the type of experience your company would usually look for in the area of LAN administration?"

This technique is something of a gamble. If your question is merely a ruse to get by Fraulein Frieda, you may end up with your foot in your mouth. But if used intelligently, it can launch you through to the Hiring Manager.

THE INSTANT BEST FRIENDS TECHNIQUE

If you are someone who has a gift for making friends with the friendless or have been known to strike up conversations with total strangers, feel free to reach out and make an instant friend. Even Fraulein Frieda is open to gabbing now and then. An especially effective tactic is to ask for her advice on how to reach the Hiring Manager. If you are sincere in your approach, you may gain an ally in the very person you previously considered your greatest roadblock.

THE BETTER THAN LEAVING A MESSAGE TECHNIQUE

Instead of leaving a message with a Hiring Manager (who may have no idea who you are), it may be better to reply:

> "I may be difficult to reach today. Could you give me a time when it would be best to reach _____?"

> WE ALL LOVE TO HEAR THE SOUND OF OUR NAME— PRONOUNCED CORRECTLY.

Then let the person know you will call back and ask if they would please let the Hiring Manager know you will be calling at that time. You are much more likely to get through.

THE BEST TIME TO CALL TECHNIQUE

If the Guardian of the Gate tells you that your target contact is in a meeting, out of the office, or otherwise unavailable, reply,

> "When do you think _____ would be available to take a call?"

If they say the target contact is very busy, ask for an approximate time. Then tell them your name (only) and let them know you will call at that time. Then make sure you do.

THE VOICE MAIL MESSAGING TECHNIQUE

With the proliferation of voice mail (automated messaging systems) in most U.S. corporations, the odds are great that you will find yourself leaving messages with this type of voice retrieval system. The good news is that almost all line managers review their messages personally (versus having a secretary review them), so you have an excellent opportunity to plant the seed for a future connection. Here is the best message:

"Hi, _____ (target's first name), this is _____ (your first name/last name). I can be reached at _____ (your phone number) between _____ and _____ today. I look forward to talking with you then."

The only modification of this is when you are calling based on a direct referral. Your message would then be:

"Hi, _____ (target's first name), this is _____ (your first name/last name). _____ (referral name) asked me to call you. I can be reached at _____ between _____ and _____ today. I look forward to talking with you then."

Then hang up. Short and sweet. This is not the time to give your full life story from the birth canal to the present. You merely need to set the hook for a callback, nothing more, nothing less. If you make the mistake of making your "pitch" on voice mail, you will lose your chance to respond to their specific needs. With minimal information given, the manager will feel obligated to return the call. Who knows? You may be a customer or supplier phoning them. In 75+ percent of the cases, they will at least attempt to return the phone call.

When you leave your name and phone number on voice mail, speak slowly, as if you were expecting the person on the other end to be taking down the information. Spell your first and last name. Repeat the phone number. Not as if you are talking to a second-grader, but as a matter of courtesy to make sure the recipient is able to write down the key information from the message. This raises the perceived level of importance attached to returning your call.

Another quick and easy response to the Guardian of the Gate who wants to take a message is to ask whether the manager has voice mail. If so, ask to be put through to it. You rather than the scribe at the other end of the line dictate what goes into your message. Voice mail is always better than a scribbled note and has greater professional obligation for action.

> IF YOU NORMALLY SHY AWAY FROM LEAVING MESSAGES ON VOICE MAIL, GET USED TO IT. IT'S THE REALITY OF COMMUNICATION IN THE '90S.

If you get no response to your initial voice mail message after at least three days, call again and leave a more detailed message based on your Thirty-Second Elevator Pitch. Give a quick synopsis of who you are and what you can provide to a potential employer. Ask for a return phone call to further discuss the employer's needs. And keep trying until you do get through.

THREE STRIKES AND YOU'RE OUT

Please, please remember that you definitely need an answering machine at Job Search Central to field calls when you are not in. Most managers will give up after three failed attempts. Even if they do get through to you on the second or third try, days or even weeks may have passed since the first attempt. Almost all managers have grown accustomed to "phone tag" and will gladly pass the baton back to you, possibly even giving you their direct line and the best time to reach them.

Chapter 14

GETTING THE OFF-CAMPUS INTERVIEW

Only those who dare to fail greatly can ever achieve greatly.
—Robert F. Kennedy

You are finally at the point of making the connection with the Hiring Manager. Now what? Your focus should be toward setting up the interview. No matter how good you sound on the phone, no matter how good you look on paper, you will not get the job without first getting the interview. Following are some of the basics.

HOW TO MAKE YOURSELF IRRESISTIBLE

Think about the last purchase you made, large or small. Why did you buy the item? Because the benefits were greater than the costs. Simple law of economics. When the benefits outweigh the costs, we buy. In reality, it's not quite that simple. We are actually making the decision based upon the *perceived* benefits being greater than the perceived costs. Yet it is only when we have a positive benefit/cost comparison that we will make our buying decision.

The same law of benefits versus costs applies to each stage of the employment process. You must convince the employer that the perceived, or potential benefits in hiring you will be greater than the perceived, or potential costs. This applies not only to the hiring decision, but also to whether or not you even get the initial interview. If I, as a Hiring Manager, do not see a benefit in meeting with you (as a potential solution for an immediate or future need) that is greater than the cost of meeting with you (giving up a half hour or hour of my time which could be used for other activities), you will not get the interview. If, however, I see a positive benefit/cost ratio, you will get the interview. While you have little control over my perceived costs in interviewing (which relate to the value of my

> INTERVIEWING IS A DIFFICULT ACTIVITY, FROM EITHER SIDE OF THE DESK.

> WHEN YOU FIRST
> CONTACT ME,
> I DON'T CARE
> ABOUT YOUR NEEDS.
> I ONLY CARE ABOUT
> WHAT YOU CAN
> DO FOR ME. WHEN
> YOU CONVINCE ME
> THAT YOU CAN MEET
> MY NEEDS, THEN I
> WILL BE INTERESTED
> IN MEETING YOUR
> NEEDS. BUT
> NOT BEFORE.

time in other areas of my work), you have almost absolute control over the perceived value of the benefits of a potential interview.

Therefore, you need to think in terms of benefits. Not yours. Not how much money you want to make. Not what a cushy job it would be for you. That has zero effect on me. If you are going to sell me on interviewing you, you will need to show how you will benefit *me* and *my company*.

To make yourself irresistible, you need to focus on what you can do to benefit my company. How you can increase our profits. How you can further develop our product line. How you can increase the efficiency of our existing systems. How you can help our business grow. How you can help our department prosper. How you can make me look good as a manager.

Many students take the attitude that I, as the Hiring Manager, should somehow magically decide what their value is and where they fit into the work world. That is not my job. That is your job. Do not expect me to figure out what your role in life will be. You know you far better than I, so do not expect me to know and understand what your greatest value is over the course of a thirty-minute meeting.

Interviewing is one of the most difficult activities to conduct in the work world, from either side of the desk. You have a limited time in which to convey value and benefit. And I have a limited time in which to evaluate that potential value and benefit. If you do your job as the transmitter, you will make my job much easier as the receiver.

Know the facts of your value and benefit, then sell others on these facts. That is what will make you truly irresistible.

WHAT TO SAY TO GET THE INTERVIEW

When you reach the Hiring Manager, you need to be fully prepared with a structured script. Now is not the time to talk about the weather. It's time for action and brevity. The best thing you can do is have a ready script that you can rely on—but don't use a script as something to read from. It is merely a dress rehearsal—to give structure to your call so that you are fully prepared to cover all the key points.

Although the basic approach can be altered, you should follow this structure to keep your calls brief, yet productive:

1. **Introduction** — who you are
2. **Purpose** — why you are calling
3. **Summary** — a brief summary of your potential benefits
4. **Action** — the step(s) to be taken

Following are two primary approaches that can be used with this structure: the direct approach and the indirect approach.

THE DIRECT APPROACH

The direct approach is generally preferred when you are targeting specific companies and are not afraid to be direct in your objective. It can be modified in "intensity" mainly by the use of alternate "action" statements. You can use either the trial close (you ask what their level of interest is) or the assumed close (you don't even ask for the interview, you just ask what day would be best). Following is a sample script:

1. **Introduction** — "Hello, Mr./Ms. _____, my name is _____. I'm currently finishing up my final year at _____ and will be getting my _____ degree in _____ in May (or August or December or whenever)."

2. **Purpose** — "The purpose of my call is to inquire about potential needs you may have within your department for _____."
Note: this is an appropriate time to mention how you were put in touch with the person in the first place; if you were referred, say so.

3. **Summary** — "My background includes . . . "
Note: state your top two or three features and potential benefits. These can include items from the Summary section of your resume and any personal attributes you feel would benefit the employer. If you have done your research properly, you should be able to customize your features and benefits specifically for your target company and target contact.

4. **Action** — "I'm planning to be in your area the week of _____ and currently have Tuesday or Wednesday open on my calendar. I'd appreciate the opportunity to meet with you and further discuss how I might serve you and your company. Is either Tuesday or Wednesday open for you?"

If you want to provide an alternative choice as your close, your last statement would be:

"Which day would be better for you, Tuesday or Wednesday?"

Remember, the key statement is the action statement. This is where you lock down on setting up the interview. One recovery statement that can be used if you get a "not interested" reply is:

"Are you aware of anyone else either within your company or at other companies who might have a need for someone of my background and abilities?"

Yes, it is a pressure release, but it can also be a cop-out. See some of the other techniques in this chapter and the next for converting a "No" to a "Yes."

THE INDIRECT APPROACH

This is preferred by those who would cringe at the idea of directly approaching a company to inquire about employment. It allows you to comfortably ask about employment without directly asking. Instead of asking a Hiring Manager about opportunities within her company specifically, ask a "Who-do-you-know" question, which could lead to one of three results: she doesn't know of anyone (or at least is not willing to give you the information if she does), she is aware of someone else who may have an interest (either within or outside the company), or she may have a direct interest herself.

You will find this to be a much more subtle approach, one that almost anyone can handle comfortably because there is none of the pressure that accompanies presenting yourself directly. If they happen to remark that they might be interested, your "Oh really?" response again takes the pressure off, since they are now coming after you instead of you going after them. A sample script for the indirect approach is as follows:

1. **Introduction** — "Hello, Mr./Ms. _____, my name is _____. I'm currently finishing up my final year at _____ and will be getting my _____ degree in _____ in May (or August or December or whenever)."

2. **Purpose** — "I was referred to you as someone who is well connected in the _____ field."

3. **Summary** — "My background includes . . . "
   Note: state your top two or three features and potential benefits. These can include items from the Summary section of your resume and any personal attributes you feel would benefit the employer. If you have done your research properly, you should be able to customize your features and benefits specifically to this target company and target contact.

4. **Action** — "Are you aware of any company that might have a need for someone with my background and abilities?"

It's low pressure, but it does come at a cost. If you are conducting a nationwide search, be aware that most referrals you will receive are local or regional at best. And with some managers, if you do not directly ask about their specific needs, you may never get the desired response.

THE HYBRID APPROACH

The hybrid approach uses the same basic script as the indirect approach (and therefore has the advantages associated with the "no-pressure" approach), but adds a crucial direct approach statement at the end of the conversation:

"And are there any areas within your company that could utilize my background and abilities?"

Although it is a direct approach, when used in tandem with the indirect opening lines, it usually makes for a very comfortable direct statement. And it can often develop more external contacts than the direct approach by itself.

Use the above scripts as basic guidelines, then develop your own standard script. Use a script only as a guide, not as a verbatim recitation. If you do, you will end up sounding stiff and lifeless. Use scripts only as your practice material, then develop a personal presentation when you are fully comfortable with your approach. Most of all, make sure you modify your script to add wording that may flow naturally when you are making your presentation. If you mention something particularly poignant during one of your phone conversations, write it down and incorporate it into your standard script. If you are asked a question for which you have no ready answer, write it down—and make sure you have a ready answer for the next time.

> **IF THE ONLY AVAILABLE ANSWERS ARE POSITIVE, YOU WILL GET A POSITIVE ANSWER.**

THE ALTERNATIVE CHOICE TECHNIQUE

Have you ever bought a car from a truly sharp automobile salesperson? You might have noticed that they don't ask questions such as "Do you want to buy this car?" since a potential answer is "No." Instead they ask, "Which color would you like, red or blue?" or "Would you rather have the automatic or manual transmission?" Why? Because the only answer options are positive.

Do the same thing in your job search. Don't ask: "Can we get together for an interview?" Instead, ask: "I have Wednesday and Thursday afternoon open for us to meet. Which day would work better for you?"

By giving a choice of two or more positive responses, you greatly increase the odds that you will get a positive response. Give them choices, but make them positive choices.

THE SOLUTION SUGGESTION TECHNIQUE

You may be aware of a product introduction or ad campaign being conducted by an employer you are interested in. Or you may be a user of their product or service. If you have a valid suggestion for improvement, drop a note to a key person detailing this information. Most executives enjoy getting this kind of feedback direct from their customers and welcome honest suggestions. "A thought occurred to me while using your product . . ."

There are plenty of potential areas of focus with any company, among which are areas where you might be able to offer a benefit for the company. Do you feel you can add value by:

Increasing sales?

Expanding market share?

Increasing efficiency?

Upgrading technology?

Reducing production cycle time?

Reducing costs?

Remember, anything you can provide as a potential benefit is reason enough to make contact—and not just increasing the positives, but also decreasing the negatives. Find a potential problem and come up with your own basic solution to present to the company. It's an extra touch that very few college students would even consider attempting. You will be head and shoulders above the crowd.

THE FAIR ENOUGH TECHNIQUE

If and when you do have to ask a yes or no question, the best technique is to frame the question in such a way that there is a "give-give" taking place and you are willing to make an up-front commitment on specific parameters, such as limiting the amount of time necessary for the initial meeting. End the request with "Is that fair enough?" or simply "Fair enough?" Why does it work? Because everyone wants to be fair, and you are appealing to their sense of fair play. Frame it properly and they will have difficulty refusing your request.

THE FIVE MINUTES AND COUNTING TECHNIQUE

"I understand you are a busy person and your time is limited. I am not asking you for thirty minutes, an hour, or two hours to meet with me. If you will give me just five minutes of your time—and not one second more—I will give you all the basic information you need to know about me so that you are ready to act when the time comes to add to your staff. You will know who I am, what I can do for you, and how I can upgrade the level of performance in your department. Five very efficient minutes. Five minutes and not a second more. Fair enough?"

If they do give you the chance to meet with them, the first thing you do is take off your watch, lay it down on their desk, and make your presentation. At exactly the five-minute point, end your presentation. You must keep your promise or this technique will fail. You need to get straight to the main points of your presentation. And if you have presented yourself effectively, they will wish you had stayed longer. Give them your Networking Business Card and ask them to call you if they have any additional questions. If they ask you to stay longer, do it! Even if they don't, they have seen you in person, you have made your initial presentation, and now it is up to you to keep the contact alive by diligently following up.

THE WE-ALL-HAVE-TO-EAT TECHNIQUE

"I realize that you are a busy person and your time is limited. Yet we all take time for lunch. I would like to make you an offer. I would be happy to treat you to lunch at the restaurant or cafe of your choice, if you will just take the time to listen to my background while you're eating. All I ask of you is that you keep your ears open. Fair enough?"

If lunch doesn't work, offer breakfast. When your offer is accepted, either order light or not at all—use your time to sell the manager on you. It will be the "cheapest" meal you will ever buy since your new contact will feel a personal obligation to assist you, either directly or indirectly.

HOW TO HANDLE THE "WORK THROUGH PERSONNEL" STALL

If you are told by the Hiring Manager to "work through Personnel," the following reply will usually disarm them:

"Oh, I'm sorry. I thought you were the Hiring Manager for the _____ area (or department)."

Even the smallest ego cannot resist proving to you that he or she is in fact the person who makes the decisions regarding hiring for the department. Even if you are forced to follow this route by some arcane company policy (they usually don't really exist), make sure you reference the Hiring Manager in your cover letter, list the person as a "CC:" (carbon copy) at the end of the letter, and forward a copy. This will enhance your image in the eyes of Personnel (since you already have the name of the Hiring Manager) and will leave the door open to this person in case you get lost in the Personnel shuffle.

> EGO IS A POWERFUL MOTIVATOR. WE ALL HAVE IT. AND WE REACT POSITIVELY TO THOSE WHO STROKE IT.

HOW TO HANDLE THE "SEND ME YOUR RESUME" STALL

One of the most common stalls in the employment world is the "Send me your resume" stall. Usually it is just a way to further stall the process and turn away those who are attempting to find their way inside the company. It also happens to be a favorite response of the Personnel Department.

In reality, it merely serves to kill the live contact that you have worked so hard to attain. The best response to this request is to let the person know that you are going to be in the area (assuming you are geographically nearby) and would be happy to hand-deliver a copy of your resume: "I understand the importance of the resume for you, so I'll stop by and hand-deliver it." This usually reverses the stall. You have now converted the brush-off into a reason to have a face-to-face meeting—even if it is just for a few minutes. Never underestimate the power of this brief meeting. Even if all you do is shake hands and pass on your resume, you have now become a person, not just a piece of paper or a voice on the phone. Any further contacts will be much warmer. And if you have a gift for conversation, don't be afraid to start talking, especially if you have done your homework on the company. It only takes a couple of minutes for an astute Hiring Manager to recognize a person who would potentially fit with the team. So use the classic stall to your advantage!

THE FAX YOURSELF TECHNIQUE

The next best way to handle the "Send me your resume" stall—especially if you are not located near the company—is to offer to fax your resume directly.

Tell the person you will fax your resume and call back within a half hour. By doing this, you accomplish two goals. First, you immediately overcome the initial stall. Second, you put information in their hands that can take you to the next step in the process: setting up the interview.

There is something truly magical about faxes. They are usually handled differently from other incoming mail. While other mail is processed through the mail room and dropped in a pile in the manager's in-basket, faxes are often hand-carried to the recipient and placed on the center of the desk. Small thing? It is not,

> **PERSISTENCE ALWAYS SCORES MORE POINTS THAN MERE EXPERIENCE.**

I assure you. Yes, they often arrive with less-than-perfect print quality and are generally unacceptable as long-term documents, but as a way to get your message across immediately, there is no better medium. Many companies are now using plain-paper faxes with a quality level approaching laser printers, so be sure to send in "Fine Mode" on the fax machine. Put it to use!

THE TRASHPROOF RESUME TECHNIQUE

Entry level candidate resumes often end up getting filed in the "circular file" (either literally or figuratively). Want to ensure that your resume will continue to see the light of day? Simply call before and after sending your resume. And when you call before, make sure you tell them that you will also be calling after. If the employer knows that the resume will be referenced again in the near future, it will be filed nearby for quick access, or, better yet, may remain on the Hiring Manager's desk, ready and waiting for you to call. So make sure you do.

THE GROUND ZERO RESUME TECHNIQUE

Instead of using your "standard" resume, take the time to create a resume from ground zero, designed specifically for the company you are interested in. Most companies assume that your resume is static, so when they see one that emphasizes the exact points that are important to them, they will be impressed.

An alternative form of this technique is to simply modify your objective to target a specific company and their needs. For example, if you are attempting to set up an interview with several companies in the insurance industry, you may want to incorporate insurance industry wording into your objective. Or if you have specific geographical areas targeted, you can modify your objective to zero in on each one of these areas.

THE I-ONLY-LOVE-YOU TECHNIQUE

Is there one company that you would really truly love to work for? Tell them so! How? Simple. By using the specific company name in the Objective section of your resume. Example:

"Staff Auditor position with Arthur Andersen."

That says it all! If you love them, tell them so.

P.S. As in love, don't go telling this to more than one (or two?) at any given point in time—otherwise you could begin to look rather fickle.

THE COMPANY LOGO TECHNIQUE

If there is a specific company you have targeted, another technique you can use is to incorporate the company logo (pardon the pun) into your objective. It takes a little creative effort (or a good scanner) to get it precise, but the effect can be quite stunning.

While I was with IBM, we received a resume with the IBM logo emblazoned into the individual's objective in imperial blue with the trademark horizontal stripes. Did we show it around the office? You bet! Did the person get the interview? Yes, he did. Did he get the job? Yes, he did.

THE LIMITED TIME OFFER TECHNIQUE

Any good salesperson will tell you that one of the best ways to close a sale is to make a limited time offer. The same applies in the employment field.

If you are having difficulty getting interviews set up, tentatively schedule a visit to the area, possibly over winter or spring break, or even during an extended weekend. Then make a new round of phone calls. This time, make sure you note that: "I plan to be in the _____ area Monday through Friday, March _____ to _____" (or whatever your time frame is). You can also utilize the Alternative Choice Technique by stating: "I have Tuesday, Thursday, and Friday open. Which of those days would be best for you?"

If they balk at the opportunity to meet with you, remind them that you will only be in the area a short time. "After that time, there would, of course, be travel expenses involved in getting together." If they have any inkling of interest, they will get the point. This is a limited time offer. If I have any interest in interviewing you, I had better do it when you are in town, or it will end up costing me $600+ for the plane/hotel/rental car routine.

This technique also works well once you have one interview set up. If you are being flown in, ask for an extra day or so to scout the area, or ask to stay over the weekend. This will give you the chance to meet with any other prospective employers while you are in town. Companies love to meet with candidates on someone else's bill. If you are staying extra on Company #1's expense account, make sure you do actually spend time looking around the area and not just meeting with Company #2 and Company #3. If that is the only reason your hotel bill is three nights instead of one, you have an ethical obligation to pick up the extra two nights' expense.

THE MULTIPLE INTERVIEWS TECHNIQUE

If you have one interview and would like to quickly generate more, simply become a name dropper. Mention the name of the company you are interviewing with as you are attempting to set up additional interviews. Most employers have a strong herd instinct that guides them in deciding who to interview. "Oh, you're interviewing with XYZ? Let me see what I can work into my schedule." It is amazing how quickly the schedule will open up for someone who is already being interviewed, especially if the interview is with a competitor.

So when you get an interview lined up, do not single-thread that process through to completion before pursuing others. You are in the very best position to set up multiple interviews immediately after the first is set up. Make the most of this opportunity.

IMPROVING YOUR OUT-OF-STATE SEARCH

If you are conducting a job search directed toward an out-of-state location, you can greatly improve your odds by establishing a local address in the target city or region. Employers are much more likely to respond to local phone numbers and addresses.

The best way to do this is to use the address of a friend or relative. Caution: if it's the home of friends or relatives with a different last name, ask them if they will answer the phone without the family name for the duration of your search. Otherwise, the caller may assume they reached a wrong number and hang up. Next best is to use a mail drop (such as Mail Boxes Etc.) and an answering service. In either case, information can be forwarded to you as often as you desire.

OUT-OF-STATE INTERVIEWS

Although almost all companies will cover your interview expenses for traveling to the company-site after an initial on-campus interview, it is not a given when you are initiating contact from out of state. When you have been invited in for a company-site interview, you should always ask the following, well-phrased question:

"Will your company be making the travel arrangements for me?"

Straight and simple. If the company is making the arrangements for you and all you have to do is pick up your tickets, it's paid for. If you are expected to make the arrangements but the company will be reimbursing, you will usually be asked to save receipts. If you are on your own, you will be advised that the travel arrangements are up to you. You should still save your receipts—the company might reimburse you at a later date or you might be able to get a tax deduction (see your tax advisor for details on deductibility).

If the company will not be paying and you cannot personally afford the trip, before passing up the opportunity you might want to weigh it in the balance—this might be a really good time to beg some money from Mom and Dad ("It's a lot better than being unemployed and living at home after I graduate" tends to open the purse strings nicely), or rich Aunt Sally, or that friend who owes you money, whomever, whatever. You can also reduce your costs by driving (if it's a drivable distance) or by flying over the weekend and staying at a budget motel. Although $500 might seem like a lot of money right now for what is not by any means a sure thing, it will seem like a pittance come graduation day if you are still without a job.

You might also consider setting up interviews with multiple companies in the area, which would help defray the "per" cost and make it a more effective trip for you.

And as a last resort, if you really can't swing it, call the employer to advise that if there were any way to make it happen, you would. But you are just a poor college student who spent your last nickel on getting this fine education—is there anything that can be done to bring you together for this meeting? Try it! Some employers will understand that you are eager to make it happen and will cover the costs. Last, last resort? Ask for Dutch treat—you pay half, I pay half. Last, last, last resort? Ask the employer to initially cover the bills, and if you are not worth every penny of the expense, you will write a check then and there. In fact, if you are confident and aggressive enough, you may want to try that technique when you first realize that the expenses might not be fully covered. Few companies would ever dare to ask for their money back from a starving college student for any reason short of fraud. As long as you are honest, this approach can be a winner.

Chapter 15

GUERRILLA INSIDER TECHNIQUES

*No one ever gets very far
unless he accomplishes the impossible at least once a day.*
—Elbert Hubbard

As your job search develops, you will likely find that the conventional ways of doing things are sometimes not good enough. Following is a collection of unconventional techniques to use in your job search. Just because they are new and different does not mean that they are difficult or impossible. If you want to succeed in your job search, you need to step outside many of the artificially imposed boundaries and seek to accomplish the impossible at least once each and every day.

THE OTHER ALMA MATER TECHNIQUE

Not interested in the companies that are coming to your campus? Not getting anywhere with the ones you have met with? Running out of options? Your next-best resource is often no farther away than the halls of a nearby—or distant—college.

Most college students limit their job search to the Career Development office of the college they are attending. Maybe it seems disloyal or even unethical to seek out the resources of another college. I assure you it is not. If you fall into one of the following categories, the Other Alma Mater Technique may be right for you:

➤ Seeking a geographical area outside of the immediate locale of your college, especially if "home" is in another part of the country

➤ Attending a small or medium-sized school with a limited number of companies coming to campus

➤ Seeking a job in a major field not currently offered by your college

➤ Wanting to interview with companies in your focus area that your school is not able to attract due to size, location, school reputation, or any of a variety of reasons

The Other Alma Mater Technique merely involves "adopting" another college—or colleges—as your own when it comes to your job search. There is nothing disloyal or unethical about it. While both private and public colleges will usually be more than happy to help you, remember that your tax dollars (or at least those of your parents) have gone to finance the state colleges. You have a right to access the information by virtue of taxes paid to fund the system. Most information is considered public information anyway, so there is no need to feel like you are robbing a bank when you ask for information from other schools.

> DON'T LIMIT
> YOURSELF TO THE
> RESOURCES OF
> YOUR COLLEGE
> ALONE.

First, you need to choose the school or schools. State schools are best, not only because of the "tax debt" issue, but also because they tend to draw a wide variety of companies both locally and nationally. And you are less likely to run into the "elitist" attitude that exists at some private schools. Unlike state schools, the private schools do not have to give you any information.

Your best choice is to choose a state school that is centrally located in the geographical area you are interested in. It doesn't have to be "State U.," although the premier state university is usually the largest and has access to the largest number of companies. You might consider contacting both "State U." and some of the smaller regional branches of the state university system.

Once you have chosen which schools to contact, there are several ways to begin drawing upon their resources. Following are some of the best:

> ➤ **Call the Career Development office at the other school directly**
> Make a call to the Career Development office and explain your situation. Ask if you can access the office's company information files. Most colleges will give you full access short of including you in on-campus interviewing and career/placement counseling. This can include access to the company listings, the jobs bulletin board, the on-campus recruiting schedule, and the company research library, including the use of CD-ROM and electronic databases. Some have even allowed outsiders to fill the open on-campus interview slots on a "standby" basis, especially if you are attending the small private college across town and have taken the time to establish a personal relationship. Better yet, take a night course at that college, which can often ensure access to the full range of career assistance available. Remember that many placement people are often overworked and underpaid, so it's possible you may not get much personal time unless you are a full-time student at the school. Don't become discouraged. Just change to a "low-impact strategy" by adopting one of the following approaches:

➤ **Attend the job fair**
This is by far the easiest way to tap into the employer pipeline. Very seldom are large state schools restrictive in job fairs. Take note that the largest schools may have several different job fairs, each with its own focus, each with a specific set of majors and disciplines in mind. So if you are an Engineering major, you would not want to attend the Teacher's Job Fair. Keep in mind that your "nonresident" status might initially throw the corporate recruiters for a loop, since they assume that everyone is from that college. Just explain that several companies at the job fair had not yet visited your school and you wanted to meet with them. You will stand out from the crowd just for your tenacity in seeking them out. These are excellent contacts since you automatically have a point of differentiation from the rest of the herd. If you present yourself well, the odds are in your favor that you will be the one who is noticed above the rest.

➤ **Ask for a copy of the on-campus interviewing schedule**
Try to get a copy of the on-campus interviewing schedule for the current semester and the previous semester. Why the previous semester? Because both listings contain companies that are hiring at the entry level. The fact that a company was on campus four months ago makes them almost as valid as the company that was there last month. If possible, you will need to find out what the companies were recruiting for. If Mobil was on campus to interview Chemical Engineering majors and you are an Accounting major, it is only a secondary contact. The best contacts are with companies that are actively recruiting in your area of interest. Contact each one of the companies, informing the contact person that you are aware that the company was recruiting at "State U." for _____, that you are a _____, that the company did not recruit at your school, and that you would certainly appreciate an opportunity to meet personally to explain why you feel you are the top candidate for the position. This is a high-probability method of scoring an initial interview.

➤ **Check out the jobs bulletin board**
Most colleges maintain a jobs bulletin board, listing those companies that are coming to campus in the upcoming weeks as well as information on various other job opportunities. The bulletin board is often in the Career Development office, but not always. Sometimes it will be in a "commons" area where students frequently pass by. Call ahead to check for the location. These are real live entry level jobs that someone will get. Why not you?

➤ **Contact the jobs hotline**
Most colleges maintain a phone number that is used for updating students on job availability. Simply call the campus operator and ask for the number. Then call as often as it is updated—usually weekly. You will get valuable information about new companies that are

coming to campus. Also, many companies that are not able to make it to campus but still have an interest are often listed on the jobs bulletin board or the job hotline.

➤ **Drop by in person**
Often the best way is to just stop in at the Career Development office and browse. If the other alma mater happens to be three thousand miles away, you may need to wait until your planned visit to the area, but it will always be a productive visit. This is where you will find the jobs bulletin board, files full of company information, and access to computers with company and job searching capabilities. Usually no one will even know you are not from the school.

In addition, you may find the library research resources of another college superior to those of your own. This is especially the case with large state schools which have access to the more expensive CD-ROM and electronic database information that can be prohibitively expensive for smaller schools. If you do find something on the shelves that you really want to take home for further reading, find out if your own college library has an interlibrary loan agreement with that library. Most do, and it can give you access to important materials not otherwise available at your own library.

The Other Alma Mater Technique will broaden your job search horizons to include companies and resources previously out of reach. Use it to your full advantage to locate and contact hiring companies and contacts.

THE POST-IT NOTE TECHNIQUE

If you have a strong advocate among your references, you may want to consider this resume-enhancing technique. Have your reference fill out a series of Post-it Notes (3″ x 3″ size works best) with the following handwritten note:

Excellent Candidate—Definitely Interview

They then sign their name (and title, if appropriate). This technique works because of the internal referral network at most companies which is supported by the Post-it Note-and-pass-along method of delegation. I receive memos and other notes from my boss with similar directions attached via Post-it Note.

An alternative would be to put "Highly Recommended—Definitely Interview" on a business card attached to the resume. Either way, it sends the very unconventional message that more people think highly of you than just you. Remember that the words of others said about you will almost always carry more weight than your words alone.

THE HIGHLIGHTER TECHNIQUE

Another unconventional method of bringing additional focused attention to your resume is to selectively highlight two or three of the most important points with a yellow highlighting pen. Again, use of a highlighter is often accepted as a means of emphasis in communications and will provide your resume with the nearly immediately eye-catching color that will draw the reader to the key areas of your background.

> IF YOU DO EXACTLY WHAT EVERYONE ELSE IS DOING, YOU WILL GET EXACTLY THE SAME RESULTS THEY ARE GETTING.

THE HIGHER CALLING TECHNIQUE

What do you say when you get through to an employer, but are given the "Sorry, no openings" line? Fumble through a timid request for "Who else do you know who might be hiring?" or some other question of the conquered? Most don't even use that line—they just give the standard "Thanks for your time" and "Bye."

One way to combat this contact killer line is to ask the manager the following series of questions:

"Since you're now fully staffed in your department, may I ask you a question? Do you feel that enough of your time is spent on the high-level duties that your job requires? Or do you find yourself having to continually tend to lower-level duties in order to get the rest of your work done?"

"Please think about that because what I would like to offer to you, now that you are fully staffed, is the opportunity to pass on some of those lower-level duties to someone else so that your time is freed up for the higher-level tasks. After all, isn't it the higher-level work that you're being paid for?"

"Please seriously consider this offer. Think about what it would be like if someone such as myself were able to give you an extra ten, fifteen, twenty hours or more per week for your higher-level duties. And also think about all those projects that you've put on the back burner because you don't have enough staff to handle the tasks. I could do that—and more—for you and your department."

"Think about it. If you have an interest, give me a call. Do you have a pen? Again, my name is _____ and my phone number is _____. And if I haven't heard from you, I'll call back in a couple of weeks to touch base. Thanks for your time."

Does it always work? No. But it works a lot better than the "Thanks for your time" and "Bye" that 99 percent replied with. You are planting a seed. It may not sprout instantly, but don't be surprised if the next time you call back, your proposal starts sounding very attractive to the manager. Your job would be to free them up for higher-level responsibilities. And your job would be one of the very best in the world because you would be directly in the middle of the departmental action from day one.

Try it!

THE UPGRADE YOUR STAFF TECHNIQUE

Another reply to the "We don't have any openings right now" response is the Upgrade Your Staff Technique. While most managers scramble to find a new person when they lose a valuable staff member, very few think about upgrading their staff when they are at full employment. Here is how it works:

> "Since you are fully staffed, now might be a good time to consider upgrading your staff. As the economy continues to grow, it will likely become harder and harder to find competent people to add to your staff. You might consider this an excellent time to make plans to upgrade your staff. Would it be correct to say that the most valuable member of your staff isn't necessarily the most skilled, but the one with the best attitude toward their work?"

> (Wait for "Yes" or "Probably")

> "Well, Mr./Ms. Manager, it's that same attitude of excellence, that same attitude of giving my all that I would bring to you and your department. I'd like the chance to meet with you and prove that I have what it takes to become a key member of your department. I am available the week of March 13th, with Tuesday and Wednesday wide open. Which day would work better for you?"

Again, it doesn't always work. But it sure gets them thinking beyond the "no openings" objection. And don't be surprised if they think about it and give you a shot. This technique plays on the vanity of the manager and their desire to be out in front of the game. Who could blame them for planning in advance? Certainly not you or I.

THE BABY-ON-THE-DOORSTEP TECHNIQUE

Baby-on-the-Doorstep is a sales technique named after the proverbial "drop the baby off on the doorstep and someone will make sure she is taken care of" method of adoption. Ever hear of a baby that was left there? Never. And that is the basic premise for Baby on the Doorstep—if I called you on the phone and asked you to adopt a child, you probably would not even consider it. But if that very same child appeared on your doorstep, what would you do? You would at least take her in and see to it that she finds a proper home.

This sales technique is used every day by energetic salespeople who call on customers unannounced, in person—many with a great deal of success. Baby on the Doorstep involves some courage on your part since you will be doing what most companies ask you not to do: show up in person without a scheduled interview. But it is actually quite simple. You just pack up your resume, head down to the company location, and try to find your way as close to the Hiring Manager as possible. Ask if the Hiring Manager is in, state your name and that you have a personal package to be hand delivered. If the person is out, ask when he or she will be in again and call at that time. If the person is in, ask to meet briefly. When and if you do get through, say that you were "in the neighborhood" and decided to drop off your resume personally. State your interest in working for the company and ask if the person would schedule fifteen minutes so that you can talk further. Do not push for anything more than that. If you are offered time right then, go for it. If not, be willing to come back at a later time that day or later that week. Remember that you are interrupting the person's day and schedule, so take only what you are given and don't push for more.

Even though you are interrupting unannounced, do not assume that you will be turned away. Managers are not continually occupied with "A" priorities throughout the day. Also, you may be stopping by at a time when hiring is an "A" priority. So know the company going in and be prepared for a potential full interview. It does happen. Be prepared.

> **GETTING YOUR FOOT IN THE DOOR IS NOT NEARLY AS IMPORTANT AS GETTING THE REST OF YOU INSIDE.**

The reality of Baby on the Doorstep is that you may only get one or two minutes face to face with the Hiring Manager. But that amount of time is quite sufficient for establishing yourself in their mind. Up to that point, you are only a piece of paper or a voice on the phone. Now you are a real person. Assuming you present yourself well, that one to two minutes has the same—or greater—initial effect as the formal interview, since you are being evaluated with very scrupulous eyes.

It's an aggressive technique, one that some may shun or shy away from. But if you are failing to get through to a company, this technique offers a solid alternative.

THE PICTURE PERFECT TECHNIQUE

Get ready for a politically incorrect (yet effective) suggestion. This one goes against almost everything written about proper resumes. But it still works in the great majority of cases.

Put your picture on your resume. Not pasted on, but scanned in as a small 1″ x 1″ graphic at the top right on the page.

I know, I know, you are not supposed to do that. And companies are not supposed to care about what you look like. But they do. Especially when hundreds or thousands of miles separate you, it can effectively communicate the vital message: "I am a real person. Talk to me."

> YES, I NOTICE YOUR APPEARANCE. NO, I DON'T CARE ABOUT THE COLOR OF YOUR SKIN. BUT I DO NOTE WHETHER OR NOT YOU HAVE BATHED IN RECENT HISTORY.

There are some caveats to this technique. If you look like the Unabomber, you might want to either shave or skip. But for 90+ percent, there should be no problem with personal appearance. Remember, this is going to shrink down your photo to less than one inch square, so complexion problems or even a large nose will not matter much.

Many large-company Human Resources Departments will screen or cover up the photo, thereby masking a small part of your resume. So only use it if your resume is going direct to the Hiring Manager or if it is a smaller company. And finally, the main reason all the books say this is wrong is because of the potential for discrimination. They are right, but only to a very limited degree. Bottom line is that there are still some rednecks out there who will discriminate against you for your race, your sex, your religion, and any of a variety of protected classes. You probably would not want to work for them anyway. Discrimination does happen. So if you are worried about potential discrimination, you have to go into this one with your eyes open. But remember that for every redneck, there are scores of professionals who will value your diversity. It is a risk, yet it is up to you to take that risk in a calculated way. If you feel it has the potential to enhance your job search, use it. If not, don't.

THE TIME IS MONEY TECHNIQUE

Want to make sure your mailed materials are reviewed? Even when your resume may be among a stack of hundreds of other resumes? Follow this simple technique: attach a crisp new $1 bill to your resume/cover letter and place a yellow Post-it note on the bill with the following handwritten note:

I know that time is money and I value your time. Would you please invest two minutes in reviewing my resume today, and in taking my phone call later this week? I appreciate your time.
Sincerely,

Your Name

It never fails to get the attention of the employer. Why? For the very same reason that our eyes are attracted to the unclaimed quarter on the sidewalk. Our eyes are naturally (unnaturally?) drawn to money. Your $1 bill will stick out in the sea of paper. And it may be what sets you apart from the crowd. And no one will throw away the $1 bill—they will either pocket it or let it sit on top of their desk until they figure out what to do with it. Either way, they will feel a guilty obligation to the original owner. Note: don't use more than $1 (such as $5 or $10). One dollar is symbolic, whereas anything more could appear to be a bribe. Not to mention the fact that at higher rates it could get very costly very quickly.

THE DREAMING TECHNIQUE

The Dreaming Technique is rather simple, yet can have a profound impact on your job search. As you dream about your potential new job, dream also about your potential dream employer(s). If you have a specific company in mind, communicate your "dream" to your potential employer. It is not enough just to dream—your dream will always be just a dream until you tell someone about it. Then it has the possibility of becoming a reality.

The key to this technique is to use the term "dream employer" when you are talking to the company. The fact that someone is currently occupying your dream job at your dream company should not make any difference. If it is your dream, say so. A typical script might be:

> MONEY IS THE NUMBER ONE VISUAL AID. IF YOU WANT TO DRAW ATTENTION, PULL OUT A LARGE BILL. IF YOU WANT TO DRAW A CROWD, DROP IT.

"I just want to let you know that your company is truly my dream employer. In all my research, in all my inquiries, I have found no company I would rather work for than yours. I realize that you may not have a need for someone with my skills at this exact moment in time. But some day, some way, I hope to have an opportunity to work for your company. I am willing to do whatever I can to help make that dream come true. Will you help me in reaching my dream by letting me know when an opening is available for someone such as myself?"

People change, companies change, and one day (possibly in the not-too-distant future) you may find yourself interviewing for that dream job. Possibly sooner than you think. It makes a significant difference to the employer to know that you see them as more than "just another job." This type of information will set you apart from the rest of the crowd when the employer considers adding new staff.

THE VIDEO RESUME TECHNIQUE

Remember the mock interview you went through at your Career Development office? Did it go well? Do you have it on tape? If not, it may be time to revisit and redo. If you are able to create a master video of your responses to some standard interview questions, that video can be duplicated and utilized as support for your job search. While you may have been somewhat unprepared for the questions in your mock interview, you should fully prepare for your video resume, and ask someone to interview you in a positive way with your preselected questions.

A video interview tape can be utilized in two ways: first, as a door opener with a select few employers you are targeting, and second, as an alternative method for moving forward a stalled phone interview process.

In preparing the video resume master for duplication, it is important to record an appropriate introduction and closing for the tape. Ideally, you can have the same person who served as your video interviewer provide the introduction and closing. Your introduction should be short and sweet, explaining who you are and the purpose and format for the tape. Your closing should provide a very specific next step for the employer to follow in making direct contact with you. Have copies made for you professionally to avoid any cheesy did-it-in-my-basement look. And label each tape with a printed label, including your name and contact information. Always include your written resume folded and attached to the videotape.

The video resume should not be utilized as a crutch for getting into nearby companies. If an employer is within a two-hour drive, it is better to press for the direct, face-to-face interview. The video resume merely serves as a distance-reduction technique to bring you closer to a company that is too far to meet with you personally. The video resume can accomplish some of the get-acquainted first steps and carry the process forward toward the eventual face-to-face meeting.

> WE ARE OUR OWN WORST CRITIC. YOU DON'T LOOK NEARLY AS BAD AS YOU THINK YOU DO.

And remember that the video resume is not a replacement for the face-to-face meeting. You will still have to perform live, in person, for the company. But it can help you in getting to the in-person interview when other techniques have stalled for you.

THE AUDIO RESUME TECHNIQUE

If you have a strong voice and would like to make a unique impact on a company, send an audio tape along with your resume. On this tape, take no more than five to ten minutes to explain why you are the best person for the job. Most Hiring Managers have a commute and a car and a tape player.

If you send me a tape, I will pop it into the player in my car on my way home that evening. And if you do a credible job, I may just call you on my cellular phone with the tape running in the background.

Make sure you stick to a tight structure and script the dialogue only as much as you need to stay focused. This is not an opportunity for you to tell your life story. It is, like your resume, an opportunity to entice me into a potential interview. Keep it short and sweet and tell me what you want me to do by way of follow-up.

THE VOICE MAIL RESUME TECHNIQUE

If you have the Audio Resume Technique mastered, you may want to place the information on commercial voice mail for playback on demand. Simply rent a voice mail number which will allow you to have a lengthy outgoing message, and record your two- or three- or five-minute introduction to you. Then publicize your voice mail via a simple postcard mailing to select companies (you can send it to as many as forty companies for under $10), which provides them with a number to call to learn more about you and your background.

Be careful to avoid the appearance that you are selling any product other than you. Make it clear that you are providing the employer with your audio resume. Many will react positively, since they are able to hear your voice and learn more about you without making the commitment to talk to you directly. And it is unique. So it will catch my attention, which is what makes it effective.

THE WEB RESUME TECHNIQUE

If you have generated your HTML (Web) resume and would like to tout it to potential employers, you can include your URL address on the postcard we just discussed for the Voice Mail Resume Technique. You can give users the option of the voice mail resume or the Web resume, or use just the Web resume.

The key is that you have to publicize its existence. It is not enough to create. You also need to promote. And postcards are an excellent (and unique) way to promote the existence of your Web resume.

THE VIDEO TELECONFERENCING INTERVIEW TECHNIQUE

With the recent advances in technology, you now have another option for the cross-country interviews. Most Kinko's stores now have a video teleconferencing center available for reservation and use. If you are here and they are there, this is your quickest way of making direct, "face-to-face" contact.

We recently interviewed an entry level candidate who was located in Louisiana using this method. We simply went down the street to Kinko's and met her via video teleconferencing. While it is expensive (approximately $300/hour for the connection on both ends), we went through an initial half hour interview for $150 and both sides had the visual image that the two hours of previous phone calls could not provide.

If you schedule a video teleconference, arrive early to familiarize yourself with the monitor and controls. You should preset yourself in front of the camera and check out how you will appear on the monitor. During the interview, do your best to focus on the camera, not the monitor. Although it is difficult to maintain eye contact with a camera, do your best to keep your attention focused in that direction.

Video teleconferencing can connect you with employers when time, distance, or travel expense are barriers to setting up an interview. It may be the needed final step to give both sides the comfort necessary to make the next-level commitment: either bringing you in for the face-to-face interview, or possibly even an immediate offer.

THE MARKETING FLYER TECHNIQUE

Depending on your chosen profession, the Marketing Flyer Technique can be a creative method for reaching your target market. The format can vary based on the type of standard communication specific to a particular industry, so it usually ties in with a specific theme. The best format is one that is standard and recognizable as an "industry format." The remaining techniques in this chapter are all variations of the Marketing Flyer Technique that have been used successfully in a variety of industries.

A marketing flyer can be highly creative and fun to work with and distribute. If well written and designed, they are often passed to several people within the target company. The key to success in development is to write for your market—what works for Satchi may not work with Andersen. If you use items with standard appeal within your chosen industry, you will be a success.

A word of caution in using this approach: some few will ridicule deviations from the standard resume/cover letter approach. If your approach is poorly conceived or shoddy in appearance, you may garner nothing more than a laugh. But if you keep to the high standards of your industry, you will get some raised eyebrows and possibly much more. It may provide you with the key for unlocking the doors that bar your entry.

Keep in mind that if you wince at any of these approaches, you should probably avoid them and stick with traditional methods. If it is out of character for you and inconsistent with the type of company you are seeking to attract, take a more conservative approach. If, on the other hand, you have a creative bent, this may give you an outlet for reaching out to your second-tier companies.

THE FRONT PAGE NEWS TECHNIQUE

This technique works well for those in publishing and other creative fields. Create a one-page newspaper with yourself as the headline and sideline stories. It requires a great deal of creativity and technical expertise; otherwise it can come off as a sappy stunt. Your objective is to create a page of professional copy, just as you might on the job. Your headline story could be your pending graduation, with sideline stories including reporter interviews with your key references, and possibly even a reference to the targeted employer in the business section of the paper.

A journalism major used this technique and re-created the exact format and headlines of the paper she was applying to. They were naturally quite impressed and granted her the interview over very heavy competition.

A spin on this technique: a graduate who was seeking a job in desktop publishing was asked by a prospective employer if she had experience with PageMaker (which was the in-house product of choice). She replied that she had extensive experience with Quark (on a

> CREATIVITY CAN OFTEN BE THE DIFFERENTIATOR FOR GETTING YOU THE INTERVIEW.

Mac) and that she was confident she could pick up PageMaker in a very short time. She trained herself on the product and developed the "Front Page News" sheet with PageMaker as proof of her new expertise, including practical illustrations of some of the more complex formatting techniques. She presented the page as a "show-and-tell" item at her interview—and had a job offer in hand before the day was over!

THE PRODUCT INTRODUCTION TECHNIQUE

This technique works well for those in the Business Administration and Marketing fields. Write a standard product introduction in the format of a press release or a product brochure. The kicker is that the product being introduced is you.

A Marketing major wrote a brochure introducing a product that was currently under production and ready to be introduced to the market, including full specifications about himself as this new product. He ended up getting a job as a Marketing Representative with a Fortune 500 manufacturer who had previously not replied to his inquiries.

THE PRODUCT ADVERTISING TECHNIQUE

A way to vary the Product Introduction Technique is to develop a product ad about yourself which follows the industry format for such an ad. This technique works well for the technical fields, such as Computer Science and Engineering.

An Information Systems major used this technique in developing a *Computerworld*-type ad about himself, including all the standard "speeds and feeds" column comparisons of his features with the competition. Who says technoids lack creativity?

THE NEW DELIVERY TECHNIQUE

> THINK LIKE THE HIRING MANAGER. WHAT WOULD YOU FIND INTERESTING ABOUT YOU?

This technique works well for those in medical-related fields. Although it's not what we might call a "professional standard" in the field, it is nonetheless a well-recognized form of communication. What is it? A birth announcement—with the major headings modified to reflect the focus. Instead of delivery hospital, list the college you are graduating from. Instead of attending doctor, list your department chair. The Vital Statistics section becomes your Vital Skills section.

A pediatric nursing graduate moving to a new geographical area wrote a birth announcement to communicate her "new delivery" to the area, including her vital statistics and abilities. She had every hospital in town fighting over who would make the best offer. Needless to say, she has arrived.

THE TOMBSTONE TECHNIQUE

This technique works very well for Finance and related majors. Write a tombstone ad similar to those you would find in *Barron's* or *The Wall Street Journal* that are used for listing an initial public offering or corporate bond offering.

A Finance major used this technique to get attention (and a job offer) from a large brokerage house in the heart of Wall Street—even though he was in Oregon!

THE AUDIT CERTIFICATION TECHNIQUE

Granted, this technique only works well with accountants seeking a career in public accounting. It is written in the same standard format as the audit certification statement made by a public accounting firm after an audit. The twist is that this is written about prospective accounting grads, "certifying" their background and skills in the industry. It is then signed by either a fictitious "Partner-in-Charge" with the firm or, better yet, the head of the Accounting Department at your college.

If you need a template for development, you will find one in nearly every annual report of publicly traded companies. Some creativity is inherent in the use of this technique, but don't get too flashy—just the concept is about as flashy as most conservative accounting firms can handle. It works best for small to medium-sized firms, which often encourage more unconventional approaches to the market and would value a true spark of creativity.

After reading through all the Guerrilla Insider Techniques, it is easy to write them off as "not applicable" to your position or profession. Yet with subtle changes, you can develop a technique that is just right for you. Creativity is all you need to be different from the piles and piles of resumes that you are competing with. Make the effort to be different. Make the effort to be unique. Make the effort to be the one who rises above all others.

INTERVIEWING SUCCESS

Chapter 16

COMPETITIVE INTERVIEW PREP

Any fact facing us is not as important as our attitude toward it,
for that determines our success or failure.
—Norman Vincent Peale

You finally have an interview! Your moment of truth has arrived. Whether your interview is on campus or off, it is important to make the most of it. Because to be successful, you should always seek to retain control of the process, and the only way to do this is to have control over the final decision. You can always walk away from a company that you later decide you have no interest in, but you need to remain in positive control to retain the power to pick and choose. Your objective in every interview should be to take yourself one step further toward generating the job offer. You can do that by doing your very best in each and every interview. Treat every interview as if it were the only one you will ever get with that company and your only opportunity to convince them that you are the right candidate for the position. Although there may be several interviews before the eventual offer, you must score positively in each interview.

Successful interviewing begins with preparation. Read this chapter and the next to be fully prepared before your first interview. And reread the information for additional pointers as your interviewing approach matures over time.

> **ATTITUDE IS EVERYTHING.**

THE MOST IMPORTANT ASPECT OF INTERVIEWING

The key element to successful interviewing is not your experience, your grades, what classes you took, your extracurricular activities, or any of the other basic necessities. Those skills are what got you the interview.

The key element to successful interviewing can be summed up in one word: attitude. If you want to rise above others with better experience, better grades, or better anything, you will need to work on developing a highly positive work attitude.

Your attitude determines whether you will "make the cut" or be discarded. Remember, there are plenty of competitors with the ability to do almost any given job—especially at the entry level. The way most employers differentiate at the entry level is by candidates' attitudes toward the job. Your attitude is what recruiters remember when the dust has settled after they have reviewed ten, twenty, or even one hundred candidates—you were the one who was sincerely willing to put forth your very best effort. If you have the attitude of wanting to do your very best for the company, of being focused on the company's needs, of putting yourself forth as the person who will be committed and dedicated to fulfilling their needs, you will likely be the one chosen.

Why is attitude so important? Because most companies already have their full share of multitalented superstars who care about no one but themselves. Ask any manager who the most valuable member of his team is, and he will point not to the overrated superstar, but to the person who has the "can do" attitude, the person who can be counted on in any situation, the person who truly strives for excellence. Give me a team player who is achieving at 99 percent and I will take her over a flashy superstar who is running at 50 percent efficiency any day of the week. And so will 99 percent of all Hiring Managers.

So don't worry if you are not "superstar" quality. If you can show me, in your words and actions, that you are ready to put forth your very best effort toward achieving excellence, you will be chosen over the superstar.

You can show your winning attitude in the way you present yourself. Incorporate the actual words "positive attitude," "excellence," and "striving to be my best" into your interview language. Then show by your stories and examples how these words positively affect your life. Show me when and where and how you have put forth extra effort above and beyond the call of duty. Show me how you beat a deadline, how you excelled in a project, or how you made a difference by going the extra mile.

If you can show me, by words and examples, your "can do" attitude, it is you I will hire, while all of the superstars will receive polite rejection letters to add to their growing collections.

THE ONE THING YOU MUST DO BEFORE YOUR FIRST INTERVIEW

Practice. Before you go through an actual interview, you should first go through a mock interview. Nearly every college campus offers access to a Placement Counselor who can take you through a mock, or practice, interview. Sadly, fewer than 5 percent of all graduating students take advantage of mock interviews. And fully 95 percent end up stumbling through several interviews before they have any practical sense of how they are doing—because that is when the rejection letters start arriving. Those rejection letters offer you nothing in the way of constructive criticism toward future improvement.

The mock interview is more than just a chance to work out your interview jitters. It is an opportunity to practice your interviewing technique and answers live. It is also a chance to hear constructive feedback from someone who (hopefully) can guide you toward improving your interviewing style and presentation.

Just one mock interview will result in a marked improvement in your interviewing skills. Why? For the same reason that a speech is not a speech while it is still on paper or just floating around in your head. It is not a speech until you give it verbally. The first time you give it in front of an audience (remember your first speech in Speech 101?), it will come out nothing like what you prepared. It is the same with interviewing. It is not enough to look at an interview question and say, "Yeah, I know the answer to that one." You need to practice your answer. Live. In front of someone else. This is not the time to talk to yourself in the mirror. Seek out a professional and practice. Ideally, have the session videotaped. That way, you will have two opinions—the mock interviewer's and your own. Remember, you get a totally different perspective from listening to yourself saying something contemporaneously than you do from the "out-of-body experience" of watching yourself later on videotape. Just as your voice always sounds different on tape, so do your answers. "Did I really say that?" Yes, you did. Aren't you glad the image is captured on tape (which can later be erased), rather than in a potential employer's mind's eye? Yes, you are.

Go through at least one mock interview. For maximum effectiveness, review your answers and then go through a second mock interview. Even if you ace the second mock interview, it will be well worth it since it will give you confidence in your first real interview.

THE INSIDER INTERVIEW PREP TECHNIQUE

The very best thing you can do to prepare for an interview with a specific company is to interview someone who is already on the inside. There are two basic methods of finding this person. The first is to use your network. If the interview was the result of a network contact, call them to thank them for helping you set up the interview, then proceed to ask for further information about the company. If you don't have anyone on your first level who works at the company, ask those first-level contacts if they know anyone who is working there. The alternative is to seek out an alum. Check with either the campus Career Development office or the Alumni Office (or both) to find out if any former grads are working at the company. The ideal is an individual who went straight out of your college into the company—the more recent, the better.

> WHEN YOU THINK YOU KNOW ALL THERE IS TO KNOW ABOUT THE EMPLOYER, YOU ARE ONLY HALFWAY THERE. ASK SOMEONE ON THE INSIDE TO GIVE YOU A REALITY CHECK.

If and when you have located this contact, call as far in advance of the interview as possible. Make sure you have done your homework so your contact doesn't have to give you all the laborious details you should already know. Ask about the person (or persons) you will be interviewing with. Personality? Likes? Dislikes? Any hot buttons (good or bad)? Next, ask them about the company. What are the primary issues of focus within the company? Profitability? Quality control and improvement? Global markets? Finally, ask about the interview process. What are the basic steps in the process?

Note that the range of questions you can ask this person is far greater than what you can ask in the course of the interview. And it will give you insider information that can make you a standout in the interview.

INSIDER COMPANY INFORMATION

Seeking further company information? Go back and reread the Employer Research Strategies chapter. Take special note of the information that can be gained from the corporate annual report. Any candidate who has read the "President's Letter to the Shareholders" will be light-years ahead of the competition. You will not only have a summary of the company's operations for the past year and plans for the year ahead, but you will also have access to all of the current lingo and buzzwords that are in play within the corporate corridors. Some companies will even have yearly "themes." Know what these are and you will score an instant hit with your interviewer. You will be viewed as a true insider for having access to (and using) information that less than 1 percent of the business market is aware of—and far less than 1 percent of the entry level job market.

DRESSING FOR INTERVIEW SUCCESS

While the college campus may be the perfect forum in which to exhibit your flair for the latest in fashion style, the interview is not the place to do so. With very few unusual exceptions (my apologies to Apple Computer), sandals and sweatshirts are out. Oxfords and business suits are still in. I don't like a necktie (noose?) any better than the next person, but it is still a fact of life in interviewing. Even though many companies have relaxed the internal company dress code, interviews still follow the conservative standard. Don't buck the trend.

> **CAMPUS FASHIONS AND WORK FASHIONS ARE TWO DIFFERENT WORLDS.**

Unfortunately, most college grads are woefully underprepared with proper interview dress. They feel they can "get by" with what is already in their wardrobe. Usually not. Dress for the world outside college is quite different from the campus scene. Remember that stylish is not conservative. You should be doing the talking, not your clothes.

This is not to say that you need to go out and buy a whole new wardrobe. Go for quality over quantity. One or two well-chosen business suits will serve you all the way to the first day on the job and beyond. Then, when you are making some money (and have a chance to see what the standard "uniform" is for the company), you can begin to round out your wardrobe. For now, no one will fault you for wearing the same sharp outfit each time you interview. If you desire some variety within a limited budget, you might consider varying your shirt/blouse/tie/accessories as a simple way to change your look without breaking your wallet.

For those of you who need a quick review of the basics, please refer to Appendix A, Guidelines for Successful Interview Dress. If you are still unsure, men should check out a copy of John Molloy's *New Dress for Success* and women should check out a copy of Diane Parente's and Stephanie Petersen's *Mastering Your Professional Image* (*New Dress for Success* does cover women's clothing, but *Mastering Your Professional Image* is much more complete). While these books may seem to have a rather conservative slant, it is the norm in most of the professional marketplace. It is almost always better to be higher than the standard than lower.

If you are still not sure how to dress for the interview, call and ask! That's right—call the employer. But this is one time when you do not want to call the Hiring Manager—instead, ask to be put through to Personnel and say:

> "I have an interview with _____ in the _____ department for a position as an _____. Could you please tell me what would be appropriate dress for this interview?"

Sure, you run the risk of someone in Personnel thinking you are a social imbecile, but that's a lot better than having the Hiring Manager distracted by inappropriate interview dress.

One final note on interview dress: while it goes without saying that your interview clothes should be neat and clean, very few interviewees give the same time and attention to their shoes. Shoes? Yes, shoes. I am aware of at least one Corporate Recruiter who forms first impressions based solely (pardon the pun) on shoes. This person does not have a shoe fetish— he subjectively judges that those who pay attention to details like shoes are also likely to be diligent in their work life. And it is not just that person's opinion. Many have said that you can judge a person by their shoes. You will find that many ex-military officers (many of whom have found their way into management positions in corporate America) are especially aware of a person's shoes. It is not enough to be clean and pressed. Make sure your shoes are conservative, clean, and polished.

ALL EYES ARE ON YOU

Your choice of eyewear can also be considered a part of your interview dress. Glasses or contacts? For those of you who have this option available, consider it wisely. There are preconceived notions (as you are probably well aware) of what wearing glasses connotes. Specific potential positives include attention to detail, focus, and intelligence. Potential negatives include awkwardness, shyness, and lack of human interaction. While these stereotypical attributes are obviously just that—stereotypes—they are still extant in our society.

If you have the option of wearing contacts versus glasses, use the following as the guideline for which to wear:

1. Contacts: people positions — consulting, sales, advertising, customer service, etc.

2. Glasses — data/things positions—accounting, information systems, engineering, etc.

If you do choose to wear glasses, wear a pair with more conservative frames. There is little you can do to change the stereotypes, but you should be aware of the potential positives and negatives and adjust accordingly.

THE MOST IMPORTANT INTERVIEW NONVERBALS

Many interviews fail because of lack of proper communication. But communication is more than just what you say. Often it is the nonverbal communication that we are least aware of, yet that speaks the loudest. Following are the top five nonverbals, ranked in order of importance when it comes to interviewing:

> **WHAT YOU SAY IS NOT NEARLY AS IMPORTANT AS HOW YOU SAY IT.**

➤ **Eye Contact** — unequaled in importance! If you look away while listening, it shows lack of interest and a short attention span. If you fail to maintain eye contact while speaking, at a minimum it shows lack of confidence in what you are saying and at worst may send the subtle message that you are lying. Do not just assume you have good eye contact. Ask. Watch. Then practice. Ask others if you ever lack proper eye contact. If they respond that they did notice, ask if it was during speaking or listening. I have met a number of candidates who maintained excellent eye contact while listening, but lacked eye contact when speaking. Or vice versa. Next, watch yourself on videotape. It does not necessarily have to be your mock interview; in fact, if you were videotaped informally (that is, you were not aware you were being taped), this will provide even stronger evidence. Then sit down with a friend and practice until you are comfortable maintaining sincere, continuous eye contact.

➤ **Facial Expressions** — it continually amazes me how many college students are totally unaware of the sullen, confused, or even mildly hysterical expression plastered on their faces during the entire course of the interview! It is almost as if four years of college has left some students brain-dead or worse. Some interviewers (not myself, of course) have been known to hang humorous labels on these students, such as "Ms. Bewildered" (who looked quizzical during the interview) or "Mr. Psycho-Ax-Murderer" (who looked wide-eyed and determined to do something, although you dare not ask what). Take a good, long, hard look at yourself in the mirror. Look at yourself as others would. Then modify your facial expressions—first eliminate any negative overall characteristics that might exist, then add a simple feature that nearly every interviewee forgets to include—a smile! Not some stupid Bart Simpson grin, but a true and genuine smile that tells me you are a happy person and delighted to be interviewing with our company today. You do not need to keep the smile plastered on for the full interview, but remember to keep coming back to it. Think about it—who would you rather spend thirty minutes with?

➤ **Posture** — posture sends out a signal of your confidence and power potential. Stand tall, walk tall, and most of all, sit tall. I don't say this to offend the "short people" of the world—in fact, I am under 5'5", which is a full 7 inches shorter than your proverbial 6-foot IBMer. Height is not what's important, posture is. When standing, stand up straight. When you are seated, make sure you sit at the front edge of the chair, leaning slightly forward, moving within an overall range of no more than 10 degrees back or 20 degrees forward, intent on the subject at hand.

➤ **Gestures** — contrary to popular belief, gestures should be very limited during the interview. So please don't use artificial gestures to try to heighten the importance of the issue at hand (pardon the pun). It will merely come off as theatrical. When you do use gestures, make sure they are natural and meaningful.

➤ **Space** — recognize the boundaries of your personal space and that of others. If you are typical of most Americans, it ranges between 30 and 36 inches. Be prepared, however, not to back up or move away from someone who has a personal space that is smaller than your own. Hang in there, take a deep breath, and stand your ground. For most of us, merely the awareness of our personal space is enough to consciously prompt us to stand firm when speaking with someone. If you have a smaller-than-average personal space, make sure you keep your distance so that you do not intimidate someone who possesses a larger personal space.

P.S. If you want to have fun at a social gathering, step inside the personal space boundary of a friend. With some practice, you can back up the person around the entire room without their even being aware of what is happening.

THE WHITES OF THEIR EYES TECHNIQUE

Eye contact is an area of importance that we often give lip service to yet fail to implement in actual practice. If you have difficulty in maintaining eye contact, try this simple technique to lock in an immediate strong first impression. Concentrate on noticing (and remembering) the color of the person's eyes as you shake hands. In doing so, you will not only show excellent initial eye contact, you will also create interest in your eyes, which will be clear and focused.

THE NOSE ON THEIR FACE TECHNIQUE

Another technique for maintaining eye contact. If you have difficulty maintaining eye contact due to discomfort at looking someone directly in the eyes, use this technique instead. Simply stare at them directly in the nose. You will not have the discomfort of direct eye contact, yet the person you are speaking with will perceive that you are making eye contact. Even though you are busily sizing up the size of their nasal openings. Just don't become so preoccupied with it that you end up being distracted from the interview.

WINNING THE BODY LANGUAGE GAME

Everybody uses body language during the interview, but very few are prepared to be a winner in the body language game. Body language is merely the smaller, less prominent nonverbal cues that we give others while communicating. Following are some typical interpretations of body language cues:

> **Openness and warmth** — open-lipped smiling, open hands with palms visible, unbuttoning coat upon being seated

> **Confidence** — leaning forward in chair, chin up, putting fingertips of one hand against fingertips of the other hand in "praying," or "steepling" position, hands joined behind back when standing

> YOUR WORDS TELL ME A STORY BUT YOUR BODY TELLS ME THE WHOLE STORY.

> **Nervousness** — smoking, whistling, pinching skin, fidgeting, jiggling pocket contents, running tongue along front of teeth, clearing throat, running fingers through hair, wringing hands, biting on pens or other objects, twiddling thumbs, biting fingernails (action itself or evidence of), tongue clicking

> **Untrustworthy/Defensive** — frowning, squinting eyes, tight-lipped grin, arms crossed in front of chest, pulling away, chin down, touching nose or face, darting eyes, looking down when speaking, clenched hands, gestures with fist, pointing with fingers, chopping one hand into the open palm of the other, rubbing back of neck, clasping hands behind head while leaning back in the chair

As you can see, there are far more negatives than positives—possibly more than we are consciously aware of. This list is given not so that you can artificially adopt the positive body language techniques, but more to help you recognize and avoid the negatives. If you have a habit of doing any of the above negatives, remove that action from your pattern of behavior before it sends the wrong signal. Concentrate on removing it now so you will not have to think about it during the interview.

And keep in mind the opposite side of the desk. As you talk with an interviewer, be aware of (although not preoccupied with) their body language and nonverbal cues. Do not try to read in more than is actually being communicated, but try to develop a sense of the interviewer's reception of you. The most obvious example is the smile connection—when your smile brings about a smile from the interviewer. Do your best to stay connected with your interviewer—both verbally and nonverbally.

THE NONVERBAL INTERVIEW TECHNIQUE

Don't just give lip service to the concepts listed above—practice them! How? With a nonverbal interview. Unlike the mock interview, this one does not require a great amount of preparation—just an observant friend. Ask the friend to ask questions, but instead of focusing on your answers, ask him to make note of your nonverbals and body language and the messages being sent. Or play back your mock interview with the sound off. The results might surprise you.

BEING SINCERELY HONEST

If you have a tendency to use phrases such as "To be honest with you," "Just between you and me," and "Well, I'll be completely honest about this"— eliminate them from your vocabulary. A person who uses such qualifiers is implying by their usage that they typically are not being honest. If you are being honest all the time (which you should be), there is no need to use these kinds of qualifiers.

THE SHOW-AND-TELL TECHNIQUE

If appropriate (the key words here being "if appropriate"), feel free to bring samples or copies of your work to the interview as concrete examples of your capabilities. Use reports, projects, photos, programs, or whatever it is that provides a tangible example of what you have done. It's one thing to say "I developed a report," and quite another to actually show the report you developed.

While the types of samples you use may vary, they can include information developed either through capstone-level classes or work projects.

Following are a few examples that have been used successfully:

➤ Programs and system design specs by an Information Systems major

➤ Complex financial analysis done by a Finance major

➤ Working product prototype developed by a Mechanical Engineering major

Be fully prepared not only "to show" but also "to tell" about your sample. Be ready to answer any and all possible questions that might come up. This should not be a casual sample—it should be an example of your very best work. It will stand as the icon of what your capabilities are. If you are extremely proud of something you have done, show me—and tell me why.

If possible, you might want to consider using your show-and-tell samples as "leave-behinds" for the company to look at later. There is usually not enough time within the course of the interview to fully explore a good show-and-tell item. This also puts another hook into the company for necessary future contact.

Although using your sample as a "leave-behind" should only be done if the item is reproducible, you might want to consider leaving behind "sample only" items with an employer, if you are truly interested. Tell them: "I'll just pick it up when I'm here for my next interview" or (if this is your final interview) "I would be more than happy to pick it up on my start date." Presumptuous? Possibly. But it may also be your golden opportunity to close the sale!

THE SNEAK PREVIEW TECHNIQUE

A variation on the Show-and-Tell Technique is to provide the company with a sneak preview of what they can expect of you as an employee. While Show-and-Tell looks backward at material you have developed in the past, the Sneak Preview focuses on the future. This technique works well when you have been given an indication (perhaps in a previous on-campus interview or phone interview) that there is a certain level of proficiency which the company is seeking. Take this as your cue to prepare for that question in advance.

> TELLING ME WHAT YOU HAVE DONE IS NOT NEARLY AS IMPRESSIVE AS SHOWING ME WHAT YOU HAVE DONE.

An example of the use of this technique comes from a Multimedia Developer, who was asked in an initial interview if he knew a particular multimedia presentation software package. While he acknowledged that he did not at the time, he promised to research the package and provide a demo of his results at the next interview.

He found the presentation software to be very similar to one he had worked with extensively. After developing a full presentation based on company marketing materials, he presented the results in the office of his future manager. He noted that the presentation was put together in his spare time with little training. The company would, of course, receive a much higher level of performance upon hiring him full-time in the position. That sneak preview not only landed him a job offer, but also expanded the scope of initial responsibilities on the job (and his overall pay).

THE PROOF POSITIVE TECHNIQUE

Another variation of the Show-and-Tell Technique and Sneak Preview Technique will provide you with a way to fill a stated need, especially in a later or final interview. The need for a required proficiency may be requested in the form of a "Have you ever . . ." question. If the answer is no, you can still show proficiency by offering to provide them with the output or results in a short period of time.

> GIVE ME A REASON TO HIRE YOU AND I MAY DO EXACTLY THAT.

This is an ideal way to answer the unanswerable question. Ask the interviewer for time to solve the problem, then take it home, do your research, prepare your result, and present your solution. Then ask for the job.

You cannot prepare for this technique as you could for the previous techniques. It is an excellent way to respond to an interview question for which you have no experience to reference. Everyone says they are a fast learner. This technique is your way to prove it.

For example, a Computer Science major who was asked if he had ever developed in HTML, the script language for Web development. He stated that he had not, but went on to say that he was a quick study, and to prove the point, he would take the corporate flyer which he had been given, put it in HTML format, and deliver the result via e-mail by 8:00 a.m. the following morning.

He went straight from the interview to the library, spent the better part of the evening reading and researching other Websites, and delivered the final product on time the following morning. Proof positive indeed!

RASPBERRY FUDGE SWIRL IN A PLAIN VANILLA WORLD

Even though you have probably already gone through this exercise in the self-evaluation phase of your career planning, it's important to go through it one more time: know how you measure up against your competition. And this time take very specific note of your competitive differences. Don't go along with the mistaken impression that you can sell based only on your own personal value-remember our discussion of product-driven marketing versus customer-driven marketing. Know what your specific advantage is for each specific employer. Be ready to articulate that advantage in very precise language.

> IF YOU ARE JUST LIKE EVERYONE ELSE, I AM NOT INTERESTED. WE ARE NOT HIRING EVERYONE ELSE.

Success in interviewing involves being fully prepared. But it's more than that—you must stand out in a world of plain vanilla job candidates. What particular strengths make you uncommon? What makes you unique? Be ready to differentiate yourself. Be ready to show your "competitive advantage." And be ready to load on the nut topping, whipped cream, and cherry if they ask for it. You have to be ready to take on the competition. Remember, your competition is sitting there in the classrooms with you. You need to know and understand your greatest strengths in relation to them. It is only by differentiating yourself that you can lick your competition.

THE INTERVIEW PSYCH TECHNIQUE

The night before the interview, spend some time with a friend or family member, telling them why you would be the best for the position. Use superlatives galore! The purpose is to put you in the right frame of mind for the interview, so that you truly believe you are the best possible candidate for the job. Why is this so vitally important? See the next item.

WHOM WOULD YOU BELIEVE?

Before you can possibly convince me as the interviewer that you are right for the job, you have to believe it yourself. It's amazing how many candidates seem tentative and reluctant to express confidence in their own abilities. Remember, you are all alone once the interview starts. No one will sell you if you don't sell yourself. How can I believe in you if you don't believe in you? I am not here to sell you on our company until after you sell me. Once you have sold me on you, I will sell you on the position and the company, but not until then. So don't expect the interviewer to tell you why you are right for the job. That is your job.

> YOUR JOB IS TO SELL ME ON YOU.

THE PYGMALION TECHNIQUE

So maybe you are the shy type who is uncomfortable talking about yourself in a positive way. There is still a way for you to prepare yourself mentally for the interview. Remember Pygmalion? No? In Greek mythology, Pygmalion sculpted a beautiful ivory statue of a woman that was given to the king of Cyprus. Pygmalion believed so strongly that the statue was real that it was eventually given life by the goddess Venus. Our TV/movie generation may know the story of Pygmalion and his statue through a modern stage/movie adaptation: Professor Higgins and Eliza Doolittle in *My Fair Lady*. Eliza is transformed from a common flower peddler to an elegant lady through the power of continuous reinforcement on the part of Professor Higgins. If others tell you that you can do something, and tell you this long enough, you will eventually come to believe it yourself and live it in your life.

To see a simple example of the power of this technique in action, notice what happens to you when you smile for an extended period of time. Think of something (or someone) pleasant or amusing that makes you want to smile. Right now, as you are reading these words on this page. And hold that smile until you finish reading this technique. The end result will be that your body will react to the smile in a very positive way. You will eventually feel like smiling naturally without having to consciously think about it. And, interestingly enough, if others walk by while you have that silly grin on your face, they will probably begin smiling also. Keep on smiling!

We create images in our mind of how things should be. If these images are believed, they can eventually become self-fulfilling prophecies. If we change the image, we change the result. So if others tell you that you are the very best person for the job long enough and sincerely enough, you will eventually come to believe this and act upon it in a positive way.

No, this is not some useless psychobabble— it really works. The key is to pick someone as your supporter who is very sensitive and willing to back you in your efforts. Significant others work great, assuming the relationship is supportive. Moms are also great for this role. Let your supporter in on the fact that you have an interview coming up, and tell them you need their help in pumping you up. Ask them to please lay it on thick, with the best praise they can muster for the occasion. This should be the last person you speak with the night before or even the day of the interview, if possible.

One final note. This is also a very effective child-rearing technique for later in life. Tell your kids they are loved and wanted and they will believe you. Tell them they are wicked and worthless and they will also believe you. Make sure you do the former.

THE VISUALIZATION TECHNIQUE

The use of mental visualization can be extremely helpful in preparing for your interview. You can, by visualization, experience your coming interview, including a rehearsal of how you would react in specific situations.

Many great athletes prepare for competition through visualization. And many of the great feats of history have been accomplished first through visualization. Sir Edmund Hillary, the first person to scale the heights of Mount Everest, was asked by a young reporter how it felt to be the first man to touch the peak of Everest. Hillary replied that it felt exactly the same as each of the previous times. What the puzzled reporter failed to see is that Hillary had already successfully scaled Everest many times through visualization.

In preparing for the interview, go through the motions in your mind. Anticipate the questions that may be asked. Visualize yourself as confident and self-assured. Not cocky, just confident of who you are and the benefit you can provide the employer. Play the part over and over again until you feel you have truly lived it. Visualize your success until it becomes reality.

> SHARE YOUR VISION WITH ME. IF I AM UNABLE TO SEE IT, LEND ME YOUR EYES SO THAT I MAY ALSO SEE. IT IS YOUR VISION, BUT YOU MUST GIVE IT AWAY FOR OTHERS TO SEE IT AND HELP YOU ACHIEVE IT.

Chapter 17

MASTERING THE INTERVIEW

*All of the darkness of the world
cannot put out the light of one small candle.*
—Anonymous

You are a special person. You know it. Your mom knows it. Your dad knows it. Your siblings know it (but probably won't admit it to anyone else). Your mom really knows it. Your friends and relatives know it. But unless you convince the interviewer of your special talents and abilities, you will fade into that great dark abyss of *Interviews Lost*.

Study this chapter. Get comfortable with the techniques and tactics before your first interview. Remember, every interview counts. Every time you interview successfully, you move one more golden step toward the job offer and career of your dreams.

THE TRUTH ABOUT INTERVIEWING

"But it seemed to go so well! We talked about everything . . . campus life . . . the weather . . . the football season. I just don't understand why I got a rejection letter . . . "

Beware the interview that gets too chummy. It may be that the interviewer has already decided to take a pass and out of politeness passes the remaining time talking about everything but you.

The truth about interviewing is that most initial interviews last only about five minutes. Oh, sure, the actual interview always takes longer than that. Twenty minutes. Thirty minutes. Sometimes even an hour. But the interview is usually over in five minutes or less. If you have not convinced the interviewer by the five-minute point that you are the right person for the job (or at least a contender who should be taken to the

> FIRST IMPRESSIONS COUNT. OFTEN FOR FAR MORE THAN IS LOGICAL.

next level), it will be next to impossible to recover. Recoveries do happen. But they are very rare.

In that first five minutes of the interview, I will have noted many critical aspects. Your appearance. Your grooming. Your handshake. Your personal presence. Your eye contact. Your articulation. And, most important, your personality. Notice that I did not mention anything about your coursework, your GPA, or your work experience. That is what got you to the interview in the first place. But it is the "soft factors" that will take you to the next level.

Having taken the right courses, having good grades (critical!), and having related work experience are all important selection criteria. But they do not matter one iota if you are not a strong personal fit for our company.

The truth is that most interviewers are seeking individuals who are able to personally present themselves well in a face-to-face interview. They are seeking to recommend those who will be a good reflection upon themselves and their selectivity. So most interviewers naturally gravitate to specific "critical success factors" that have worked for them consistently.

THE PERSONAL CONNECTION TECHNIQUE

No matter how good you look on paper, no matter how well you present yourself, no matter how well you answer their questions, you will not get the job unless you make a personal connection with the interviewer. I need to know from the very start that you are someone I can trust to represent me and my company. How do you establish that trust? Simple. At the very beginning of the interview, when the introductions are being made, concentrate on looking directly and solidly into the interviewer's eyes, giving them your sweetest and most endearing smile. I tend to think of it as a "shy smile," or, if we can venture into the bounds of cuteness, a "cute smile." The bottom line is to make it a warm and friendly smile. Then think about the fact that you are truly pleased to be there in the presence of this person. Establish that personal connection both physically and mentally with the interviewer.

How do you know when the connection is made? When they return your smile in a comfortable, relaxed manner you are connected and ready to communicate on a personal level. Remember, I only hire people I am comfortable with. If the connection is not made, I won't hire. So take the time to establish that personal connection.

TEN CRITICAL SUCCESS FACTORS NEARLY EVERY COMPANY IS LOOKING FOR

With all the different questions being flung about, you may wonder what exactly the employer is looking for. And I will tell you.

Following is the list of ten critical success factors that nearly every employer is looking for:

1. Positive attitude toward work
2. Proficiency in field of study
3. Communication skills (oral and written)
4. Interpersonal skills
5. Confidence
6. Critical thinking and problem-solving skills
7. Flexibility
8. Self-motivation
9. Leadership
10. Teamwork

Show your competence in as many of these critical success factors as possible and you will rise above the competition.

THE THREE-STEP INTERVIEW PROCESS

In its most simple form, the interview consists of three distinct steps:

1. Establish rapport
2. Gather information
3. Close

It is vitally important to understand these basic steps in order to be successful in your interviewing. Each step carries with it a different focus and emphasis. Each step has its own protocol and requirements. And successful completion of each step is critical if you are to go on to the next step in the process, whether another interview or the actual job offer.

It is important to note that there is a dual responsibility for successful completion of each of these steps. The employer has a responsibility to follow through in each step, yet you have a greater responsibility. If the employer fails in his responsibility, the company will potentially fail to hire a qualified candidate. But if you consistently fail in your responsibility, you will fail to be hired. So you need to take personal responsibility for your side of the interview process.

The establishing-rapport step is where the vital first impressions are formed. Some employers will claim to be able to make a decision about a candidate in thirty seconds or less. The truth is that

> IF YOU TRY TO CONTROL ME IN THE INTERVIEW, YOU WILL BE REJECTED.

you will set the tone for the interview through your physical appearance and initial responses. If you start off poorly, you can recover, but only after a herculean effort. Your personal appearance speaks volumes before you ever utter a word. Many interviewers are analyzing you in reference to the company culture. Does this person fit in? Would this person represent our company well? Would others feel I made a good selection in recommending? And the small talk is actually big talk, since it will greatly affect how you are perceived in the eyes of the interviewer. It's not necessarily the words you say, but how you say them. Your verbal articulation and vocabulary will be noted, especially any variance, positive or negative, from the standard. If you have done your interview homework and have fully researched the company, the words will flow smoothly. If not, it will show. This is where your positive attitude and confidence will establish the tone for the interview. And this is the step during which you have the opportunity to make your personal connection with the interviewer.

> SMALL TALK IS FINE IF IT'S SINCERE; IF NOT, YOU HAVE JUST TALLIED POINTS AGAINST YOU.

In the gathering-information step, the employer will be asking questions and matching your answers against their critical success factors. Some of the questions will be closed ended, such as "What was your GPA?" Others will be open ended behavioral questions, such as "Can you give me an example of a time when you had to make an unpopular decision?" While preparation is important, your honesty and sincerity in answering should be evident. Most interviewers are keenly aware of when they are being snowed. The questions in this step will usually be probing questions which drill deep into your background, attempting to get past the interview veneer. Although you may have presold the interviewer in the establishing-rapport stage, you will need to solidify the employer's view in this stage. The outward questions are designed to answer the inner doubts. You will be judged on attitude (is she always this pleasant or is there someone evil lurking beneath the surface?), work ethic (will he really work hard or is he just looking for a cushy job?), intelligence (does she really understand the industry concepts or is she reaching?), and honesty (is he really this good or is he just acting?).

You will be subject to the individual whims of each individual interviewer. Often not by design, but due to lack of training. The only individuals who have truly been trained to interview (Human Resources) usually do not make the hiring decision. So the Hiring Manager interview is usually less structured and more subjective. And in the end, an imperfect decision will be formed from an imperfect interview process. If you have not sold the inter-viewer by the end of this step, you will have great difficulty in resurrecting.

In the close step, the interviewer will set the hook for the next step. If you have succeeded to this point, the conversation will center around the interviewer selling you on the company and the next steps in the hiring process. If you have failed to this point, the conversation will center on the football team, the weather, or any other neutral subject that provides for a clean disengage. If your interview was successful, there will usually be an indication of future steps. You may be given further company information which is reserved for only the select few. No matter what your view of the interview to this point, it is important to personally close the interview by establishing continuity of the process. Understand what the next step will be. "We will be reviewing all of the candidates and getting back to you" is not necessarily a close-out, although it is the standard when there is no in-terest. Make certain you understand the next steps and be prepared to follow up on your side. Always pursue each interview as if it were your last. You can always back away from it later if you truly have no interest, but you cannot back away from a company that you failed to impress.

Understanding the basic steps of the interview is only the starting point. You need to be fully prepared for different personality styles, dif-ferent interview styles, and different questions. You need to master your ability to present the very best you.

THE PERSONALITY MATCHING TECHNIQUE

This technique is the secret to successful interviewing. If you read nothing else, read this technique. There is a simple key to success in interviewing that very few people utilize. It is the process of mirroring the personality of the person to whom you are speaking, a process that I refer to as "Personality Matching." It is based upon the proven fact that we like people who are like us. It is the halo effect in action—anyone who is like me must be a good person. Result? Instant rapport.

Any good salesperson is aware of this simple technique. Want evi-dence? The next time you get a call from a telemarketer, do not hang up. Instead, stick with them a few minutes just to hear their pitch. You will probably know pretty quickly if you are dealing with a "greenie" who is reading from a script or a seasoned professional. If it's a greenie, give them a polite "no thank you" and hang up. But stick with the pro through the entire call. Why? Because now we are going to have some fun.

In the beginning of the call, talk to them in a very quick and upbeat voice, possibly somewhat higher in pitch. If they are good, they will follow right along

with you, matching your tempo and pitch. If not, they are still a greenie, operating in their own little world. End the call. But if they follow along, here comes
the fun. Gradually slow down your rate of speaking and lower your voice in
both volume and pitch. Guess what? The true pro will follow you all the way
down. Surprised? Don't be. Just as a telemarketing pro is trained to do this (and
at this point may not even be conscious of what they are doing), any good mar-

> # MAKE AN EFFORT TO MEET ME AT MY LEVEL AND I WILL ATTEMPT TO MEET YOU AT YOURS.

keting person does the exact same thing.
Whatever the industry, the most successful
salespeople are the ones who meet you (the
customer) at your level.

In the same way, the best interviewees are the ones who have the ability to
meet the interviewers at their level. "Wait
a minute, shouldn't that be the job of the
interviewer?" No! The only interviewers
who have actually been trained at interviewing (Personnel/Human Resources) are usually not the ones who make the final hiring decision. Even
some of the best interviewers are totally unaware of this technique or are
unwilling to apply it.

So how does one do this "personality matching" thing? First match
the voice and then the physical characteristics of the interviewer. In
matching the voice, the most important aspect is to match the rate of
speaking (tempo); then match the pitch. In matching the physical characteristics, it is most important to match (or at least reflect) the facial expressions, then the posture (sitting back or forward, etc.). Although you
should not be trying to "mimic" (like a mime in action), you should attempt to closely match him or her.

To be effective with this technique, you need to first understand your
own personality range. For some of us, it is quite wide and variant. For
others, it may be more narrow. As an example, I consider myself to have a
very wide personality range—I am very comfortable in matching both the
very flamboyant and the very subdued. Each type is at an extreme end of
my personality range. Most people, however, operate in a somewhat nar-
rower personality range. The key is to be able to identify your personal
bounds of comfort.

So what do we do if the person we meet with is talking a mile a
minute? Should we try to artificially match that person, if it is outside of
our personality range? Quite simply, no. To attempt to act like someone we
are not would be "faking it." It's better known as being two-faced and in
the business world it can be a real killer. Some people end up getting

sucked into this trap in order to get the job, then go through a continual living hell as they are forced to fake it for the duration of the job. Don't do it. But you should be aware of what your personality range is and be willing to move fluidly within that range to accommodate the personality of the individual with whom you are meeting.

Personality matching does not mean perfect matching (it never is). It does mean that we should do our best to come as close as possible to matching the other person's personality within the bounds of our own personality range. Keep in mind that there is no "perfect personality" (or perfect anything on this earth, for that matter). What is perfect to one will always be lacking in some way to another. Perfection is relative to the recipient. Remember that.

As a side note, think about someone you truly dislike. In most cases, it's because the person is outside your personality range, usually in the upper extreme (too loud, too pushy, too cocky, too egotistical, too stuffy, etc.)—they are "too much" of something that you do not embrace in your own personality. If you have a "too much" area in your own personality, you are best advised to bring it under strict control, not only in interviewing, but in your life in general.

If you put into practice this one technique, you will likely increase your chances of success dramatically, and not just in interviewing. Personality matching is a technique you can use in virtually all areas of human communication.

THE HANDSHAKE MATCHING TECHNIQUE

Apply the same principle of the Personality Matching Technique to handshakes. Don't get confused by the "too hard" or "too soft" handshake psychology baloney. There is no absolute when it comes to handshakes because the effectiveness of the handshake is defined by the recipient. So is the handshake unimportant? No. But it would be wrong to attempt to come up with "the perfect handshake." There is no such thing, since each person receiving your handshake has their own definition of perfection. It's relative to the person who has your fingers in their grasp. Therefore, a truly effective handshake is going to be a "mirror" of the handshake being offered. Match the person's handshake the same as you would their voice or posture.

While personality matching is dynamic and takes place over an extended period of time, the handshake lasts just one to two seconds. So how do you adjust? Use a medium-grip handshake, and then squeeze down on the gorilla or lighten up on the softie, as necessary. Don't get into a wrestling contest. Again, just as in personality matching, you don't have to match the extremes. Just move to that end of your "handshake range." Practice a few times with a friend. Or better yet, practice with a loved one.

THE FIVE TYPES OF INTERVIEW QUESTIONS

Interviewing is not a science. Nor is it an art form. It is simply an imperfect form of human communication designed to increase the predictive validity of potential employer-employee relationships. And it is very imperfect.

There are basically five types of questions you may face during the course of an interview:

1. **Credential questions** — these questions include "What was your GPA?" and "How long were you at..." Their purpose is to place objective measurements on features of your background.

2. **Experience questions** — these questions include "What did you learn in that class?" and "What were your responsibilities in that position?" Their purpose is to subjectively evaluate features of your background.

3. **Opinion questions** — these questions include "What would you do in this situation?" and "What are your strengths and weaknesses?" Their purpose is to subjectively analyze how you would respond in a series of scenarios. The reality is that "Tape #143" in your brain kicks in and plays when you recognize the question and play back the preprogrammed answer.

4. **Dumb questions** — these questions include "What kind of animal would you like to be?" and "How many ping pong balls could fit in a Volkswagen?" Their purpose is to get past your preprogrammed answers to find out if you are capable of an original thought. There are no right or wrong answers, since they are used primarily to test your ability to think on your feet.

5. **Behavioral questions** — these questions include "Can you give me a specific example of how you did that?" and "What were the steps you followed to accomplish that task?" Their purpose is to anticipate future responses based upon past behaviors.

> INTERVIEWING IS A GAME IN WHICH I DEAL THE CARDS, BUT YOU HOLD ALL THE ACES. IT'S UP TO YOU TO PLAY THEM.

Of all the questions, only behavioral questions have a predictive validity for on-the-job success that is higher than 10 percent. And 10 percent predictive validity is the same level that is generated from a simple resume review. Behavioral interviewing, on the other hand, yields a predictive validity of 55 percent. Still far from perfect, yet much more reliable for most interviewers. Interestingly, the first four question types are still the favored approach by most untrained interviewers, simply due to lack of experience.

Behavioral interviewing is gaining greater acceptance by trained interviewers because past performance is the most reliable indicator of future results. Companies such as Andersen have modified this approach with specific critical behavioral interviewing to target those behaviors that provide the highest correlation for predicted positive results.

THE BEHAVIORAL ANSWERING TECHNIQUE

From your side of the desk, the behavioral interviewing approach can appear somewhat difficult at first. The interviewer will be consistently drilling down to specific examples in your past. When you have difficulty coming up with a specific example, a well-trained behavioral interviewer will not let you off the hook, but will provide you with a prompt to continue thinking until you can provide an example. The dreaded silence that follows can be uncomfortable. Very uncomfortable. Unless you are prepared in advance.

> EVERY INTERVIEW IS A NEW OPPORTUNITY.

As you consider the variety of questions that can and will be posed over the course of a series of interviews, keep in mind that you will not always have the right answer to every question. But if you are well prepared, you will have a variety of examples to draw from which will give you the background to formulate your answers.

The Behavioral Answering Technique involves answering questions with specific examples, whether or not you have been asked to provide them. This technique works in lockstep with an interviewer who is following a behavioral interviewing approach, yet it works even better with those who are not. Because you will always be providing examples and stories which make you a real person. With real experiences. Real experience that can benefit a future employer.

So as you go through the exercise of interview preparation, carefully consider all questions in an "example" format. Keep in mind the "Can you give me an example..." follow-up that is the cornerstone of the behavioral interviewing approach. Be prepared to use examples from your work, classes, and extracurricular activities. And be ready to offer up not just any example, but your very best example.

THE COMPELLING STORY TECHNIQUE

Once you have grown accustomed to the Behavioral Answering Technique, you can expand your answers by turning your examples into compelling stories. Instead of

> DON'T TELL ME HOW YOU WOULD DO IT; TELL ME HOW YOU DID IT.

merely providing an example that suits the question, weave the example into a compelling story with personality, flair, and interest. Captivate your audience by providing the details and nuances that bring your story to life.

Consider yourself the author of a piece of fiction. As you put your plot into words, you must give life and meaning to the characters and surroundings. Do the same in telling your compelling stories. Build the framework and background for the story. Add the elements of interest and intrigue. Give the plot twists. And show how our hero (you) saved the day in the end.

We all have compelling stories in our past. We tell them to our friends, our family, our loved ones. We laugh. We cry. And our hearts yearn for more. Yet we sometimes lose these stories over time, or bury them in our long-term memory bank, only to dredge them up at reunion time.

The key to retaining these compelling stories for your interviewing is to write them down. Go over the questions and bring to mind the stories you can weave to provide your example in living color. And as another compelling story occurs to you, or as you find yourself in the telling of another interesting tale, ask yourself if the story will provide substance in your interviewing. If so, write it down.

After a period of time, you will have a collection of compelling stories to guide you through your interviews. As you become proficient in angling these stories to fit your needs, you will find yourself steering to these stories to illustrate your points.

> # WE ALL LOVE TO HEAR A GOOD STORY.

One example of a compelling story was told to me by a recent grad, who answered my question about her organization skills by telling me how she planned and organized the alumni dinner during homecoming weekend, including full details of the management of twenty different student volunteers and coordination with six different campus departments. The event was a resounding success, but there were several challenges she needed to overcome. And each of these challenges provided a compelling story of its own, as she was able to show her ability to plan, organize, and develop a team toward eventual success. In the end, she received a personal letter of recommendation from the President of the university, which she presented to me as validation of her extraordinary efforts.

Another compelling story was given to me by a current student in reference to a question about his lower-than-expected grade point average. He related to me the amount of work he had put in to finance his college education, averaging thirty hours per week and occasionally putting in as much as fifty hours per week. He was eventually promoted to department manager, even though the employer knew he would be leaving after completing his degree. He recounted the story of the meeting with the employer in which he tried to back away from the management responsibilities, asking that one of the other department employees be promoted. The employer called in the four other workers in the department, who each personally asked that he take on the job as their manager. This student successfully shifted the focus from his lower-than-expected grades to his outstanding performance on the job by the use of a compelling story.

How do you know if your story is connecting with the interviewer? By eye contact. This is where the interviewer will show their interest. If you are not connecting with your story, decrease the amount of detail and drive home your point quickly. Depending on the personality type of the interviewer, you may need to adjust the length of the story, yet compelling stories work with all personality types. With the extreme driver or analytical personality types, you will need to keep the details to a minimum, while quickly making your point. Usually two or three shorter stories are better than one long story. At the other extreme, for feeling personality types, you will perform better with a longer story and more details. How do you detect the difference in personality types? By continuously striving to stay personally connected with the interviewer. If this connection appears to be lost or fading during the telling of a compelling story, shorten the story and come to your point quickly. On the other hand, if you have a captive audience who is hanging on your every word, provide all the necessary details.

The key to using compelling stories is that stories are remembered. Stories are what make you human. Stories are what put a face on you in the mind of the interviewer. And stories are what they will come back to when you are being sold to others internally. When that time comes, you have given your interviewer ammo for helping others to see why you should go on to the next step in the hiring process. Or be offered the job.

THE PREGNANT PAUSE TECHNIQUE

If you are succeeding in presenting a series of compelling stories during the interview, you will likely develop a rapport which places the communication on a more interactive level.

However, as you are presenting information during the interview, you may need to test the waters with the length of your answers. This can be done easily with the Pregnant Pause. As you are telling a story or example, pause at the conclusion of the story. This will be the cue to the interviewer to take back control with another question or redirection of the original question. But if the interviewer continues eye contact during the pause, use this as a cue to go on and provide another example.

Interviews do not have established ground rules, agendas, or programs. It is always a good idea to keep your answers within a two-minute maximum. But you will have no idea at the outset if the interviewer has two questions or twenty. By proper use of the pause, you give the interviewer the opportunity to stick with their plan and schedule. And, if appropriate, you can continue to give further details or an entirely new example.

A side note to the pause is the converse reaction—an interviewer should not have to interrupt your answer. If you are interrupted, give control back to the interviewer. Take it as a tip that you will need to shorten and tighten up your following answers.

One additional side note: never interrupt or finish a sentence for an interviewer. Even if they talk extraordinarily slow, be patient. Remember, they are the one who holds the ticket for admission.

THE QUOTABLE QUOTES TECHNIQUE

If you want to add credibility to what you say about yourself, tell the interviewer what other people have said about you. The best quotes are not words that others have said about you to you, but about you to others. The best way to provide this information is to quote the other person, referring to yourself in the third person:

> "My boss always said that if something needs to get done, give it to Jane and you know it will not only be done right away, it will also be done right."

> "My professor once told my academic advisor, 'Tim is the one person I can continuously count on to give a 110 percent effort in every class.'"

> "My coach called me 'The Dave' and coined the phrase, 'Give it to The Dave' when he had a game that needed saving. Even now, after I'm no longer on the team, he still uses 'Give it to The Dave' as his way of saying that it's time to put in the reliever."

When you can quote what others have said about you, you have elevated the view of who you are to the shoulders of others. From that vantage point, your value increases substantially. Take note of what others say about you. And be ready to quote the quotables.

THE HERO TECHNIQUE

Has there ever been a time in your life when you saved the day? "Hero" stories almost always make compelling interview stories. Was there a time when you put in the above-and-beyond effort? Or maybe a time when you did something that dramatically changed the course of events (for the positive, of course). Or perhaps even a time when you were a true hero, by saving someone's life or an act of great bravery? If so, work the story into your collection of compelling stories.

The difficulty with true hero stories can be in finding a successful bridge to the story. But with careful thought, you will find ample opportunities.

A recent interviewee told of the time when he literally saved someone from drowning in a lake, while cutting his feet on sharp objects trying to get to the drowning victim. This story came after a question about reaching goals in his life. Not sure how he got there? His bridge (after telling about his career goal of working for our company) was to say that he was very strong at keeping focused on the goal and not letting side issues deter him from achieving the objective. And he then went on to tell the story of how he saved the drowning victim, in spite of injuring himself in the process. He only realized he had cut his feet after he had carried the girl out of the lake. Thus, his focus is confirmed and the story is now ingrained in me, probably for posterity.

Another interviewee told of the time that she was given a surprise party by a customer of the company she worked for. They were all so appreciative of the hard work that she put in that they gave her a going-away party when she went back to school. This story was given in response to a question about how responsive she was to the needs of others.

Another interviewee told of the time he hit the game-winning RBI in the final game of a softball tournament. He told the story in response to a question about teamwork and did it in a way to show that all the members of the team had contributed to the final outcome, even though he was the one carried off the field by his teammates. He used it as an example to show how he valued the bonding of the team and how each member was able to perform at a much higher level than would have been possible individually.

And finally, another interviewee told the story of sinking the 8-foot putt for victory on the first hole of sudden-death playoff in golf. He was asked a question about his ability to handle pressure, and he used the story to show that he actually thrived on pressure and performed at his peak while under pressure.

Hero stories play well in the minds of interviewers. We all love to hear a good story and hero stories are often some of the best. Think about the times in your life when you were the hero. And begin to weave your hero story (or stories) into your interviewing answer repertoire.

THE SUCCESSFUL VAGABOND TECHNIQUE

There is a very simple key to successful interviewing which I learned from a couple who successfully traveled around the world on a sailboat. While not requiring a great deal of money for their journey (most of their needs were supplied by the wind and the sea), they did occasionally have need for provisions. So when they made a stopover in the port of a distant land, they would often seek short-term work, usually just enough to replenish their supplies. To compound the difficulty of this task, they were always foreigners in a foreign land, seeking limited-term work, and asking at or above the local prevailing wage. Yet they were always successful.

> BE CONFIDENT IN WHO YOU ARE AND WHAT YOU CAN BRING TO THE JOB AND POSITION. THEN PASS THAT CONFIDENCE TO ME, SO THAT I MAY SHARE YOUR LEVEL OF CONFIDENCE WITH OTHERS.

Their secret? Confidence. Simple confidence. Confidence in who they were. Confidence in what they could do. "I can do this job and do it well." They did not go begging for work. They would walk into a company with confidence that they would be able to make an immediate contribution. Confidence that they would be profitable employees. And their confidence came through loud and clear. They found work in every port, near and far.

Every company, whether in the United States or abroad, looks for confidence when hiring new employees. If you lack confidence, you will be refused. If you show confidence, it will cover a multitude of shortcomings in other areas. Lacking work experience? Confidence will overcome. Confidence is the great counterbalancing factor for entry level college grads.

When I am interviewing college students for entry level opportunities at my company, one of the first things I look for is confidence. The confidence factor is one of the most quickly recognized skills in the brief on-campus interview and one of the most highly reliable predictors of future performance.

So how do you gain this confidence? Through preparation. Knowing who you are and what you can do. And practicing. Over and over. Until you are both confident in yourself and able to project that confidence to others. I must also be confident in your ability to do the work. Then, and only then, will I be willing to invest in you.

HOW TO NEVER BE NERVOUS AGAIN

If even the thought of interviewing makes you nervous, it's important to get that emotion under control. The interview is your opportunity to be at your best. If you allow nervousness to control your presentation (or lack thereof), your image may be forever shrouded in the cloud of nervousness that will block the interviewer's total view of who you are.

Why do we get nervous? Because of the unknown. We are seeking approval, but we are unsure of ourselves and how we will be perceived. We are afraid we won't get approval, which makes us nervous. And to compound the problem, our increasing nervousness makes it even more difficult to gain that approval, thereby compounding the basis for our fears. Uncontrolled, nervousness can destroy our ability to effectively interview.

But it doesn't have to be that way. The following is a simple technique you can apply to overcome your nervousness in any interviewing situation. It is a technique that I personally use in overcoming my own nervousness, and it will work equally well for you.

THE ROWBOAT TECHNIQUE

In my public speaking, I am often confronted by crowds of hundreds and sometimes even thousands. Do I get nervous? You bet. Every time. Is anyone aware of my nervousness? Not unless they see me in the few minutes before I go on stage, before I have successfully applied the Rowboat Technique. This simple technique allows me to overcome my fears and successfully speak before thousands of people I have never met before. And it will help you in meeting with and speaking to people you have never met before in the interviewing situation.

The Rowboat Technique is a simple contraction of the abdomen in combination with rhythmic breathing that allows you to fully overcome your nervousness in any situation. To understand how to use this technique, sit forward in a chair, arms outstretched, as if you are grabbing oars in a rowboat. Take a deep breath, then slowly pull back your arms and contract the abdominal muscle just below the rib cage. As you continue to let out air, roll the contraction of the muscle downward, just above your pelvic region, centering on your navel. Keep your muscles tight until all of the air has been expelled. Count to three (don't breathe in yet!), then inhale deeply. Repeat this simple process two or three times and you will find that your body is completely relaxed.

To better understand the Rowboat Technique, stop by the gym and sit down at one of the rowing machines. You will gain a firsthand feel for the relaxation brought on by the series of muscle contractions and deep breathing that comes naturally during this type of workout.

So how can this apply with interviewing? Obviously, you don't want to go through all the visual animations in front of the interviewer, but you can still effectively apply this technique. Simply take in a deep breath through your nose, then contract your abdominal muscles in the "top to bottom roll" discussed above as you slowly exhale through slightly parted lips. Hold it at the bottom, take in a deep breath, and you are ready to go. If you are still nervous, simply repeat the technique one or two more times. Even if you are not nervous at the time, it is always a good idea to use this technique as you wait to meet with your interviewer. During the interview, you can use it while the interviewer is speaking to keep potential nervousness in check.

> A CERTAIN LEVEL OF NERVOUSNESS IS TO BE EXPECTED DURING ANY INTERVIEW. BUT HOW YOU REACT TO IT WILL DETERMINE THE OVERALL IMPACT.

What if you are overcome by nervousness while answering a question? Simply pause, take a deep breath, exhale and contract, then continue. Your nervousness will be noticeable to the interviewer (due to the pause in your answer), but the five-second drill will also show that you are seeking to control your nervousness. If you are able to successfully overcome, I will never hold that pause against you. I will admire your self-control and the positive, proactive action you took to put the interview back on a successful track.

This technique is virtually unnoticeable to anyone nearby. I make it a habit to apply this technique several times before going on stage, whether I am feeling nervous or not. You could be seated next to me and be completely unaware of what I am doing. Yet I will effectively put away all my nervousness and prepare myself for a dynamic presentation. You can do the same in preparation for your interview.

Why does it work? Very simply, the muscle contractions prevent the introduction of chemical imbalances into your system that can cause nervousness. The deep breathing helps to dissipate any chemicals that have already been released. It forces the body to prepare physically for the upcoming task. The body begins to focus on producing the positive endorphins needed for the anticipated "rowing" ahead. And this exercise will give your mind the opportunity to focus positively on the actual task of interviewing.

You can use this technique in a variety of circumstances in which you need to focus your mind and body: overcoming anxiety, anger, fright, tension, nausea—even a simple case of stomach butterflies. You can overcome interviewing nervousness, and much more, just by using this simple technique. If you haven't already done so, give it a try right now!

TEN TOUGH INTERVIEW QUESTIONS AND TEN GREAT ANSWERS

Mental fear of the unknown is often what produces the physical symptoms of nervousness. In addition to preparing yourself physically, you need to prepare yourself mentally. The best way to prepare mentally is to know what may be coming. Fear of the unknown can only exist when there is an unknown. Take the time to understand some of the "standards" when it comes to interviewing questions.

The following are some of the most difficult questions you will face in the course of your job interviews. Some questions may seem rather simple on the surface—such as "Tell me about yourself"—but these questions can have a variety of answers. The more open ended the question, the wider the variation in the answers. Once you have become practiced in your interviewing skills, you will find that you can use almost any question as a launching pad for a particular topic or compelling story.

Others are classic interview questions, such as "What is your greatest weakness?" Questions most people answer inappropriately. In this case, the standard textbook answer for the "greatest weakness" question is to give a veiled positive—"I work too much. I just work and work and work"— which ends up sending the wrong message. Either you are lying or, worse yet, you are telling the truth, in which case you define working too much as a weakness and really don't want to work much at all.

The following answers are provided to give you a new perspective on how to answer tough interview questions. They are not there for you to lift from the page and insert into your next interview. They are there for you to use as the basic structure for formulating your own answers. While the specifics of each reply may not apply to you, try to follow the basic structure of the answer from the perspective of the interviewer. Answer the questions behaviorally, with specific examples that show that clear evidence backs up what you are saying about yourself. Always provide information that shows you want to become the very best _____ for the company and that you have specifically prepared yourself to become exactly that. They want to be sold. They are waiting to be sold. Don't disappoint them!

1. **Tell me about yourself.**
    My background to date has been centered around preparing myself to become the very best _____ I can become. Let me tell you specifically how I've prepared myself . . .

2. Why should I hire you?

Because I sincerely believe that I'm the best person for the job. I realize that there are many other college students who have the ability to do this job. I also have that ability. But I also bring an additional quality that makes me the very best person for the job—my attitude for excellence. Not just giving lip service to excellence, but putting every part of myself into achieving it. In _____ and _____ I have consistently reached for becoming the very best I can become by doing the following . . .

3. What is your long-range objective? Where do you want to be ten or fifteen years from now?

Although it's certainly difficult to predict things far into the future, I know what direction I want to develop toward. Within five years, I would like to become the very best _____ your company has. In fact, my personal career mission statement is to become a world-class _____ in the _____ industry. I will work toward becoming the expert that others rely upon. And in doing so, I feel I will be fully prepared to take on any greater responsibilities that might be presented in the long term.

> MAKE MY JOB EASY FOR ME. MAKE ME WANT TO HIRE YOU.

4. How has your education prepared you for your career?

As you will note on my resume, I've taken not only the required core classes in the _____ field, I've also gone above and beyond. I've taken every class the college has to offer in the field and also completed an independent study project specifically in this area. But it's not just taking the classes to gain academic knowledge—I've taken each class, both inside and outside of my major, with this profession in mind. So when we're studying _____ in _____, I've viewed it from the perspective of _____. In addition, I've always tried to keep a practical view of how the information would apply to my job. Not just theory, but how it would actually apply. My capstone course project in my final semester involved developing a real-world model of _____, which is very similar to what might be used within your company. Let me tell you more about it . . .

5. Are you a team player?

Very much so. In fact, I've had opportunities in both athletics and academics to develop my skills as a team player. I was involved in _____ at the intramural level, including leading my team in assists during the past year—I always try to help others achieve their best. In academics, I've worked on several team projects, serving as both a member and team leader. I've seen the value of working together as a team to achieve a greater goal than any one of us could have achieved individually. As an example . . .

6. **Have you ever had a conflict with a boss or professor? How was it resolved?**
Yes, I have had conflicts in the past. Never major ones, but certainly there have been situations where there was a disagreement that needed to be resolved. I've found that when conflict occurs, it's because of a failure to see both sides of the situation. Therefore, I ask the other person to give me their perspective and at the same time ask that they allow me to fully explain my perspective. At that point, I would work with the person to find out if a compromise could be reached. If not, I would submit to their decision because they are my superior. In the end, you have to be willing to submit yourself to the directives of your superior, whether you're in full agreement or not. An example of this was when . . .

7. **What is your greatest weakness?**
I would say my greatest weakness has been my lack of proper planning in the past. I would overcommit myself with too many variant tasks, then not be able to fully accomplish each as I would like. However, since I've come to recognize that weakness, I've taken steps to correct it. For example, I now carry a planning calendar in my pocket so that I can plan all of my appointments and "to do" items. Here, let me show you how I have this week planned out . . .

8. **If I were to ask your professors to describe you, what would they say?**
I believe they would say I'm a very energetic person, that I put my mind to the task at hand and see to it that it's accomplished. They would say that if they ever had something that needed to be done, I was the person who they could always depend on to see that it was accomplished. They would say that I always took a keen interest in the subjects I was studying and always sought ways to apply the knowledge in real-world settings. Am I just guessing that they would say these things? No, in fact, I'm quite certain they would say those things because I have with me several letters of recommendation from my professors, and those are their very words. Let me show you . . .

9. **What qualities do you feel a successful manager should have?**
The key quality should be leadership—the ability to be the visionary for the people who are working under them. The person who can set the course and direction for subordinates. A manager should also be a positive role model for others to follow. The highest calling of a true leader is inspiring others to reach the highest of their abilities. I'd like to tell you about a person who I consider to be a true leader . . .

10. **If you had to live your life over again, what would you change?**
That's a good question. I realize that it can be very easy to continually look back and wish that things had been different in the past. But I also realize that things in the past cannot be changed, that only things in the future can be changed. That's why I continually strive to improve myself each and every day and that's why I'm working hard to continually increase my knowledge in the _____ field. That's also the reason why I want to become the very best _____ your company has ever had. To make positive change. And all of that is still in the future. So in answer to your question, there isn't anything in my past that I would change. I look only to the future to make changes in my life.

In reviewing the responses, please remember that they are samples. Please do not rehearse them verbatim or adopt them as your own. They are meant to stir your creative juices and get you thinking about how to properly answer the broader range of questions that you will face.

FIFTY STANDARD INTERVIEW QUESTIONS

It is not enough to have solid answers for only the above questions. You need to be prepared for the full spectrum of questions that may be presented. For further practice, make sure you go through the required mock interview (see the Competitive Interview Prep chapter); and for further review, look at some of the questions listed in Appendix B, Fifty Standard Entry Level Interview Questions. Don't just read the questions—practice them. Don't let the company interview be the first time you actually formulate an answer in spoken words. It is not enough to think about them in your head—practice! Sit down with a friend, a significant other, or your roommate (an especially effective critic, given the amount of preparation to date) and go through all of the questions. Make the most of every single interview opportunity by being fully prepared!

ONE INTERVIEW QUESTION THAT NEARLY EVERY COLLEGE STUDENT FAILS

Here it is. The one question that nearly every college student fails to answer properly (and will continue to send students to their interview ruin) is:

"Why did you choose to attend this college?"

You have spent the last several years knocking the college—the professors, the administration, the dorms, the food in the dining halls, whatever—and now you need to come to its defense. And if you have not thought of an answer before the interview, you definitely will not come up with a valid one on the spot.

So think about it in advance. What is the real reason you are attending your college? Is it because of the academic program? Is it because of extracurricular programs? Athletics? Close to home? Party school? Great dating opportunities? Everyone else turned you down?

Once you acknowledge your true reason for attending, you will need to temper your response with some directed reasoning—tie in what it is about your college that makes it worthwhile from the perspective of the employer. Your response should emphasize what it is about the school that makes it an attractive training ground for this employer. You need to talk about your college as the ideal training facility for becoming a _____ with that company.

You might find it best to give a "process answer" such as:

> "I originally decided to attend State U. because of its strong general academic reputation and its close proximity to my home, which gave me the opportunity to continue working at my part-time job. During the years I have spent here, I have come to truly appreciate the depth and breadth of the _____ curriculum. It has given me an excellent foundation for becoming an immediate contributor in the _____ field."

Lay on the superlatives, but don't get mushy. You will come to appreciate your time at college later in life, but for now, a few well-chosen words about why it is number one for you in your career will suffice.

DON'T COMMIT ONE OF THE WORST INTERVIEW SINS

One of the worst "sins" an interviewee can commit is to speak in generalities rather than specifics. It is not enough to say, "I'm a very goal-oriented person." You have to back it up with specifics. For example: "I'm a very goal-oriented person. In fact, I regularly update a list of personal and business goals with specific time frames. Since I started keeping this goal list three years ago, I've successfully reached or surpassed over 95 percent of these goals. I'm confident that the other 5 percent are also within reach in the coming year."

> DON'T FORCE ME TO CONTINUALLY PROMPT YOU FOR FULL ANSWERS. I WILL SOON GROW WEARY OF THE PROCESS AND GIVE UP.

If you are prone to using generalities, a sharp interviewer will usually follow with the behavioral question "Can you give me a specific example?" So beware! In fact, a favorite dual interview question of mine is: "Do you consider yourself to be goal oriented?" (which to date has been answered 100 percent of the time with "Yes"), followed by: "Can you give me a specific example?" It's amazing how many people could not answer the second question or (worse yet) attempted to snow their way past it. The best answers came from those who didn't even need the prompting of my second question, but gave specifics in response to my initial question. That is what a good interviewer will be looking for.

An important aspect of being specific is to use the quantitative approach. Don't just say, "I increased productivity." Instead use, "I increased staff meeting productivity 25 percent in one year within my department by implementing a video teleconferencing system for participants at our other location, thereby reducing unnecessary travel time. And as a by-product of this focus on the needs of our employees, meeting attendance is up over 10 percent. In fact, the teleconferencing system was showcased in the August newsletter. Let me show you a copy."

THE PARROTING TECHNIQUE

If a question is unclear to you, it is entirely appropriate to ask a clarifying question or paraphrase the question to make sure you understand. "Parrot back" the question in your own words to make sure you have the correct meaning. Don't assume or make a "best guess" of what the interviewer is looking for. They are the only ones who truly know what they want, so a well-placed "Just so that I understand, what you are asking is . . ." response will serve you far better than treading down an unknown path.

> THERE ARE NO PERFECT QUESTIONS AND THERE ARE NO PERFECT ANSWERS. JUST COME AS CLOSE AS YOU CAN.

The Parroting Technique will also serve you well as a temporary stall when you do not have a ready answer.

THE SAFETY VALVE TECHNIQUE

What do you do when you have been asked a question that you know you have a good answer to, but cannot think of it immediately? Don't get caught using the typical "I know the answer to that and I will give it to you as soon as I can remember what it is" line that is most often blurted out (either figuratively or, I'm sorry to say, literally by some). Instead, use the Safety Valve Technique. Basically, this technique "allows some steam to escape" while you formulate your answer. If handled well, it will appear almost seamless to even the most experienced interviewer.

Here is how it works. The interviewer has just asked you a question for which you know you have a good answer, but you just cannot think of it at that moment. First of all, repeat back the question with the Parroting Technique. This will buy you a few precious seconds before going on to the next level. If you still cannot put together the answer, you have two "safety valves" left. First, comment on the importance of the question and its context—"I understand the importance of this in regard to . . . " If you still haven't formulated your answer, turn the question back to the interviewer for comment—"Can you tell me how _____ (subject area) specifically plays a role within your company?"

This technique takes some practice to avoid the "snow job" look, but if you practice it enough (try attending some MENSA meetings to watch the professionals perform), you will find yourself quite ready and able to squeeze precious seconds out of even the most seasoned interviewers.

THE REFRAMING TECHNIQUE

The word "control" is often used with regard to interviewing. Often it is used incorrectly, by giving the interviewee the impression they should attempt to take full "control" over the questioning in the actual interview. This is, quite simply, a terrible mistake. If you attempt to take one-sided control of the interviewer and the interview, you may win the battle, but will certainly lose the war.

The right use of "control" in the interview is your ability to control both the context and perspective of your answers. You can do this effectively by utilizing the Reframing Technique. To do this, you should always attempt to answer the questions as straightforwardly as possible initially, but then reframe the original question to illustrate an area of your background that can further enhance your overall image. This requires a thorough understanding of your strong points so you have a planned direction and course. By properly using the Reframing Technique, you will find yourself covering the same core topics (which reflect your greatest strengths) in nearly every interview, regardless of the questions used as the launching point.

For example, if you are asked who your favorite professor is, you might give a short answer about a particular professor, then reframe the question by telling why that professor is your favorite. "She has the ability to tie in all of the classroom theory with practical business applications; in fact, it was her inspiration that encouraged me to participate in a two-week internship over winter break, where I combined my classroom knowledge with practical experience in the field of _____."

Reframing can take many forms, but at its best there is always a solid connection between the original question and the reframed emphasis. If the reformatting of the original question goes into a totally unrelated topic area, it will be counted against you. The key is to stay within the same general frame and use the question as a launch pad in a new, yet related direction (the reframed question). When done smoothly, the interviewer will not even be aware of the slight shift in focus. And you will have the opportunity to put forth your strongest points. Know your strong points and all the bridges you can use to reach them so that you can use reframing to your advantage in the interview.

THE EXPERIENCE OF A LIFETIME TECHNIQUE

One of the most difficult questions at the entry level can be the "experience" question. If you have applicable work experience in your chosen occupation, great! Make the most of it and capitalize on this area to differentiate yourself from your competition.

But what if you don't? What if your experience consists primarily of flipping burgers at McDonald's? Don't answer apologetically, as most do, that you really don't have any real experience to speak of. Instead, use the Experience of a Lifetime Technique to solidify your background and confirm your ability to do the job:

> YOU HAVE
> FULL CONTROL
> OVER YOUR
> ANSWERS. MAKE
> CERTAIN THEY ARE
> GOOD ONES.

"Thank you for asking me about my experience. I understand the need to review my past experience to determine whether or not I'm able to accomplish the tasks necessary for this job. I have, in fact, had a lifetime of experience that is directly related to this job. For example, I've learned . . ."

Then go on to relate life experiences and what those have taught you or how they have prepared you for this job. These responses can include the generic, which would apply to any position ("I've learned the ethics of hard work and seeing a job through to completion, whatever the cost, during my summers working for my uncle on his farm. One summer, my uncle broke his leg, and the entire family counted on me to . . ."), to the specific ("I've learned through my classes how to utilize object-oriented development tools to efficiently develop modular systems that can be used across a series of platforms. In fact, in the capstone project in my final year . . .").

Then close by detailing your personal attributes: "I've learned that for a company to succeed, it needs people who are ready and willing to put forth their very best effort. People who aren't afraid to work hard. People who are dependable. That is the experience that I bring to you and your company."

Modify the above to suit your own needs, but please don't regress to the "I really don't have any experience" line. The interview is as good as over the minute you say it.

THE ARTICULATION FACTOR

The ability to articulate your background is a combination of good preparation (which you have full control over) and vocabulary/enunciation (which you have practiced control over). Your "smartness," "sharpness," "quickness," "aggressiveness," and "brightness" are all attributes that are evaluated based upon your articulation. If you have "lazy lips" you may want to practice enunciating and forming your words more clearly. And whatever you do, don't continually reach for elusive words to perfectly portray your thoughts and feelings. Any practiced interviewer prefers an individual who is comfortable within their vocabulary level than one who is always searching at the level above.

> USE WORDS YOU KNOW AND ARE COMFORTABLE WITH. DON'T USE WORDS YOU THINK I THINK YOU SHOULD KNOW.

In practicing your articulation, take careful note of the "quickie" words which we tend to develop in our everyday speech pattern. Words like "gonna" and "yeah" and "y'know" and "kinda" are all killers. They can make you sound uneducated and coarse. And they have a habit of repeating. We have all probably had a parent (or sibling) point out the use of "y'know" in our speaking. In addition, you may have particular words or phrases you use for emphasis which can become particularly pronounced in the interview. These would include "to tell you the truth" and "truthfully" and "basically" and "OK, well" and "Like, . . ." As a side note, I once counted the number of times a candidate said "to tell you the truth" after it became particularly repetitive. She said it over fifteen times. And I began to question her truthfulness.

Make sure you are fully prepared for the interview, reviewing both your own background (nothing will kill an interview quicker than someone who cannot recall personal events) and the background of our company. Proper research will help you formulate your answers in a clear and succinct manner.

THE DIRTY DOG THEORY

We all love the dog, except when he needs a bath. Same with interviewing. I have conducted countless interviews where things seemed to be going just fine, when suddenly the interviewee began a series of complaints about others. And suddenly the spotless interviewee has become hopelessly stained.

Is there anything worse than a complainer? Nope, nothing worse. We all know one, and we all want to distance ourselves from that person. Corporate or otherwise. So remember that the interview is not your forum for griping. If you gripe about your current or past employers or professors or make note of any shortcomings in your life of missed expectations (even though they may be few!), you have just relegated yourself to the position of "complainer." And complainers are all too common already within most companies. Why would any company hire new complainers? They won't. Be positive about everything. Case closed.

THE ABRAHAM LINCOLN TECHNIQUE

It goes without saying that talking down the competition is a no-no. But talking about the competition can be quite different—if handled appropriately.

When Abraham Lincoln was arguing a case in court, he would usually argue both sides of the case to the jury. He would first take the opponent's side of the issue and then his client's side. But note: he was always very precise in bringing out more favorable facts for his client than for his opponent. Both sides were covered on a positive note, although his client's side was always more favorable.

> DON'T MAKE EXCUSES FOR SHORTCOMINGS. INSTEAD, POINT TO YOUR STRENGTHS.

At IBM, we followed this same principle. We were not allowed to talk down our competition. We could acknowledge them and their products, yet we never put them down. We were required to sell IBM on the strength of IBM, not on the weakness of others. Our customers appreciated our willingness to accept the competition and seek to rise above on our own merits rather than try to push the competition down to a lower level. So if you are confronted with a comparison to your competition, be prepared to fully acknowledge the strength of your competition, then follow with what you feel are your own greater assets.

An example in applying this technique is how to handle the potential negative when the interviewer asks why you are lacking in a particular area (be it grades, work experience, extracurriculars, etc.). You need to first speak well of the others. Then you need to establish your own case, which can also include using the Reframing Technique. An example would be in response to a question about a low GPA:

"I'm sure that there are many who have put more time and energy into their GPA than I did—and I congratulate them on their efforts. Grades are important, but my overall focus has been to develop myself as the very best accountant I can become. For me, this has involved not only time in the classroom, but also time in applying these skills in real-world situations. Because of that focus, I have spent fifteen to twenty hours per week working as a bookkeeper during my final two years. While I was not able to devote myself full time to pure academics, I feel the combination of academic and work experience has more fully prepared me for the accounting field than full-time academics alone."

Honest Abe would be proud of you.

THE PRIDE OF OWNERSHIP TECHNIQUE

Not sure how you are doing in the interview? Want to greatly increase your odds? You can do both with the Pride of Ownership Technique. To use this simple technique during the course of the interview, simply start giving your replies and asking your questions in terms of ownership—as if you are already part of the company. One way is to formulate the last part of your response to a "Teamwork" question with, "What kind of departmental structure will I be working in with your company?" Note the important difference. You are not asking, "What kind of departmental structure does your company have?" This is detached. You need to attach yourself—take pride of ownership—in the company.

Why? Two reasons. First and foremost, it establishes the link between you and the company. This is critical in helping the interviewer visualize you actually working for the company—the offer will never come if they cannot get past this step. Second, it provides you with instant feedback as to how you are doing within the interview. If the interviewer balks at your question or reshapes it by unlinking—especially by adding the "if" word in restating your question—you have a pretty good indication that you have not fully sold them on you. But if they accept your language and begin talking about you as if you are a part of the company, you are probably in a good position to close the sale.

THE COMPETITIVE POSTURE TECHNIQUE

It's important to maintain a competitive posture in the interview. The employer should be aware that they are not your only suitor. There is a delicate balance between letting the employer know that you really want to work for them and that if they don't make an offer, you will go with another company. The best way I can illustrate it is with the dating game. Sure, you love him/her and only him/her, but if things don't work out, there are plenty of other hims/hers banging on your door asking for a date. Right? Well, maybe it doesn't equate directly to your personal life, but you get the drift.

This posturing is very simple to incorporate into your interview language. Frame it in the form of a simple 1-2-3 engage/disengage/re-engage statement. Example:

1. "After what I've heard from everyone here at the company, I'm more convinced than ever that I would be an excellent contributor to your team. Just say the word and I'm ready to come to work for you."

2. "Of course, I do still have several other interviews pending."

3. "But at this point in time, you're the company I would most like to work for."

If you feel comfortable with closing the sale, you can add the "Are you ready to make an offer?" question to the last statement above. The point is that you have put a limited time offer on your enthusiasm—if they want you, all of you, they better move quickly and decisively.

THE ONE QUESTION TO ASK EVERY INTERVIEWER

THE PERCEIVED VALUE OF ANY PRODUCT IS DIRECTLY PROPORTIONAL TO THE NUMBER OF PEOPLE FIGHTING FOR IT.

The opportunity for you to ask a question often comes only at the end of the interview. In fact, you are typically offered the chance when the interview is over: "Are there any questions that I can answer for you?" However, there is a question you should ask of every interviewer as early as possible during the course of the interview: "Can you tell me about the position and the type of person you are seeking?"

Properly positioned, this question can provide you with your single greatest opportunity for understanding more about the job and your ability to fill the role. The answer can show you the specific areas of need you should address during the course of the interview. So it is important to inject this question into the interview as early as possible. You can do this with an out-take question. As you finish an answer, use it as a lead to your question. Be careful not to use this technique as an attempt to control the interview. You merely need to use this technique to inject this critical question.

For example, in answering a "What do you know about our company?" question, you can answer directly with what you know about the company (you have done your research, right?), then state that you do not know as much about the specific position. Turn your answer into the out-take question: "Can you tell me more about the position and the type of person you are seeking?"

Find the strategic opportunity to inject this question as early as possible in the process. Then, as appropriate, frame your answers around what they are seeking in the person to fill the position. Stay within practical and ethical bounds in directing your answers, yet keep in mind the perspective of the interviewer and seek to meet their needs for the position. You will be further ahead in the interview than if you merely take shots in the dark, hoping for your answers to magically hit the mark.

QUESTIONS TO ASK THE INTERVIEWER

Following are additional questions you may want to consider asking at an appropriate point in the interview:

> "Why did you personally decide to work for this company?"

> "What are the three most important attributes for success in this position?"

> "What are the opportunities for growth and advancement for this position?"

> "How is your company responding to competition in the _____ area?"

> "What is the anticipated company growth rate over the next three years?"

Limit yourself to no more than one or two questions during an on-campus interview and no more than two or three questions during each company-site interview. Even if you are not able to get answers to all of your open questions before the offer is made, you will have one final opportunity at that point.

THE MONEY RESPONSE TECHNIQUE

If the "money question" is asked early in the interview (as it often is), the best response is: "What would a person with my background and qualifications typically earn in this position with your company?" The best response if asked late in the interview process is: "I am ready to consider your very best offer." This is one time you don't want to be specific. If you give specifics, you lose— you will be either too low or too high, costing yourself thousands of dollars or possibly even keeping yourself from getting the job.

That said, if you are pressed by the interviewer for specific numbers, don't put them off with more than one "end run" response. First, make sure you have done your homework on the expected salary range for your field. The salary surveys usually are skewed toward the high end (possibly because only the best-paid graduates responded, while those with average or low pay did not want to admit what they were earning), so take them with a large dose of conservative adjustment. The best surveys are from those who graduated within the last year in your major from your school. You can possibly locate such information through your campus Career Development office, Alumni Office, or your personal network of contacts. A business grad from Stanford is going to be earning a lot more than a business grad from Podunk U. Know the "going rate" for your major, your school, and the field that you are considering entering. And make sure you know it before you get propositioned with the money question.

> # THERE IS MORE TO LIFE THAN MONEY. BUT MONEY DOES PROVIDE A GOOD START.

Armed with this information, ask the interviewer: "What is the general salary range for new hires in this position?" If the entire range is acceptable, respond with: "That would be within my expected starting range, depending on the entire salary and benefits package." If only the top end of the range is acceptable, respond with: "The upper end of the range is what I have been discussing with the other companies that are currently interested." If the range is below your expected starting salary range (be careful!), respond with: "The other companies I am currently speaking with are considering me at a salary somewhat higher than that range. Of course, money is only one element and I will be evaluating the overall package." Do your best not to get pinned to specific numbers, but if they do mention a number and ask if it would be acceptable to you, respond by saying: "I would encourage you to make the formal offer. What is most important is the opportunity to work for you and your company. I am confident that your offer will be competitive." Remember, don't do any negotiating until you have a formal offer in hand.

When that finally happens, go straight to the Successful Job Offer Negotiation chapter for guidance on shaping it into the best offer.

THE LOCKDOWN TECHNIQUE

If you are truly interested in the job, one thing you should do at the end of the interview is recap: (1) why you feel you are the best candidate for the job (give two or three of your strongest attributes and/or qualifications), and (2) restate your interest in the position by asking for the job. Don't expect the employer to make the first move. Let them know of your interest and desire to work for them.

It is interesting to note that fewer than 1 percent of all college students actually ask for the job. It's almost as if they assume it to be a given. But it's not. So those who take this extra step will put themselves far be-

> **IF YOU WANT THE JOB, TELL ME SO.**

yond the rest of the competition. If I know that you want the job—that you really want the job—it makes my job as the interviewer that much easier and will greatly increase the odds of an offer either on the spot (it does happen) or in the very near future.

Remember that you cannot close the entire sale except with the person who can actually make the entire purchase. So if you are interviewing with Human Resources, close by asking to move forward to the next step in the process, which will likely require meeting with the Hiring Manager. When you interview with the Hiring Manager, you are ready to close on generating an offer.

WHAT TO DO IF YOU ARE ASKED AN ILLEGAL QUESTION

The interview is going along smoothly. You are psyched that "this may be the one." And then it happens. Out of nowhere. "Are you considering having children?" Or, "How long has your family been in this country?" Or, "Your people place a high value on that, don't they?" Or, "You've done amazingly well for someone in a wheelchair. How long have you had to use one?"

On the surface these questions may seem innocent enough. And most of the time, they are truly asked in innocence. Yet the structure and format of the question is entirely illegal. So what do you do? How do you respond?

First of all, it is important to understand the difference between an illegal question and a criminally liable question. Even though a question or comment may have been stated in an illegal form, it does not necessarily mean that a crime has been committed. There is a difference between criminal liability and civil liability. For there to be criminal liability, it requires establishing a motive or intent. Most illegal questions are asked in ignorance, not with malicious intent. Yet there can still be civil recourse, even when there was no criminal motive or intent.

In our politically correct society, we often cry "foul" at the slightest deviation from the accepted standard. But the reality is that most illegal interview questions are asked in true innocence. Or, better stated, in true ignorance. Ignorance of the law, ignorance of what questions are proper, ignorance of how the information could be used by others in a discriminatory way.

Ironically, most illegal questions are asked when the untrained interviewer is trying to be more friendly and asks a seemingly innocent question about your personal life or family background. Therefore, any attempt by the candidate to assert their constitutional rights will merely throw up the defense shields and put an end to mutual consideration. Warning lights go on, sirens sound, and the interviewer begins backing down from what may have been an otherwise very encouraging position.

So what is the proper response? The answer is up to you, but my recommendation is to follow one of two courses of action: answer in brief and move on to a new topic area, or ignore the question altogether and redirect the discussion to a new topic area. The interviewer may even recognize the personal misstep and appreciate your willingness to put it aside and go on.

Unless the question is blatantly discriminatory—and yes, blatant discrimination does still take place—your best option is to move on to other things. But if it is blatant and offensive, you have every right to terminate the interview and walk out.

While laws vary from state to state, there are some definite taboo areas with regard to interview questions which employers should avoid. For a brief list of some of the questions that employers should not be asking, see Appendix C, Illegal Interview Questions.

Chapter 18

ON-CAMPUS INTERVIEWING SUCCESS

The average person puts only 25% of his energy into his work.
The world takes off its hat
to those who put in more than 50% of their capacity,
and stands on its head
for those few and far between souls who devote 100%.
—Andrew Carnegie

Consider the on-campus interview for a moment. You will be spending twenty to thirty minutes in a tiny cubicle with a total stranger. This person will subsequently decide whether you will ever have the chance of working for their company. The best you can hope for is to avoid being disqualified, which only takes you one step further into the interviewing maze. One little mistake, one little error, and you could be history.

Actually, the entire process seems rather absurd, except for the fact that you will not get a job without playing the interviewing game. And on-campus interviewing is often the starting point for the interviewing process.

On-campus interviewing is not simply meeting with three or five (or even ten) companies and then picking the one you want to work for. To maximize your on-campus interviewing success, you need to first maximize both the quality and quantity of the interviews, and then maximize your interview efficiency. It is not enough to just "show up" for the interviews and hope that someone will miraculously offer you a job. You have to perform at your peak to gain mileage from on-campus interviewing. So don't just read this chapter, read all of the chapters related to interviewing.

THE COMPANY'S INTERVIEWING PROCESS

From my side of the desk, there are four distinct steps we go through in our entry level hiring process:

1. **Marketing** — getting the company name out on campus

2. **Screening** – reviewing a candidate's qualifications against our basic criteria

3. **Assessing** – reviewing a candidate's behaviors against our critical behavior profile

4. **Selling** – encouraging chosen candidates to choose our company over the competition

The first two steps take place on campus. The final two take place at our company-site interview. It is the fourth step where you want to find yourself—where you are being courted as the employee we want. But before you get to that stage, you will need to pass the first three steps. And the opening steps are right there on campus.

KNOW YOUR COMPETITION

They are sitting there in class with you. They will also be sitting there in the interview waiting room or shaking hands with the interviewer in the time slot just before (and after) yours. All those students you have been competing with for grades are now your direct competition for jobs—at least for the jobs that come calling to your campus. They are the same ones who blew the top end of the curve on the last test. But keep in mind that this is not the chemistry final. It is not how much you know, but how well you communicate. The 4.0 student who cannot interact with anything outside a test tube will have as much (or more) difficulty finding a job than others.

> WELCOME TO THE COMPETITIVE WORLD. WELCOME TO REALITY.

Know your competition and what they have to offer. Know yourself and what you have to offer. Be ready to differentiate and sell yourself based upon your unique skills.

WHAT TO BRING TO YOUR ON-CAMPUS INTERVIEW

Yourself, your 9" x 12" portfolio/folder, two copies of your resume, copies of your top three letters of recommendation, any company information you have gathered, and any show-and-tell information you may want to use (but it better be outstanding, or leave it home). Nothing more, nothing less. And do not take notes unless you are specifically asked to take an action that you need to record for memory. Remember who is interviewing whom.

THE WAITING ROOM PREPARATION TECHNIQUE

The on-campus interviewing waiting room is your initial face-to-face connection point with your potential employer. Use this waiting room area as the preparation location for your interview. Always, always, always arrive at least ten to fifteen minutes early. This will give you the time necessary to do a quick final review before the actual interview. Get a drink of water on the way there, to avoid the cotton mouth syndrome.

When you arrive at the waiting room, check in with the secretary or administrator. If you do not already know the name of the interviewer, find out and write it down. Ask if there was anyone on the schedule before you. If not, or if that person canceled, be prepared for a potential early start. This can work strongly to your advantage, since it gives both you and the interviewer additional time. Ask how long the interview is scheduled to take, so you have an idea of how much time you will have. While waiting for the interviewer, take out your resume and review it one last time. Know it front to back. Visualize and mentally rehearse some of the standard answers. Think through some of your compelling stories to utilize in your behavioral answering.

I may be drinking coffee and sometimes will ask you if you want some. Refuse my offer. You will need your hands and mouth free to accomplish the task at hand. I am merely being polite. And avoid candy and gum, or you will be marked off my list even before we enter the interviewing room.

> A SMILING FACE
> CAN WORK
> WONDERS WITH
> A WEARY
> INTERVIEWER.

THE ANTICIPATION TECHNIQUE

As you wait for the interviewer to greet you in the waiting room, prepare to make your very best initial impression. Choose a seat that is facing the door or hallway where the interviewer(s) will approach. There will likely be several companies interviewing concurrently for a variety of different positions, so there may be several other anxious students seated in the waiting area. Be constantly conscious of the entryway, and when you see an interviewer approaching, make immediate eye contact and smile. Anticipate each interviewer as if he or she is the one who will be interviewing you. The interviewer will normally walk into the waiting room and announce the name of the next interviewee, or possibly check with the receptionist. Even though you may end up making eye contact with several interviewers who will be interviewing someone else, treat each one as if they are your interviewer. By anticipating this initial contact, you will be sharp and alert when you do make your connection. And their first impression of you will be of someone who has a high level of anticipation and readiness.

THE BRAGGING POINT TECHNIQUE

After the initial introductions are made, there is usually a long, silent walk back to the interview room. It may be a short period of time, but it can often feel like a death march. Instead of walking silently behind the interviewer, take the opportunity to establish a basic level of rapport. As you begin "the walk," whether it is 5 feet or 500 feet, comment to the interviewer, "I appreciate the opportunity to meet with you today." Wait for a response, then prompt with a well-selected bragging point about the interviewer's company, showing that you have done your research. A bragging point is something the employees of the company would be particularly proud to note. It can usually be found in the President's letter to the shareholders in the company's annual report. An example would be: "I understand that your company has been growing at over 30 percent per year for the last five years. It must be an exciting time to be working for XYZ." Always choose what you feel will be the number one bragging point for the company. Turn the tables and look at it from the employer's point of view. What would be their selling point in attracting new employees to work for their company? When you show that you have detailed knowledge of the company in one area, it will be assumed that you have even greater knowledge about the company. Set up this bragging point as an opener on your way to the interview room and you will not only show your knowledge of the company, you will also set a level of rapport that will guide you through the course of the interview.

HOW TO IMMEDIATELY IMPRESS AN ON-CAMPUS RECRUITER

If you have done your job well in researching the company, carry the company information with you to the interview—not packed away in your folder, but out where it can be seen. Most recruiters will notice immediately that you have an advanced edition of what they may have been giving to others at the end of the interview. It shows that you have done your homework.

Where to get this information? Your Career Development office usually has a company folder with materials gathered from past visits. Don't worry if the information is six months or a year out of date, since it will give the recruiter the opportunity to update you on the latest.

Make sure you know the information inside and out. This is not just a prop for show, since you will be expected to know more about the company if you have it. Be ready and willing to demonstrate your basic understanding of the company when asked. Good preparation will always impress an on-campus recruiter, whose day often consists of explaining, over and over, what their company does. Finally, someone who understands in advance. You have made a connection.

ACE YOUR ON-CAMPUS INTERVIEW

Do not take your on-campus interview lightly. Although it was "free" to you and easier to come by than direct contact with the company, the competition is intense.

To ace your on-campus interview, you will need to read (and study) all of the information contained in the Interviewing Success section of this book. If you treat every interview as if it were your last (in both a positive and a negative sense), you will be more focused on affecting the end result. On-campus interviewing is a gift. Spend it wisely.

SECURING THE COMPANY-SITE INTERVIEW

We all know the feeling. You have just completed an on-campus interview with a company you are truly impressed with. You really want to work for this company. It's almost like falling in love all over again—well, maybe you don't spend every waking hour thinking of them, but the butterflies in the stomach seem fairly familiar.

So you sit back to wait for them to take the next step. And then it happens. The infamous "Dear John" letter (and your name isn't even John!). How could this happen? How could they possibly fall for someone else when you are the only one for them? How could they possibly give their heart to another?

In job search as well as romance, you cannot sit by the phone waiting for it to ring. You snooze, you lose.

> **ON-CAMPUS IS ONLY THE FIRST STEP. YOU NEED TO PASS THE COMPANY-SITE INTERVIEW BEFORE AN OFFER WILL BE MADE.**

Just going through the motions of the on-campus interview is not enough to secure the company-site second interview. And in almost all cases, the second interview is the next step toward the eventual prize of the job offer (and meaningful life after college).

The first and most important step toward securing the second interview is to establish continuity at the end of the first interview. The typical "Do you have any questions?" should leave you open for two select questions about the company (remember to do your research in advance so that these questions are appropriate and specific to the employer). You might even test the waters with a Pride of Ownership Technique question to establish the connection between you and the company.

Then on to your final series of closing questions: "From everything I have heard today, combined with my research about your company, I am very interested in going on to the next step. Please let me know—are you interested in me?" I know, it sounds rather bold. But remember, you are in love! Now is not the time to woo from afar. Let them know where you stand, which gives you the right to ask the reciprocal question. Assuming they have at least a mildly encouraging response, ask your final question: "What is our next step?" Take careful note of the actions that need to be taken. This will be the chart for your course in securing that vital company-site second interview.

THE ON-CAMPUS FINAL IMPRESSION TECHNIQUE

Want to leave an excellent final impression? Write out your "thank you" note immediately after the interview and hand-deliver it before the interviewer leaves at the end of the day. Final decisions for company-site callbacks are usually made the same day, so strike while it still matters. If you were not the last interview on their schedule, sit down in the waiting room and scribe your response on the "thank you" stationery you brought with you. Then give the card to the receptionist and ask that the card be passed on to the interviewer. If you are the last interview of the day, write a quick note and get it to your interviewer before he or she leaves (most recruiters spend a few minutes organizing the accumulated information before departing). You can even have part of the note (the "thanks for your time" opening) written ahead of time. Then track the person down before he or she leaves the building (beware of alternate escape routes!).

If you are unable to get your "thank you" card to the interviewer, call the office and ask for the interviewer's voice mail. When messages are checked that evening, your personal "thank you" will make a lasting impression.

By taking these simple steps, you will definitely stand out from the crowd.

Chapter 19

PHONE INTERVIEWING SUCCESS

The man who goes farthest
is generally the one who is willing to do and dare.
The sure-thing boat never gets far from the shore.
—Dale Carnegie

Many people do not think of phone interviewing as interviewing. "It wasn't an interview, it was just a phone call." It was still an interview. And it could affect your potential career with an employer. So treat it with all the respect due a full interview.

THREE TYPES OF TELEPHONE INTERVIEWS

There are three basic types of telephone interviews:

1. You initiate a call to the Hiring Manager and they are interested in your background. The call from that point forward is an interview.

2. A company calls you based upon a previous contact. You will likely be unprepared for the call, but it is still an interview.

3. You have a preset time with a company representative to speak further on the phone. Also an interview.

TELEPHONE INTERVIEW PREPARATION

In preparing for your phone interview, there are several things you can do. To prepare for an unexpected contact:

➤ Tape your resume to a wall in view of the phone. It will be there for the call and will be a constant reminder for your job search.

➤ Keep all of your employer research materials within easy reach of the phone.

➤ Have a notepad handy to take notes.

➤ Keep a mirror nearby (you will see why in the next few pages).

If the phone interview is to occur at a set time, there are additional steps you can take:

➤ Place a "Do Not Disturb" note on your door.

➤ Turn off your stereo, TV, and any other potential distraction.

➤ Warm up your voice while waiting for the call. Sing an uplifting song to yourself.

➤ Have a glass of water handy, since you will not have a chance to take a break during the call.

➤ Speaking of breaks, if your phone interview is at a set time, make sure you answer nature's call first.

➤ Turn off call waiting on your phone.

THE PHONE PERSONALITY MATCHING TECHNIQUE

A variation on the previously discussed Personality Matching Technique (in the Mastering the Interview chapter) is to apply the same basic principles within your phone interview. Although you obviously cannot match the interviewer's physical characteristics, try to match the interviewer's speaking rate and pitch. Remember to stay within your personality range, but venture toward that portion of your range that most closely matches that of your interviewer. This is an excellent way to establish rapport quickly over distance and phone lines.

THE OPEN AND AVAILABLE TECHNIQUE

You have a major advantage in a phone interview that does not exist in a face-to-face interview. Namely, you cannot be seen. Use this to your advantage.

Have all of your materials on yourself and the company open and available on your desk as you are speaking on the phone. This includes not only your resume, but also a "cheat sheet" of compelling story subjects you would like to introduce. It can also include a cheat sheet about the company, including specific critical points describing the company and their products.

As I am speaking with you on the other end of the phone, I have no idea that you are actually being prompted from a document as you are speaking. All I can hear is a well-informed, well-prepared interviewee. Keep in mind that this preparation is not "cheating" at all. It is preparation, pure and simple.

So have your materials open and available when you are preparing for a phone interview. They are there to support you and enhance your value to the employer, who will greatly respect your ability to answer questions with focus and meaningful content.

THE STAND AT ATTENTION TECHNIQUE

Here is a simple technique to increase the enthusiasm and positive image you project over the telephone: stand up. Whenever you are talking with a potential employer on the phone, stand up. It gets your blood flowing, improves your posture, and improves your response time.

It's interesting to note that many telemarketing companies have come to realize that standing can actually improve their sales, so they often provide the telemarketers with hands-free headsets that allow them to stand and pace back and forth. It helps give an action perspective to an otherwise passive activity. So apply this technique in improving your telephone presence.

> KEEP YOUR MIND FOCUSED ON YOUR PHONE CALL. REMOVE ALL DISTRACTIONS FROM YOUR LINE OF SIGHT.

THE VANITY TECHNIQUE

When I was in college I had a roommate who enjoyed flexing his muscles in the mirror. He could do it for hours at a time. A little vain? Well, I am going to ask you to do the same thing (except leave out the flexing muscles part). In prep for a telephone interview (or any telephone contact), make sure you have a mirror within view. Why? Because I want you to look into that mirror consistently throughout the phone call. And smile. You will improve your telephone presence 110 percent just by using this simple technique. You will find yourself coming across as much friendlier, more interested, more alert. If you are at all self-conscious about seeing yourself in the mirror, you can use the mirror as an occasional checkpoint. But for most of us, seeing oneself reflected back gives us the kind of feedback necessary to make instant modification toward a more positive presence.

Remember, you are standing, so a wall mirror usually works best. You can pick up a small wall mirror for a limited amount of cash. It's worth it.

Try it the next time you are on the phone. But don't do it with your roommate around.

Chapter 20

COMPANY-SITE INTERVIEWING SUCCESS

If one advances confidently in the direction of his dreams,
and endeavors to live the life which he has imagined,
he will meet with a success unexpected in common hours.
—Henry David Thoreau

The company-site interview may be scheduled after successfully passing the on-campus screening interview, or it may be the first and subsequent interviews that result from contacting off-campus employers. Either way, the company-site interview is often the required final step in the interview process before an eventual job offer. However, you first need to survive the close scrutiny that comes along with it. Instead of meeting with just one person, you may be meeting with three or four. Instead of a simple half hour interview, you may be subjected to a half or full day of interviews. And tests. But with all the anticipated rewards now dangling within view.

The company-site interview is also your final opportunity to evaluate the company. You will be given the opportunity to see the inside of the company and meet with some of the key people. Possibly some of the people you will be working with. And you will gain a better understanding of the true work environment.

THE SPONSOR PREPARATION TECHNIQUE

Your sponsor has a vested interest in your doing well at the company-site interview. This person, who may have initially been a screener, is now an includer. You will be the personal representation of what they view as a potential new employee. In a way, their professional reputation is on the line whenever a new person is brought back to the company-site. No one wants to hear the dreaded, "Why did you invite that person back?"

So take advantage of this turn of the tables. The person who was against you is now for you. Be prepared to ask some questions:

"Who will I be meeting with?"

"What is this person's background?"

"What will they be looking for in the interview?"

"Will there be any other activities scheduled during the day?"

"What can I do to prepare myself further for your company?"

"Can you send me additional material about your company?"

You have a free opportunity not only to ask the questions, but to ask for recommendations. You will get a true insider view of what it takes to be successful at your company-site interview. Your sponsor is now your advocate. Build your personal connection to your mutual benefit.

FINAL ARRANGEMENTS

Your sponsor will be taking care of setting your schedule and providing you with advance materials. If you have not already filled out an employment application, ask if one will be required. If so, ask to have it sent out in advance, so you can fill it out neatly and completely. Note that "See Resume" is not an appropriate answer on an employment application. Make sure you print your neatest, since you will be judged by your penmanship (and you thought your second grade teacher was crazy for giving you such a hard time about your sloppy writing skills).

Your sponsor will also have the responsibility of coordinating your travel arrangements to and from the company-site, although the actual details might be delegated to an office assistant. And yes, you probably will have to skip some classes to interview. It's allowed.

There are four categories of travel expenses that can be incurred in your visit to the company-site: travel (air, train, or auto), local transportation, lodging, and food.

In most cases, your arrangements will be made for you by the employer. The general rule is that the higher the expense and further the distance, the more likely the employer will be to make the arrangements for you. However, if you are just across town, it may be presumed that you will find your own way without any expectation of compensation for the minimal expense incurred.

If you are flying to the interview, the flight expense is usually booked directly through the employer. Your tickets will usually be delivered to you via overnight courier, unless the time frame is tight, in which case they will be held for you at the check-in desk. If you are traveling by train, you may be expected to purchase the tickets and fill out an expense report for reimbursement. If traveling by personal auto, you will usually be given a set amount per mile, so be sure to reset your trip odometer before starting on your journey. When you fill out the expense report, you simply double your one-way mileage.

> **DON'T ASSUME ANYTHING IN YOUR ARRANGEMENTS. GET ALL THE DETAILS AHEAD OF TIME.**

If you will be taking a plane or train, know what your local transportation arrangements will be. The most convenient is to use a cab and save receipts, but if the company is not located in a large population center, they may have a rental car for you or may even have a company car pick you up at the airport or station. If you are taking a cab, always ask for receipts. With a rental car, make sure you have the collision damage waiver. If the company is expecting you to pay for the car, you will need a credit card. Keep receipts for your gas and parking for later reimbursement. If the company is sending someone to pick you up, know the designated connection point and signals. Usually the pickup person will be standing with a company sign with your name on it.

Overnight lodging may be required, especially if you are traveling from a distant location. Again, this is usually taken care of by the employer. Most employers have arrangements with local hotels for out-of-town visitors. You may be required to use a credit card if you want to use any of the extra services in the hotel. It is not advisable to indulge in either the locked liquor refrigerator or the pay-per-view movies. Go to bed early and wake with enough time to fully prepare. Traveler's note: if you are flying, bring your interview clothes in a hanging bag and hang it in the storage area just inside the plane door. Never check it with your luggage, or fold it over, or store it in the overhead bin.

Food is always a covered expense when you are with the company representatives. However, most other meals, including breakfast and dinner, are usually on your own. Many hotels offer a continental breakfast included with the room. Always make sure you have eaten before your interview. You will need the extra energy for what can sometimes be a grueling schedule.

Know where and when you will be meeting with the employer. Get accurate directions and a map if you need assistance. If you are arriving the night before, an excellent psych-up activity is to drive by the company location and visualize your interview the following day. Always plan for the unexpected, especially when it comes to traffic. Plan to arrive early. Keep in mind that it may take ten minutes to get from the parking lot to the front door and another five to ten minutes to get to the department location, so allow plenty of extra time. No one will fault you for being up to ten minutes early, but do not be earlier than that. Your target is five minutes early. If you have extra time, spend it reviewing company materials, your resume, and any additional information. Take a restroom break before you leave for the company, since many companies do not have restrooms available until you reach the inner sanctum. If there are restrooms available, stop by for one final visual and mental check. Look yourself straight in the mirror and say, "I am the very best person for this job. My job today is to convince the company of that fact."

THE VOICE WARM-UP TECHNIQUE

Have you ever been awakened by the phone in the middle of the night? "Hello?" And you wonder where that froglike voice comes from? Your vocal cords are simply not warmed up yet.

The same thing can happen at the company-site interview. You have little opportunity to actually speak until you arrive at the company-site. And then you are expected to talk nearly nonstop for the remainder of the day.

Take the time to warm up your voice on the way to the interview. If you are driving, turn on a radio station you enjoy and sing along. Top of your lungs is just fine. If you are taking a cab, either spend time talking with the cabbie (they have some of the most interesting stories you will ever hear) or ask to have the radio turned on. Again, sing along—although a little more quietly than if you were in your own car.

In any case, use and stretch your vocal cords before beginning your day of interviewing. You will benefit with a clear and resonant voice.

THE LOBBY WAITING TECHNIQUE

As you arrive at the company, take note of the surroundings. If this is the corporate headquarters, take note of the grounds and buildings. These are often major sources of pride for image-conscious companies.

When you arrive in the lobby, you should step up to the receptionist, state your name (present one of your networking business cards if you have them), who you are there to see, and the time of the appointment. Note that you should say you have an "appointment," or "meeting" scheduled, not "an interview."

The receptionist will phone your contact and will inform you of your status. "Jane will be with you in just a few minutes. Feel free to have a seat." Do not sit down. Instead, walk around the lobby, looking first at the walls for plaques and awards. Read them all. And if there is a product display, study it closely. Next, look for employee newsletters or other internal documents which may be displayed by the waiting room table. Finally, take note of the industry trade magazines that are being displayed.

This information will give you a very practical feel for the corporate culture, as well as an excellent starting point for rapport-building small talk throughout the day.

THE COMPANY-SITE INTERVIEW PROCESS

Usually you will initially meet with your sponsor. Depending on the company, you may have a published agenda for the day. This may include simply names and times of scheduled interviews, or additional information, such as titles and departments for each person, and the purpose of each interview.

The interviews can range from peer level to potential managers to executives. Many companies will have you meet with several different managers, any one of whom could be your potential manager. At the peer level, you may be given the opportunity to meet with one or two recent graduates who have just begun work with the company in the past year or two. The purpose of this interview is to give you a feel for what the company and the position are really about. But do not let down your guard in this interview or get too chummy. Even peer interviews have input into the final decision. Interviews with managers two or three levels above your entry position are usually designed to give the executive the final rubber stamp.

You may also be asked during the course of the day to take an exam or test. These tests are used to bring a level of objective standardization into the hiring process.

EXAMS AND TESTING

Be prepared to take an exam or a test. Asking your sponsor if there will be other activities scheduled when making the final arrangements is designed to alert you to the possibility, yet it may still come up

> THIS ISN'T THE THIRTY-MINUTE ON-CAMPUS INTERVIEW WITH ONE PERSON. YOU WILL SPEND THE BETTER PART OF A DAY MEETING WITH SEVERAL PEOPLE WHO WILL DETERMINE YOUR FATE.

unannounced. Being asked to take a test is a good sign, because employers do not waste time and money testing someone they are not interested in.

Following are the five basic types of tests you may encounter:

1. **Intelligence/Mental Ability Tests**
   These tests are designed to test your critical thinking skills, including problem solving, mathematical aptitude, and memory. They are usually structured in a format similar to the SAT/ACT.

2. **Work Simulation Tests**
   These tests are designed to provide you with example work scenarios or problems which you must work through to a satisfactory result. For example, a test for a Programmer position may ask the person to develop the program logic for a bank statement program.

3. **Specific Skills Tests**
   For many highly specialized professions, they will test your skills in specific areas. Many of these tests are tied into certification, such as the CPA or CNE. A subset of these certification tests is the specific skills test. These tests are designed to ask questions at a detail level. They are very specific and very accurate. You will be more likely to encounter these tests in technical professions, such as engineering or information technology.

> DON'T TRY TO FOOL A PERSONALITY TEST. IT IS FAR SMARTER THAN EITHER YOU OR I.

4. **Personality Tests**
   These tests are often the best indicator a company has of someone's personality. If you are familiar with the Myers-Briggs Type Indicator (MBTI), you will understand the type of comparison questions: "Would you rather fly a kite or read a poem?" or "Would you rather read a book or fly an airplane?"

5. **Honesty Tests**
   These tests are usually reserved for jobs in high-security areas or where there will be access to trade secrets, merchandise, or cash. Many of the questions are repetitive comparisons ("Do you like chess better than poetry?" and "Do you like poetry better than chess?"), although some will ask for absolutes ("Have you ever told a lie?"). You know the answer. And the test knows if you are telling the truth.

While these tests are all an attempt at standardization and greater objectivity, they are all lacking to a certain degree. They still have a subjective element. Be prepared, both mentally and physically, for these tests. I am aware of at least one company that does not begin salary negotiation until after the person has completed the series of tests. The theory is that they are so beaten down that they will accept almost anything that is offered.

Following are certain points to keep in mind with quantitative (math, numbers, reasoning, objective) and qualitative (opinion, viewpoint, comparison, subjective) tests:

QUANTITATIVE TESTS

- Get yourself mentally psyched. Clear your mind of all else and focus on the test.
- Take time to fully understand the instructions before you begin.
- If it is a timed test, forget about the time. Simply stay concentrated on the test.
- If you have no idea, it is usually best to skip the question.
- If you are unsure of your answer, it is usually best to answer the question.
- If you can skip questions, skip the more difficult ones and come back to them if you have time.

QUALITATIVE TESTS

- Prepare yourself mentally for taking the test. Get into a positive frame of mind.
- Take time to fully understand the instructions before you begin.
- Do not try to fool the test. Always give your best answer.
- Answer as the professional you, not the personal you.
- Answer from the employer's point of view.
- Incorporate qualities that have made you successful into your answers.
- Resist any impulse to lie about who you are.

With any test, keep in mind that the purpose is to further qualify you for the position. Put forth your very best effort and do not show discouragement when you finish the test. If asked about the test, make a comment about it being "challenging" (for quantitative) or "interesting" (for qualitative).

MEAL INTERVIEW DO'S AND DON'TS

You may find yourself on a breakfast, lunch, or dinner interview (or "eating meeting") during your company-site visit. This is usually a good sign that you are under strong consideration. Following are some of the basic do's and don'ts:

Do:

- Wait for your host to gesture the seating arrangement
- Place your napkin in your lap as soon as you are seated
- Remember everything your Mom taught you about table manners
- Order light; you are there to interview—eating is only the sideline
- Know what you are ordering; avoid exotic items
- Chew and swallow before you speak; no airborne food particles, please
- Be polite to waiters and waitresses, but not chatty

- Keep your elbows off the table
- Thank your host for the meal

Don't:
- Bring your briefcase; your portfolio is plenty
- Open your menu until your host has done so first
- Become lax in your presentation style; it is still an interview
- Drink alcohol, even if your host offers
- Be indecisive in ordering—make a decision and stick with it
- Begin eating until everyone is served
- Attempt to pay the bill or split the cost; it will be covered by your host
- Smoke, even if your host does
- Criticize the meal or the restaurant
- Order a doggy bag

SEVEN THINGS TO NEVER ORDER AT A MEAL INTERVIEW

1. Spaghetti
2. Pizza
3. French onion soup (see French Onion Soup Technique below)
4. Most expensive item on the menu
5. Least expensive item on the menu
6. Any fish with the head or bones still attached
7. Any food that requires fingers or a bib

SMOKING OR NON?

The question is asked every time we enter a restaurant. And I will always turn to the interviewee and ask, "Which do you prefer?" Whether you smoke or not, always respond, "It's up to you." And if you do smoke, do not smoke, even if your interviewer smokes.

Smokers beware. Smoking is at an all-time low on the acceptance scale. You are not a protected minority—and you are definitely in the minority. Even the smell of smoke on your clothes can count against you. If you smoke, do not smoke the day of the interview. In fact, do not smoke after your last shower prior to the interview. And wear fresh clothes that are free of the tobacco smell. Tough rules? Possibly. But there are enough sensitive noses and prejudiced minds out there that you should do your very best to avoid any and all potential negatives. And smoking is one area that most of society looks down on.

If you do smoke, there will likely be an advantage to kicking the habit before you begin work—ideally, before you begin interviewing, given the potential negative impact it can have on the job search process. Most companies now force employees to smoke either in a designated smoking room or outside the building (which can be especially rough in northern climates). The amount of time necessary for even the average pack-a-day smoker to

> **SMOKING COULD BE HAZARDOUS TO YOUR CAREER HEALTH.**

get their nicotine fix can amount to over 10 percent lost productivity. This fact is not quickly ignored by the average manager. And it may eventually work against you, either in your job search or in your professional career.

If you have been looking for an incentive to quit, this may be your opportunity.

THE FRENCH ONION SOUP TECHNIQUE

College students are often under the mistaken impression that they must conduct themselves perfectly in an interview. If they make a mistake, they've had it. Interview over. Give it up. History.

In truth, that point of view often becomes a self-fulfilling prophecy. But it doesn't have to be that way. Occasional "stumble errors" do happen. But if you use your error as an opportunity for well-placed humor, you can actually increase your odds.

Let me give you an example. I was on a luncheon interview with three partners from the firm I hoped to work for after college. I made the foolish error of ordering French onion soup. Why an error? Well, it wasn't just onion soup—it was French onion soup. So it also had that chewy, crusty piece of French bread smothered with mozzarella cheese buried in the steaming broth. Still don't see the problem? Let me describe it to you graphically—every time I tried to take a spoonful of the soup, I also brought with it a two- to three-foot strand of stringy cheese. As hard as I tried, I could not get that cheese to separate from the bowl on the way to my mouth. So there I was, trying to convince

> **A MANAGER REJECTED A CANDIDATE AFTER HIS MEAL INTERVIEW. WHAT HAPPENED? THE CANDIDATE SPILLED SOUP ON HIS TIE. MISTAKES DO HAPPEN. BUT THIS CANDIDATE PROCEEDED TO LICK OFF HIS TIE...**

these managers that I would make an outstandingly graceful consultant, when I could not even gracefully handle the soup sitting in front of me.

So what did I do? I took the spoon out one last time, lifted it high into the air—with all eyes at the table fixed on the three-foot strand of cheese—and stated calmly, "I promise you that I will never, ever again order French onion soup for as long as I work for this firm. One of my greatest assets is that when I make a mistake, I recognize it, change, and never make that mistake again!" We all broke into laughter. That broke the tension and made everyone feel comfortable again.

P.S. I got the job.

So if you make an obvious error, use self-deprecating humor to remove the tension—and the error—from the situation. It shows that you can admit to your own mistakes and laugh at yourself at the same time-two valuable traits for any company employee.

> MISTAKES CAN AND WILL HAPPEN. ALWAYS LEARN TO MAKE THE BEST OF A BAD SITUATION, WHETHER DURING THE INTERVIEW OR IN YOUR FUTURE CAREER.

I was told another story of a student who arrived for the company-site interview minus his luggage (containing his interviewing suit), which apparently chose to take an alternate flight to Los Angeles. Others might have considered calling off the interview in disgust, but he showed up in his blue jeans, sweatshirt, and tennis shoes. As he met each new person during the interviewing process, he began by assuring them that he really did own a blue pinstripe suit. Everyone got a good laugh and he got the job.

FRIENDS IN HIGH PLACES

One of the worst mistakes you can make in your job search is to treat the secretary poorly or on an inferior basis. The secretary usually has a great deal of influence over whether or not you will be hired—believe it. One of the first things I do after an interview is ask my secretary what she thinks of the person. If they were rude to her or treated her disrespectfully, they are automatically eliminated from consideration! That's right—no matter how well they did in the interview, if they were not equally impressive to my secretary, I know that the person was a fake and was just putting on a good show in the interview. The secretary is one of the best "friends" you can have within the company. But do not go beyond standard business protocol. I have also disqualified some for coming on to my secretary. Be professional.

One other important tidbit is to always take note of the secretary's name. It's a scary thought, but you might be face to face with the Guardian of the Gate, the person you will need to get past when you call the manager again at a later date.

SUCCESS SIGNALS

Following are some of the signals that an offer may be near:

➤ You are introduced to employees other than those you interview with.

➤ You are given a facility or plant tour.

➤ You are given information about the local area, including apartment rental guides.

➤ You are given relocation information.

➤ You are given employee-only materials, such as benefits guides and handbooks.

➤ You are given anything that you will be expected to return at a later date (such as CD-ROM training or expensive software).

➤ You are introduced to or interview with your potential boss's boss.

FROM INTERVIEW TO OFFER TO JOB

Chapter 21

AFTER THE INTERVIEW

Nothing in the world can take the place of persistence.
Talent will not;
nothing is more common than unsuccessful men with talent.
Genius will not;
unrewarded genius is almost a proverb.
Education will not;
the world is full of educated derelicts.
Persistence and determination alone are omnipotent.
—Calvin Coolidge

It's not over 'til the fat lady sings. In the case of interviews, don't get lulled into thinking that your final "good-bye" is the end of the opera. Far from it.

THE TWO MOST IMPORTANT POST-INTERVIEW ACTIVITIES

There are two simple steps you can take to make a lasting impression after your interview and greatly increase your odds of success.

The first is to call the interviewer to thank them for their time. If possible, you may want to add additional information which was not discussed in the interview. An example would be: "I noticed in speaking with the receptionist that Microsoft Office is your corporate software standard. I just wanted to mention that I'm also fully proficient in each of the tools in the Office suite." This phone call should ideally take place the same day. If you are unable to reach the interviewer directly, leave a voice mail message.

The second activity is to immediately write the interviewer a short note, thanking them for their time and re-emphasizing your interest in the position. Then do your best to get it to them as quickly as possible. Fax it, hand-deliver it, messenger it, use overnight mail, whatever. But be sure they have it before the end of the following day. Ideally, you want to get it in their hands by the end of the day of the interview or first thing the following morning. Why? Because the quicker your letter arrives, the greater the likelihood of a positive outcome.

Doesn't everyone follow up like this? Hardly. Virtually no one calls after an interview and few take the time to write a "thank you" letter. Those who do write letters generally send them via the postal service, which can arrive as much as a full week after the interview. The simple gestures of a phone call and "thank you" letter can make a big difference in separating you from your competition.

> A "THANK YOU" NOTE MAY SEEM OBVIOUS, BUT I CAN ASSURE YOU THAT THE MAJORITY OF STUDENTS DO NOT SEND THEM.

And if you interviewed with multiple individuals, make sure each "thank you" letter is unique. Common language is acceptable, but do not simply change the name at the top of the letter. Your application, resume, and other materials will likely be stored in a single file, usually in the possession of the person guiding you through the hiring process. Your "thank you" letters will eventually find their way back to this central file. Yes, we do compare notes. And what seemed to be a unique and original note can actually work against you if there are two or three duplicates collected together in your file. It has taken a great deal of effort to get this far. Take the extra time to make this final impression a positive one.

THE THIRD-PARTY RECOMMENDATION TECHNIQUE

If you want to make a lasting impression on a potential employer, ask the individuals who supplied you with letters of recommendation to either call or write to the employer, giving an additional recommendation. This technique will instill confidence in the employer that they are making a wise decision in hiring you.

Obviously, this technique works for you only if you have a strong sponsor (or two) among your references. And it has the potential for abuse—you do not want to burden your reference in every interviewing situation. However, when you truly believe "this is the one," it may be time to cash in some chips.

Do not give in to the temptation of using a "fill in the address" prewritten letter from your reference. It should be unique and original, printed on letterhead or stationery. This technique works because it shows that others think highly enough of you to take the time to call or write. There is truly no higher compliment your references can pay you. So remember to thank them—in words now, and with a card and a small gift when the offer comes.

GENERATING JOB OFFERS

Once the "thank you" letter has been sent, your role in the job search is to work toward an offer. By staying in close contact (at least once a week) with your primary company contact, you will be continually aware of the process. And the contact will be continually aware of your interest.

Always make sure you know the next step in the process. How? By asking directly.

> IF SOMEONE ELSE ALSO THINKS YOU'RE GREAT, GIVE THEM A KEY ROLE ON YOUR JOB SEARCH TEAM.

"I am very interested. What is the next step?"

If you are straightforward and direct, the contact will keep you posted as to your progress. If you are no longer under consideration, you will be informed. If there are further interviews pending or your background is being reviewed by others, you will be informed. If the company is getting ready to put together an offer, you will be informed. Stay close to your contact and be ready to act on a moment's notice.

EARLY OFFERS

A rather nice situation—yet still perplexing—is to receive an "early offer" from one of the companies you have interviewed with. By "early," I mean in relation to other potential job offers. You may have had eight interviews in the last month, three of which resulted in second interviews, but one of which resulted in an immediate offer. Worse things can happen.

Yet it still creates a dilemma. Sure, if the offering company is your first choice, accept the job and send the others your regrets. But if not, then what?

THE PRICE OF MEMBERSHIP THEORY

The first thing you should do when you receive an early offer is to make the other companies immediately aware of the offer. Your stock will go up markedly the moment you have been "put into play." It is simple human nature to covet what others have, and the price of membership has just gone up for those who want to join in the fight for the coveted prize. What is difficult to obtain always holds greater value. Interested players are now required to react immediately or lose you. If they are truly interested, they will react. If they have just been stringing you along with a load of others, they will cut you free. Be prepared: you may be isolated with your lone offer. But if you are good, you may receive multiple offers.

The second thing to do is ask the company that made the initial offer for as much time as possible to make your decision. The amount of time you request may depend on the other pending offers (have an idea as to when they might be ready to respond). One week to make the decision is common and you might be able to get as much as two weeks. But this is not the time to go out and start new contacts from scratch. It's time to wind down your search and cash in your chips.

> THE ONLY THING BETTER THAN GETTING YOUR FIRST JOB OFFER IS GETTING YOUR SECOND ONE. AND THE ONLY THING BETTER THAN YOUR SECOND IS YOUR THIRD.

THE MULTIPLE OFFER TECHNIQUE

If you are willing to entertain offers from other companies, it is your personal obligation to inform these companies of your offer as quickly as possible. You may have only one or two others that are even in the running. If so, restrict these multiple offer tactics to them.

Contact the person within the company who would be your Hiring Manager. Let that person know that you have received a competitive offer and tell the manager which company made the offer. The reason for giving out the company name is that you usually will not have to disclose the dollar amount, since most industry insiders have at least a general idea what others in the field are paying. Don't be surprised if the manager suddenly backs off, because they may realize that their company cannot match the other company's wage/benefit package or other perks. If you have scored your initial hit with an industry leader such as P&G in Consumer Products, Boeing in Aeronautical Engineering, Arthur Andersen in Accounting, Microsoft in Software, or another market leader, you may find it difficult to draw a second offer. The giants are tough to beat. It takes time to put together a competitive offer and some companies may be just as willing to back away as fight. If this happens and you have a true preference for the secondary company, let them know in very direct terms that you are still more interested in them than the company that made the initial offer.

You will find that once the first offer comes in, it is often quite easy to generate others. If you have done an excellent job of developing yourself differentially from your competition, employers will know they have to react quickly to sway you to their side.

You may have the uncommon luxury of choosing whom you want to work for. While others are scratching and begging for an offer—any offer—you actually have the difficult (?) decision of deciding which company you like best. Keep all the negotiations open and honest. You will find that honesty is not only "the best policy," but also your greatest competitive advantage. If one

> LISTEN TO YOUR HEART WHEN DECIDING BETWEEN MULTIPLE OFFERS. IT USUALLY KNOWS WHAT IS BEST FOR YOU. YOUR HEAD WILL ALMOST ALWAYS CHOOSE THE HIGHEST DOLLAR OFFER. YOUR HEART WILL CHOOSE THE BEST EMPLOYER.

company comes up $2000 short of what you would accept, discuss it with the appropriate party. The company would much rather shoot at a specific target. For more specifics on negotiating your offer, see the Successful Job Offer Negotiation chapter.

THE REFUSED OFFER TECHNIQUE

If someone you know receives multiple offers, you should congratulate them immediately. And if they are in your field, make sure you immediately contact the losing suitors. The refused offers will leave behind employers with jobs that have not yet been filled. Strike quickly and decisively. Even if it's not a company you have met with yet, there may still be time if you are willing to move quickly.

Chapter 22

SUCCESSFUL JOB OFFER NEGOTIATION

Who is wise? He that learns from everyone.
Who is powerful? He that governs his passions.
Who is rich? He that is content.
Who is that? Nobody.
—Benjamin Franklin

In the excitement of the actual job offer, the tendency for many grads is to make the costly error of accepting the first offer that comes their way. However, the time frame from when the initial offer is made to when you accept is a golden opportunity for negotiation. If these two events are simultaneous, you will lose a chance to negotiate that you may never have again.

ARE YOU REALLY READY TO NEGOTIATE?

Remember that you are not in a position to negotiate money (and/or any of the other attachments) until after the "sale" is made. So the information in this chapter should be utilized only if you are truly ready for salary negotiations.

How do you know when you are ready to negotiate? You are ready to negotiate when you have a "ready buyer." You are ready to negotiate when you hear anything from "We are ready to make the offer" to the formal letter offering you the job. Until that time, you are not ready to negotiate the "whats" of the offer. Until then, you are only negotiating the "ifs" of the offer. It is always the best negotiating posture to wait until you have the actual job offer in hand. In writing, if possible. Get the offer first, then begin your negotiation.

To steadfastly put forth your "I am ready to consider your very best offer" response when the employer shows true interest at the end of the interviewing process should lead to the best possible initial offer from the company. I say "initial" because it is exactly that. Very few companies have offers that are "cut in stone"—even those that say they do often give in to many of the perks that are requested.

OUTSTANDING QUESTIONS

No, I am not referring to questions that are wonderful. I am referring to questions that are still outstanding, questions not yet fully answered. If these questions still exist when the offer is made, you have two choices: ask them at the same time the offer is made (best choice) or add them to your list of potential concessions you will request when you accept (see the Acceptable Offer Negotiation Technique later in the chapter). You should always be ready for the offer to come through—at any time, under any circumstances. If you are not prepared in advance, you will miss the opportunity to ask some "free" negotiating questions that can give you additional career commitments above and beyond what has already been given. These questions are invaluable since they cost you virtually nothing from a negotiating standpoint.

> ASK THE QUESTIONS NOW. YOU MAY NOT GET ANOTHER CHANCE.

So if you are on your toes when the offer is made, you can ask these key questions (if yet unasked in the interview process) at little or no risk:

"What are the promotional opportunities of the position?"

"To what position/level?"

"How and when will my performance be reviewed?"

"Will this include a salary review?"

"What kind of salary progression would be expected in the first three to five years?"

Be sure to take careful notes of the answers and who gave them. These may be the most "liberal" responses you ever hear with regard to your position. Don't be afraid to refer to these promises and guarantees later when they become important in your work. But realize that they are not true job offer negotiations. They are "gifts" given to you at the time of your job offer, possibly never to be uttered again. Take careful notes.

JOB OFFER NEGOTIATION

If you have a true job offer in hand, the first thing you need to do is decide whether the offer is acceptable to you in its present form. In other words, if this is the very best you can negotiate, will you still accept the job? If not, you will need to take a different tack.

In either case, it is always important to know who is pulling the strings. It is usually the Hiring Manager, but not always. Hiring authorization may actually come from a level above the Hiring Manager. There may even be input from a Salary Administrator

> # JOB OFFERS DO COME. REALLY, THEY DO!

in Human Resources, although they are usually there for input, not for absolutes. The key is to know who makes the decisions. If you don't know, ask. Ask the Hiring Manager, the person you will be working for. Remember, it is always in their best interest to make this happen. Now that they have made you an offer, you have one foot in the door to their company. You have access to information you didn't have prior to the offer.

EVALUATING THE TOTAL PACKAGE

While salary is certainly the most important element of a job offer, it is by no means the only point of consideration. The total package includes all of the benefits and other perks that are provided to you as an employee of the company. One of the biggest errors many college grads make in evaluating an offer is to look exclusively at salary as the measure of acceptability. Benefits seem to be an ethereal element that will never actually be used. The Invincibility Factor ("I'll never be sick, disabled, die, or need to get my teeth cleaned") runs high among most new grads. If you have not been provided a formal benefits package to review by the time the job offer is made, ask that it be sent to you. If you are given the information verbally, take copious notes and ask clarifying questions on any areas you do not understand.

EVALUATING YOUR BENEFITS PACKAGE

Benefits are not just for the twilight of your career. While we typically think of benefits as basic insurance coverage, a good benefits plan can include many additional perks that offer true tangible gains in relation to the competition. Following are some of the basic elements of benefit plans and what to look for:

> ➤ **General Coverage**
> Find out if there are any monthly or per-pay-period costs for the overall benefits plan (which will make an immediate and tangible dent in your take-home pay), who is covered (does it only cover you or does it also cover other family members and future family members), when each component of the benefit actually begins (some will begin the first day of work, some after thirty days, and some

after one year of employment), and whether any of the benefits are taxable (life insurance is an example of a benefit that you can end up paying taxes on at the end of the year). If the benefits are provided cafeteria-style (where you can pick and choose which you will enroll in), find out if you can add benefits at a later date and what restrictions would be involved.

➤ **Medical Insurance**
Consider the type of plan (Preferred Provider Option, Health Maintenance Organization, Blue Cross/Blue Shield, etc.), what expenses are covered (HMOs will often pay for preventive care expenses that others will not, etc.), deductibles (annual deductibles, per-office-visit deductibles, etc.), co-pays (percentage the company pays versus the percentage you will pay), exclusions for pre-existing conditions, and whether or not the plan has open enrollment (including medical exams or other evaluations that may be necessary for enrollment in the plan).

➤ **Dental Insurance**
Consider whether preventive care (exams, cleaning, X rays, etc.), surgical care (root canals, etc.), and orthodontic care (braces, etc.) are covered and to what extent (deductibles, co-pay, annual, and lifetime maximums).

➤ **Vision/Eye Care Insurance**
A great benefit if you need it. A great benefit even if you don't currently need it (most of us need it eventually). Evaluate what expenses are covered, what the deductibles are, and what the annual and lifetime maximums are. Many companies now offer an "up to" amount of coverage that can include exams, eyeglasses, contact lenses, and even disposable lenses.

➤ **Life Insurance**
Although you are likely not planning your funeral arrangements yet, this benefit will become increasingly important as you add loved ones to your life. In the meantime, it may cover the basic expenses in the event of unexpected tragedy. Some companies will also allow you to purchase additional blocks of term insurance, frequently at or above the going market rate. It is usually better to purchase additional insurance separately, but evaluate the costs—especially if the rates offered are stable for the duration of your employment.

➤ **Accidental Death Insurance**

As if it somehow matters how you die, some companies pay more if your death is of a more spectacular nature. If they offer it for free, take it. Don't buy additional amounts.

➤ **Business Travel Insurance**

Another variation on the accident insurance theme. Companies sometimes provide their employees with insurance to cover accidental death or dismemberment while traveling on business. Again, if they offer it for free, take it.

➤ **Disability Insurance**

One of those benefits you will never ever care about until you need it. Disability insurance is usually divided into short-term disability (which can sometimes include an allocation for sick pay) and long-term disability (which usually kicks in after six months to a year). Note the percentage amount, how that percentage may change over time, and what that percentage is based on.

➤ **Vacation**

Consider how many days are allowed in your first year, when they begin accumulating, when they may be used (can days be taken before they are earned?), how many days are allowed in future years, and the maximum number of days. Most companies provide two weeks (prorated from the hire date) during the first year and one additional day per year of service thereafter, with a maximum of four weeks vacation. Some companies, however, do not provide any vacation during the first year. Note also whether vacation days accumulate according to the calendar year or work year (based on your date of hire).

➤ **Holidays**

There are six standard holidays that nearly every U.S. company covers (New Year's Day, Memorial Day, Independence Day, Labor Day, Thanksgiving Day, and Christmas Day). In addition, most cover the day after Thanksgiving, and some cover additional days such as Presidents' Day and Martin Luther King Day (and then there is the U.S. government, which is a member of the Holiday-of-the-Month Club). Many companies will offer six or more "set" holidays plus one or more "floating" holidays that can be used at the employee's discretion. In this case, these floating holidays usually end up being treated much the same as vacation days.

If the company offers floaters and you are starting midyear, note how many will be offered to you during the first year.

➤ **Sick/Personal Days**

While most companies have moved away from having formal sick days for salaried staff (which encourages the more slack employees to take them in spite of lack of actual illness, since they are already enumerated), some companies still provide for a certain number of personal days. Again, these can be thought of as pseudo-vacation days. But remember that when you take time off work to visit your sick Aunt Martha in Idaho, it will likely be applied against this time allocation.

➤ **401(k) Plans**

Your company's 401(k) plan can help you begin building a tax-deferred retirement nest egg early (start

> ## START YOUR 401(K) EARLY AND MAX IT.

now and you will really be able to enjoy your retirement). Consider the amount of company matching (if any), and the maximum amount of matching and employee contributions. Also check the amount of time it takes to vest the company matching amount and whether there is a partial vesting during the interim.

➤ **Pension Plans**

The ultimate yawner benefit for twenty-two-year-olds, these can and will make a difference to you later in life. Usually the company puts an amount into an account that silently accumulates for you over time. An excellent benefit that many companies are either cutting back or replacing with 401(k) plans.

➤ **Profit Sharing**

Profit sharing can be an outstanding benefit, assuming the company is profitable and expected to continue in the black. However, the amount of profit sharing provided is often at the discretion of executive management and may be stated as an "up to" amount or percentage. If it is unclear what that amount is, ask what the company has paid, historically, for the last three years to individuals in a position similar to the one you are being offered. Forget any promises that it will likely be greater in the coming year(s). Even when you are dealing with historical figures, don't plan to spend the money until you have the check in hand. Anything can and will happen with the profit-sharing wild card, even in the most conservative companies.

➤ Stock Options/ESOPs

Once the domain of executive management, stock options have recently been filtering down into the rank and file of companies through ESOPs, or Employee Stock Ownership Plans. While different from true stock options (you usually have to buy the stock at regular intervals at the prevailing market price), it gives the advantage of buying company stock at a discount from market value. Although the discount varies, it is usually in the 10 to 15 percent range, which means you make an immediate 11 to 17 percent profit (since you are buying at a discount). The stock purchase is often free of broker commissions or fees. Some companies will allow you to sell the stock commission-free through their investment banking firm. Most will also allow you to reinvest your dividends commission-free to buy more stock. It is an outstanding benefit and you should immediately sign up for the maximum allowable (usually 5 to 10 percent of your base salary). Unless you have little faith in your company's financial performance (in which case you should ask yourself why you are working there in the first place), let the money grow as your career and employer continue to grow.

➤ Tuition Reimbursement

An especially important perk if you plan to pursue an advanced degree during your evening and/or weekend hours. Consider what types of coursework are covered, the tax impact of the benefit (usually the IRS will consider the benefit tax free only if you are studying within your current field), how the benefit is paid (some companies pay 100 percent for an "A," 75 percent for a "B," etc.), and the yearly maximum.

➤ Health Clubs

As part of the trend toward taking care of all of your worldly existential needs, some companies now offer free or reduced-rate memberships in health clubs. Some larger companies even offer on-site facilities so that you can work out in the morning, at lunch, or after work without having to leave the company location. It's a nice perk, depending on whether the facilities meet your personal needs.

➤ Dependent Care

As companies adjust to the work force of this decade and beyond, they are examining the role of providing dependent care for their employees. This can include providing on-site child care facilities or allocating specified amounts for child care and elder care. Some companies, while not paying directly for these costs, will offer programs for allocating funds for these expenses from pretax funds. Although this benefit may not mean much to you now, probably one of the very best benefits to have is the ability to drop off your kid(s) next door to work in the morning, have lunch with them, and take them home with you in the evening—the parent of the '90s.

➤ **Employee Assistance Programs**
Some companies have a formal program designed to aid employees in need of assistance. While this can sometimes be for mainstream needs (such as financial planning and tax assistance), it can also include drug/alcohol counseling and other types of crisis support. Just one more way to let you know that you are not on your own when you are in need of help.

➤ **Overtime/Travel Premiums/Comp Time**
While salaried employees are usually not paid overtime, some companies will compensate for time above and beyond an expected standard (about forty hours per week). This can take the form of overtime or bonus pay, a premium above and beyond standard pay for hours worked at out-of-town locations, and/or comp time (which converts extra hours worked into extra time off).

➤ **Parking Reimbursement**
This often overlooked perk can amount to a great deal over time, especially if you will be working in one of the high-cost parking (and living) cities such as New York, Chicago, or Los Angeles. This $50–$100/month tax-free benefit can easily amount to $1000–$2000/year in salary equivalence.

➤ **Commuting Cost Reimbursement**
Few companies will pay you for the commute to and from the office. Some companies in high traffic/smog congestion areas, however, will provide company van service, a car pooling allowance, or commuter train/bus allocations to encourage their employees to use environmentally friendly means of transportation.

➤ **Expense Reimbursement**
Almost all companies will pay you for direct business-related costs that you incur. However, how that cost is calculated often differs, with you picking up the difference. For example, using your car for business travel (above and beyond your standard commute) might be covered at anywhere from six cents to thirty cents per mile. That ends

up being quite a difference if you are racking up the miles. Also, items such as business entertainment may only be reimbursed up to 80 percent. So if your job requires incurring business expenses, know what will be covered and to what extent.

SALARY COMPARISON CALCULATOR

Is an offer for $40,000 in New York City better than a $28,000 offer in Des Moines? While there are a variety of cost-of-living comparisons available, one of the best is provided on the Web at a site called Homefair:

http://www.homefair.com/homefair/cmr/salcalc.html

This cost-of-living calculator will allow you to compare the actual cost of living in over one hundred cities throughout the United States, giving you a better understanding of the true value of your offer. You simply select the base city, enter a salary, then a target city. The salary calculator will respond in seconds with the comparable salary in the target city. You will find yourself playing out

> PAID OVERTIME REALLY MAKES A DIFFERENCE WHEN YOU'RE WORKING FIFTY TO SIXTY HOURS PER WEEK.

several "what ifs" throughout the country at this very well designed site. You can also get there through the Interviewing/Offer page at the College Grad Job Hunter Website:

http://www.collegegrad.com/intv

And in answer to the original question, $28,000 is worth more in Des Moines than $40,000 in New York. But New York is a lot more fun than Des Moines. But Des Moines is a lot safer than New York. So it all evens out in the end.

ITEMS YOU CAN NEGOTIATE

If you feel the offer is unacceptable to you, you must determine what will make it acceptable. Remember that the answer is not always more money. Real estate agents are great at "restructuring offers" to make them more attractive, while the

> MONEY ISN'T EVERYTHING. 401(K) MATCHING AND STOCK OPTIONS ARE NICE TOO.

bottom-line dollars remain virtually unchanged. The point is, there are more things than money that can make a deal happen. Following are some of the basic areas of job offer negotiation:

Monetaries	Near-Monetaries	Non-Monetaries
Base Salary	Benefits	Title
Promised Increases	Overtime/Comp Time	Training/Education
Yearly Bonuses	Company Car	Access to Technology
Signing Bonuses	Travel Awards	Reviews
Profit Sharing	Relocation Assistance	Travel Assignments
Stock Options/ESOPs	Expense Coverage	Home Equipment Usage

Although there are many different areas subject to negotiation, it should also be noted that money is the first issue that needs to be resolved. If you are seeking $30,000, and they are offering $20,000, there is a major discrepancy. But it is quite different if they are offering $29,000 and you want $30,000. Is a $1000 differential going to keep you from accepting the position? Is it truly unacceptable? How do you determine what is acceptable and what is unacceptable?

THE BALANCE SHEET DECISION TECHNIQUE

There is an easy way to determine whether an offer is acceptable. The method was originated by one of the wisest men in the history of our country—Ben Franklin. The name of the technique? The Balance Sheet Decision Technique. He probably never called it that, but good old Ben used it just the same. In weighing a difficult decision, he would take a sheet of paper and draw a line down the middle. Then he would put the heading "Reasons For" on the left side and "Reasons Against" on the right side. He would proceed to list the positive aspects of the decision on the left and the negative aspects of the decision on the right. Once everything was down on paper, the answer usually became obvious to him. Use the Balance Sheet Decision Technique in evaluating the initial offer. Important: do not evaluate the position against what you want. Instead, evaluate it against the next-best alternative. For some, that may be your present job. For others, it may be another job offer. And for others, it may be unemployment and continuing the job search.

Whatever you do, don't get caught in the "hope trap"—comparing your offer against what you hope another company will offer. Until you have it in writing, you are comparing against vapor. Make sure all of your negotiations are on firm, solid foundations. Otherwise, you may find it all slipping out from

> # YOU CANNOT NEGOTIATE THAT WHICH YOU DO NOT HAVE.

under you. Objective number one is to get the job offer. Then, and only then, can you begin to negotiate that job offer.

If the job offer is still truly "unacceptable" per the Balance Sheet Decision Technique, continue with the Unacceptable Offer Negotiation Technique which follows. Otherwise, what you really have is an acceptable job offer that you were hoping would be better. Read the Acceptable Offer Negotiation Technique for advice on how to potentially improve this type of offer.

THE UNACCEPTABLE OFFER NEGOTIATION TECHNIQUE

If your offer is truly unacceptable, you must communicate this fact in no un-certain terms to the decision-maker while keeping the outlook for resolution positive. Example:

> "I am still very interested in working with you and your company; however (never use the word "but"), at this point I am not able to ac-cept the offer for the following reason: (state your reasoning suc-cinctly and what part or parts of the offer are lacking). If you were able to _____ (give your proposed solution), I would gladly accept the po-sition immediately. Are you in a position to be able to help?"

Let's make note of some of the key elements of this approach. First, you are putting at risk the job offer made to you since you are asking for a different offer. In terms of contract law, you have just made a counteroffer, which technically invalidates (or rejects) their initial offer. But if the initial offer is unacceptable to you, you need to be willing to accept the consequences.

Second, you need to communicate what is specifically lacking in the initial offer. Is it the position? The role and responsibilities? The money? Insurance? Vacations? You must name it specifically.

Third, you must provide a proposed solution. Tell them exactly what can be done to make things "right." You need to make it understood that if this could be changed, you would be willing to accept the position. Immediately. On the spot. They will be much more willing to go to bat for you if they know that this is the last roadblock. Don't play the "you shot low so I'll shoot high" game. Be straight with them as to what it will take to make it happen.

Lastly, you need to appeal to their position and their vanity. "If it is in your power" is a positive challenge to the true power of the manager. If they really want you and your request is attainable, this will ice it. Very few managers like to admit they are powerless to get what they want. So if it can be done, they will make it happen.

It's a given that the company wants you by the very fact that they made the initial offer. However, this does not guarantee that they will be able to respond to your request. Several factors may come into play. First, can they adjust the offer at all? Some companies (although very few) have rigid "first offer is last offer" policies. And in most companies, salary administration is more rigid at the entry level since comparable parity (what they are paying others with similar backgrounds and skills) is much easier to define. If they cannot adjust the offer under any circumstances, you are wasting your time and theirs and they will probably tell you so. If they are fixed on the monetaries, you might want to consider attempting to negotiate the near-monetaries or non-monetaries since these usually allow for some flexibility. But if the offer is still truly unacceptable, give them a polite "Thanks, but no thanks" and take your leave of them.

Second, what is the magnitude of your request? There may be restrictions regarding pay level within the position or benefits offered (only VPs get company cars, etc.) that cannot change. Be ready to consider alternatives if necessary (example: a hiring bonus or relocation assistance in lieu of higher pay).

Third, what are their alternatives? If you are the only person in the world who can fill this position, they have very few alternatives and must work to make the impossible happen. But if they have two others "waiting in the wings" in case you balk, they may not have much desire to negotiate.

Again, this negotiation technique is the best approach when the offer is truly unacceptable, but it does run the risk of the entire deal falling through if you cannot come to terms. So use it with caution.

> ACCEPTING THE OFFER DOES NOT RELINQUISH YOUR ABILITY TO NEGOTIATE.

THE ACCEPTABLE OFFER NEGOTIATION TECHNIQUE

In attempting to sweeten an acceptable job offer, the best approach is to play upon the ego and power of your new manager. Not in a negative way, but giving him a chance to "show his strength" within the company. You need to realize that you are in one of the strongest political positions you may ever be in with your new employer. Utilizing this technique can have the side effect of enhancing your future power within the organization—if used correctly.

The key to using this technique is to empower your new manager. You give him power in two ways: (1) by accepting (yes, I said "accepting") the position, you give him power because he has added the desired person to his team; and (2) by asking him for his assistance in meeting your further needs, you give him an opportunity to show his power within the organization. How to do this? Consider the following example:

> "_____ (name of boss), I'm calling you with some very good news. I would like to accept your offer and I'm looking forward to working with you and becoming a valuable member of the team. (Wait for their positive response.) I am committed to working with you, and as my future boss there is (are) a (two, three, some) minor issue(s) about the offer that I want to make you aware of. I don't know if you're able to make changes in this (these) area(s), but I'd surely appreciate your looking into that possibility. Namely, would it be possible to _____ (name changes)?"

The beauty of this technique is that it provides two things. First, it locks in your acceptance of the job and takes that acceptance out of the negotiating. Second, it leaves open additional concessions that may be given to you at no cost. Please note that most books and articles on negotiating would argue against "giving away" your greatest negotiating chip—acceptance of the position. But this argument is correct only if you can afford to lose this chip. If that's the case and you truly want to "spin the wheel," you can use the information under the Unacceptable Offer Negotiation Technique outlined above. But you risk losing the job offer entirely if you choose that approach. By closing out the offer acceptance portion, you have locked down the one thing you cannot afford to lose, yet you leave open other areas. Your retained negotiating chip? The hoped "show of power" on the part of your future boss. Even if your boss is not able to deliver, the fact that you "turned over" your request to your boss will make him/her more willing to help you in any future needs. Even if all you get is exactly what was originally offered, you are given by default a future negotiating chip.

Why does this technique work? Simple. It's a win/win situation. The key to successful negotiation is that each side should stand to benefit. In this example, the worst case scenario is that you will have the new job you want and the company will have the new employee it wants. The best case scenario is that your new boss will feel personally and professionally satisfied because of his ability to immediately enhance your new position. Even if your boss is not able to get all (or any) of the concessions, he will feel privileged that you brought him this issue to handle, and will then feel an obligation (due to guilt?) to help you in any future requests.

The greatest benefit of this negotiation technique is that it has zero risk (by securing the job offer acceptance), yet invariably gets most managers to give in to some or all of the concession requests. Why? Plain and simple—ego. Your new manager wants to show that he has the power to make things happen. At this point, you are both on the same side, working for the same goal. Later in your career your goals may conflict with your manager's, but at this time, if you can convince your manager of the value of your request, you will have a strong advocate on your side.

So if there are areas of the offer you are seeking to "redefine," this is a safe, effective way to test the waters. The risk is minimal, while the payback can be significant. It should be noted that this technique cannot be used for significant offer changes. If you need to make changes of great magnitude, you will probably have to follow through with the Unacceptable Offer Negotiation.

Good luck! If you successfully applied these negotiation strategies, you likely just paid for this book—possibly many times (even several hundred times?) over. So why not use your newfound wealth to send for several more copies of this book to give to all your starving and unemployed college friends who haven't found a job yet? Or at least pass on your copy to a friend in need.

THE FLOOR MATS TECHNIQUE

A modification of the above techniques is a negotiating technique my father taught me about purchasing a car, which I call the Floor Mats Technique. It goes something like this: you are sitting there in the car dealer showroom, having worked out all the major details (like options, price, delivery date, etc.), you pick up that magical pen as if ready to sign on the dotted line, then look up at the salesperson and say, "By the way, I assume you don't mind throwing in a set of those nice custom floor mats with the deal, right?" At which point the salesperson begins (again) to rant and rave about how much money he is already losing on this deal (aren't they wild?) and how he cannot possibly afford to throw in the floor mats, which cost over $50 (retail, that is), which is more than he is even making on this entire deal. You calmly put down your pen, reply, "I'm sorry we couldn't make the deal happen," and head for the door (for the third time that day). The salesperson stops you just before you get into your car, calls you back in, tells you he will give you the floor mats for the discount price of $25, and you get up to walk back out the door again. He stops you again and says, "All right, you can have the floor mats!" (which cost the dealership a total of $7). He gives you the pen, you sign, he gets the sale, and you get your floor mats for free.

Great, you say, now I know how to get another $50 thrown in when I go to buy my next car—but what does this have to do with job offer negotiation? Simple. Just as my father knew that once the deal was "made" it was still possible to get a minor concession, the same thing applies to job offers. The only difference is that you don't have to walk out of the showroom and your new boss probably won't be ranting and raving like a lunatic car salesperson. You simply present a minor (it must be minor) negotiating factor in the "By the way, I assume _____, right?" format as if you assume it's okay. Examples:

> "By the way, I assume my taking a week to spend with my family in Tennessee before starting would be okay, right?"
>
> "By the way, I assume the plans that my family has made for vacationing at Disney World in late August won't be a problem, right?"
>
> "By the way, I assume that my cell phone expense while on the road will be covered, right?" (even if their employees don't typically have or use cell phones)

Please take note: the only way this approach is "no risk" is if you are willing to give in, no matter if their response is yes or no. Because even though dear old Dad was on his way out of the showroom over some stupid floor mats, he always would have gone back in and signed, even if they didn't go get him (he didn't want to start all over again, either). Sure, it's a fun way to play a final bluff. But my Dad has always gotten his floor mats-they always gave in. Why? Because the cost of the floor mats is insignificant in comparison to the overall deal. So make sure it's insignificant and be ready to back off if your bluff is called.

But even if you get a "we can't do that" response, they will usually feel guilty that they couldn't and may even offer other concessions in exchange. Boy, this negotiating stuff sure is fun, eh? Yeah, it sure is—just don't get carried away. It is truly a once-in-a-job opportunity.

SALARY NEGOTIATION

While there are many potential points of negotiation, salary is usually the primary issue. Keep in mind that any discussion of salary negotiation might reach the unacceptable range and put the offer at risk. So tread carefully through salary negotiation.

Many companies have a fairly tight (although not airtight) salary range at the entry level. If you are able to show extraordinary educational or work experience, you may be able to extend the top end of the scale. Yet the magnitude of salary differentials will always be smaller at the entry level than at higher-level positions. So do not get carried away, even if you have multiple offers in hand.

When discussing salary, always state that you are "hoping" for more, instead of "expecting" more. Companies are always more willing to fulfill your hopes than your expectations. And keep your personal budgetary needs out of the equation. Having a larger personal budget does little to inflate your worth from a company perspective.

To better establish the acceptable range for the position, ask what the hiring range and pay range is. Most larger companies will have set ranges to work within, although many medium to smaller companies may have more flexible market-driven ranges. Following are some sample questions to ask in salary negotiations:

"What is the salary range for the position?"

"What is the hiring salary range for the position?"

"Do you ever pay higher than that range? If so, for what reason?"

"What is the average increase being given? After one year? Two years? Three?"

"How often is the employee reviewed? For performance? Salary?"

In attempting to modify salary, you may find that the best you can achieve is a promise for tomorrow. If so, be sure to get it in writing from a person with authority to make it stick.

And in the end, do not let salary be your only guide. You are much better off making $15,000 a year and happy than $50,000 a year and miserable. The money will take care of itself over time when you are doing work that you love.

THE FRIENDLY ADVICE TECHNIQUE

What do you do if you find yourself attempting to negotiate with someone who does not have the authority to negotiate or make changes? Do not attempt to negotiate, just simply ask for their advice. "What would you recommend . . . ?" or "How would you recommend . . . ?" questions will allow you to seek the individual's advice and counsel, without putting them in the uncomfortable position of not being able to respond.

Take careful notes of the steps you are recommended to follow. Even though the individual may not have a great deal of personal authority, they may be willing to give you the keys to unlocking some of the doors in negotiating. These answers are being given to you without cost. Yet the value and payback can be substantial.

RELOCATION EXPENSES—YOURS OR THEIRS?

Yours. Don't even think about getting into the higher-level relocation perks at the entry level. The best you can hope for is that they will pay for the cost of a U-haul or Ryder truck rental and/or your mileage in getting to your new location. Beyond that, you are on your own. Full-service movers, house buyouts, realtor fees, mortgage buy-downs, and other perks will be out there for you in five-plus years. Until that time, everything but the most basic moving and relocation expenses will likely be yours.

MAKING YOUR FINAL COMMITMENT

In the end, you will need to make a commitment. It should be a commitment that you are willing to stand behind. Companies spend money, commit resources, allocate training time, and shape schedules around your commitment. In addition, they will also be sending the "Dear John/Dear Jane" letters out to all of the "second-place" finishers. So make sure you are willing to stand behind your commitment.

COUNTEROFFERS

So you have finally worked out and accepted the offer. If you are leaving the ranks of the unemployed or underemployed (or never employed), it's an easy decision. Yet many of you may be working full-time in your field while completing your degree. Or you may have gone back to school to complete a higher degree.

If you are currently employed and are ready to move on to your new company, the time has come to tell your boss that you are leaving. And guess what? Now is probably not a good time for you to be leaving. In most cases, when you decide it's time to go is not the time your company wants you to leave. So what happens? The company may try to make a counteroffer in an attempt to keep you from leaving.

Remember this: companies concerned with the best interests of the employees rarely make counteroffers. Only those companies that place corporate interests ahead of personal interests are likely to make counteroffers.

Why do counteroffers happen? Simple. Because while you have been planning to leave, the company has probably not been planning for you to leave. In most multitask jobs, you will almost always find yourself in the middle of a project or assignment that is important to the company and to your boss. It never looks good for a boss to have someone leave, unless the boss is the one who decided it would happen. Your leaving may "reflect poorly" upon your boss.

Picture the scene: you have just "broken the news" to your boss that you will be leaving. What does she think about? Your happiness about your new position and new company? Or does she think about your current job, how difficult it will be to fill, and how she cannot afford to lose you right now. And so she breaks into the "I didn't realize you were unhappy here" speech and begins probing to find the reason you are leaving. More money? Higher position? More perks? Then guess what? We will offer you the same or better position if you will stay! Wow! Great! Right? *Wrong!* Remember this—unless you are a true gambler (the kind who likes playing the odds ten-to-one against winning) you should never accept a counteroffer. Why? Because counteroffers are almost always temporary! It's a temporary "solution" provided by your boss so that she can remain in control. It buys her time. Time to get your project finished. Time to get you to tell others in the company about all those key areas that only you know. Time to find someone to replace you. Time to train someone to replace you. And time for your boss to decide when you will leave the company. Don't buy it. Ever.

Why do people accept counteroffers? Usually for simple comfort. To go to work for someone else we have to step outside our comfort zone. The counteroffer gives us the benefits of the new offer with the comfort of staying right where we are. But there are several fallacies in that line of thinking. First, the reasons for leaving still exist—some of those reasons may be temporarily altered by the counteroffer, but they are still there. Second, it should not have taken an outside offer to prompt the change. Third, and most important, by giving in to the counteroffer, you lose control over your destiny and hand it over to someone else.

Some will say, "Oh, but they're giving me $10,000 more per year—I was only making $25,000 before. They really want me to stay because I'm so valuable and important to the company." But remember—$10,000 more per year is only $2,500 more out of your boss's budget if she can find someone to replace you within three months, when you may be either demoted or fired ("you're too expensive for us to keep"). "They wouldn't do that to me. They love me." Oh yes, they would. And no, they don't. This has nothing to do with love or any other emotion. It is strictly business. At the first mention of cutbacks, your head is already clearly marked for the chopping block. The money spent to retain you temporarily is worth not having to train someone from scratch.

Some bosses even play the "We were about ready to promote you/increase your salary/give you a company car" game in matching your offer, like it was going to happen all along. Don't believe it.

Here is the real zinger. If you do accept a counteroffer and then do leave at a later time (probably just a few months later), you no longer have that great job offer in hand. You might even be out on the streets. "They wouldn't do that to me!" Oh yes they would! Just by virtue of the fact that you have "gone looking,"

> IF YOU THINK NO ONE VALUES YOU IN YOUR WORK, WAIT UNTIL YOU SAY YOU ARE LEAVING.

you are no longer considered to be "loyal to the team." You are expendable from the very moment you accept their counteroffer!

So what is the best course of action if and when a counteroffer is made? Simple. Just smile and say, "Boss, I'm flattered that you consider me important and would like to keep me as part of the team. But I've made up my mind, I've made my commitment and I'll be leaving in two weeks. Please tell me what I can do to make the transition as smooth as possible."

Some companies may even resort to such bullying tactics as getting the boss's boss or even the boss's boss's boss to try to talk to you. Don't give in. Remain calm and professional. When they know you are unshakable, they will back down.

Some companies, when they see you won't accept the counteroffer, may try to pressure you into staying far beyond your planned departure date. For example: "You can't leave now—we're in the middle of . . . " or something to that effect. They may try to make you feel guilty: "You're leaving us at our greatest moment of need." Or they will play on the "training the new person" theme: "You need to give us time to replace you, and then train the new person." They will try to stall for time by asking you to stay longer than planned. It's your life, but my strong recommendation is never to ask your new employer to make a change to accommodate your old employer. Your loyalties are now with your new employer. The general industry standard is two weeks' notice, so you should in no way feel obligated to go beyond that. By changing your start date, you run the risk of putting your new job in jeopardy and artificially delaying your career. If you are even considering delaying your start date, talk to your new company first. If there is any hesitation on their part, stick to the planned start date. Many companies have set start dates due to classes and training, so don't jeopardize your new job on account of the old one.

Remember, under no circumstances should you give in to a counteroffer, no matter how tempting it may seem. And only under extreme circumstances should you consider altering the "terms of departure," and only after first checking with your new employer.

GIVE PROPER NOTICE

One of our tendencies in accepting a new position is to want to move right away. But even if the position is vacant at your new company, no ethical employer would ask a person who is already employed to start immediately. It's just not done. Even if you aren't happy with your current employer (see "Don't Burn Those Bridges" below), you owe them the professional courtesy of proper notice.

How long? Two weeks is standard in almost every industry. Your current employer may wish it were longer, but two weeks is the standard and is all that you are obliged to provide. In certain situations, an employer might decide to immediately dismiss an employee who is leaving. While federal and state laws vary as to whether they are required to pay you for your two weeks' notice, your best defense in this situation (if you believe it is a possibility) is to notify your new employer of the possibility: "Given my current situation at ABC Co., it's possible that when I give notice they may ask me to leave immediately due to _____ (competitive reasons, just finished project, etc.). If that were to happen, would you like me to start with you right away?" This approach is especially useful if the position is currently vacant.

Remember, don't get bullied into giving more than two weeks' notice unless you are absolutely sure this will fit your new employer's schedule. Only in extreme cases should you consider remaining more than four weeks after giving notice, unless, of course, your start date is later than that, which can often be the case with entry level hiring.

DON'T BURN THOSE BRIDGES

No matter how awful your previous employer was, no matter how terrible your boss was, no matter how evil your coworkers were, never ever burn your bridges behind you! I don't care if you were the victim of sexual harassment or threatened with human sacrifice—take it up with the courts, but don't take it out on your boss or coworkers in person before you leave. The "take this job and shove it" attitude will get you absolutely nothing except a temporary feeling of superiority. Even if you were treated unfairly, don't sink to their level to get even. The most respectable thing you can do *(especially* when it was rough) is to leave with honor and dignity. Keep your head up and keep your mouth shut. You will leave with respect instilled in your character rather than disgust instilled in your heart.

And yes, burned bridges do come back to haunt you—in ways you least expect. I knew of one man who felt he had every right to tell his boss exactly what he thought of him—and did exactly that. Imagine his shock and horror when this former boss was hired by his new company over four years later—as his new boss! Needless to say, he lasted only a few months before he moved on to a new company. Another young woman who told off her boss when leaving the company found herself having to work with her less than a year later on a committee as part of her professional association.

> # There is never a perfect time to leave one job for another.

Remember, no matter how large your geographical view of the world is, it's a very small work world out there. Even if your former bosses never have any contact with you, they may very well talk about you (negatively) to others— sometimes at every opportunity they get. So keep it civil and professional.

Look forward, not backward. If you really want to throw them for a loop, sincerely thank them for all the help they have given you. Do your very best work in the time you have remaining with the company, and make them realize what a gem they are losing.

Chapter 23

WHEN THE OFFER DOES NOT COME

*It's not whether you get knocked down,
it's whether you get back up.*
—Vince Lombardi

There is no worse feeling in your job search than finding out you didn't get the job. Whether by mail, phone, or fax, the message always seems the same (and probably is, since most companies use form letters for candidate rejection).

But all is not lost! Before you start papering your walls with rejection letters, consider the following "resurrection" ideas.

THE REJECTION REVERSAL TECHNIQUE

You go to your mailbox, hoping for mail. And there it is. A thin envelope bearing the return address of the company you interviewed with last week. A rejection letter. Not exactly the kind of mail you were looking for. Rejection can be difficult to bear, especially when it comes from the employer you were most interested in. However, you can use this as an opportunity to grow, learn, and possibly reverse the rejection.

Upon receipt of a rejection letter, immediately call the person who wrote the letter and request feedback. "What was I lacking in meeting your needs?" Then listen closely. If you are provided with a valid area of lacking, take note of it and politely thank the manager for taking time to speak with you. However, if the answer is based on an incorrect assumption, you may have an opportunity to correct the error. For example, if the manager states that you did not have a high

> WE ALL LOVE TO GET MAIL. EXCEPT FOR THE KIND THAT BEGINS WITH "IN SPITE OF YOUR EXCELLENT CREDENTIALS…"

enough GPA for their requirements and you simply failed to put your GPA on your resume, you have the potential for a turnaround.

A recent example of a turnaround occurred when a student friend of mine received a form letter rejection after the company-site interview. She was very interested in the company and had been certain that an offer would be made. When she called to inquire as to the reason, she was told that the position required that the person be available for travel in the first two years. "But I am available to travel. In fact, I would love to travel." Her contact seemed puzzled, but promised to get back to her. When the contact called back, he explained that one of the managers had written on an interview form, "Will not travel or relocate." She explained that while she wanted to stay in the metropolitan area, she was more than willing to travel. What had been a simple interview misunderstanding had almost cost her the position. The company reassessed and made the offer by the end of the following day.

> "NO" DOES NOT ALWAYS MEAN NO. SOMETIMES IT MEANS "NOT NOW."

As difficult as this call may seem, it can produce excellent results. Minimally, you can learn about an area of deficiency which you can correct for the next employer. Maximally, it can provide you with the opportunity to reverse what would have otherwise been a dead end.

THE ISOLATION TECHNIQUE

If you are not sure you are getting the real reason(s) from the employer for your rejection, you can test the validity by isolating the specific reason given. For example, if you were told that you were rejected because of low grades, ask, "If my GPA were higher, would you have been willing to consider hiring me?" If GPA is the only issue, the answer will be affirmative. If not, other issues may come creeping out. This technique can become especially valuable when the primary answer is simply a smoke screen for something the employer is not initially willing to share with you.

A recent graduate, Peter, was rejected after final interviews due to what was termed "high salary requirements." He told the manager his salary range was flexible and asked, "At what salary range would you be willing to hire me?" "Actually, salary is not the only issue. We also received a rather poor report on you from one of the recent graduates from your school." Ah, the truth comes out! The "poor report" had come from a graduate now working at the employer who had difficulty working with Peter on a team assignment at school the prior year. Peter had not spoken with him in over a year, but it was now making the difference in getting the job he wanted. Peter took the initiative to contact the former classmate and invited him to lunch. Apparently, much of the

> YOU CANNOT REFUTE THE UNKNOWN.

"poor report" had to do with the classmate's view of how Peter would fit into the company culture. Peter used to have a beard and wore tattered jeans to class. All that had since changed, but that was the last image the classmate had of Peter. Peter brought him up to date on his accomplishments and even convinced him to write a letter of recommendation. Does all of this seem like a lot of extra effort? Possibly. But the bottom line is that that company did eventually hire him.

Isolate the real reason. And change it if you can.

THE KAMIKAZE TECHNIQUE

A more aggressive version of the Rejection Reversal Technique and the Isolation Technique is to commit yourself to turning the situation around and getting another interview. The Kamikaze Technique works well when you have been closed out at an early point in the process, especially with on-campus interviews that have gone awry.

What happens if you blow the initial interview with Human Resources or some other non-hiring manager? End of the line? Roll over and die? Not necessarily. Try going kamikaze. It's not necessarily crash and burn, although it does help if you have rather daring tendencies to help make it work. Allow me to explain.

What you need to do is contact the Hiring Manager (not the person you wowed—or bow-wowed, as the case may be—in the initial interview) and explain the situation. You have already met with the personnel-type person and they have informed you that your background is very interesting, but not what they are looking for at this exact moment. Standard blowoff. If you sincerely had a bad day (illness, recent brain surgery, dog was being held for ransom, etc.), let them know. Valid excuses do

> YOU CANNOT LOSE THAT WHICH YOU DO NOT HAVE.

count. The key is to let them know that you really want to go to work for their company and you would be willing to fly, drive, hitchhike, whatever, to be there and meet with them, even if just for fifteen minutes. "Would you please give me the chance to prove myself with you personally?" You can even play to what is hopefully a giant "I am the manager" ego with the "After all, you are the Hiring Manager, right?" line. Let them know you truly want to work for their company and will do whatever is necessary to make it happen.

Crash and burn? Sure, it happens. But remember, you have already taken a direct hit. So why not go kamikaze? The results might surprise you.

A recent college grad used this technique to secure a company-site interview after he got the standard rejection letter based on the campus interview. He called the Branch Manager, told him he would be in the Chicago area the following week, and asked for further consideration so that he could show his full experience level, including a recent project he had completed. The manager agreed to bring him in and put him through the paces. He aced the company's aptitude test, impressed all the key managers, and had a job offer in hand by the end of the week!

Yes, miracles do happen. Especially when you do your part in helping them to happen.

THE SECOND-PLACE TECHNIQUE

> I HAVE HIRED MANY WHO WERE INITIALLY "SECOND PLACE" BUT LATER UPGRADED.

If you are told that you were "second place" or "second choice" in the hiring process, don't despair. Call the company back in two to three weeks to emphasize again that you are interested in working there. Why? For two reasons: (1) their first choice may not have worked out (the new hiree may have gotten a counteroffer, a better offer, or just plain cold feet), and (2) it keeps you under consideration for any other position or future position that may come available.

The reality is that for every one hired, they may have told as many as five to ten others that they came in "second place." But if that is what they told you, take them on their honor and give it a shot.

THE SQUEAKY WHEEL TECHNIQUE

One of the more difficult situations in conducting a job search is attempting to move the process forward with a less-than-enthusiastic employer. You can get caught in the waiting game, hoping for the phone to ring. Your job search is your number one priority, but it may be far down the list for the employer. And most job seekers simply give up. Do not include yourself among the quitters. Many jobs have been found through simple diligence and consistent follow-up.

If you have an employer who is unwilling or unable to move forward, continue to make regular contact with them. You may find yourself on a weekly schedule of calling only to hear a "nothing has changed" response. If their interest in you has not changed, but has simply stalled, continue your efforts to move the process forward. It may be at the lowest point that the wheel begins to turn.

> CALL ME AND I WILL RESPOND. DON'T WAIT FOR ME TO CALL. I AM TOO BUSY RESPONDING TO THE OTHERS WHO CALLED.

We recently interviewed a college student who did not meet our initial profile. In fact, we sent her an immediate rejection letter based on her resume. She had only an Associate degree, and we usually hire only Bachelor or Master degree graduates. To make it even more difficult, her degree was ten years old. However, she kept in touch with us and asked what she could do to prepare herself for work in our field. I suggested further training to update her previous schooling. After she completed this training, she called me back, asking to take our computer-based test to measure her increased knowledge. She did well, but we still had no immediate openings for someone with her limited skills. Bottom line, she kept in touch with us until an opportunity became available. Instead of starting a search for available candidates from scratch, we went forward with the simple solution: we hired the squeaky wheel. And now she is on her way in the job of her dreams. But only because of her tenacity. Her rejection letter proves that "No" does not always mean no. Sometimes it simply means "Not yet."

Chapter 24

GRADUATION AND STILL NO JOB

If opportunity doesn't knock, build a door.
—Milton Berle

I do not envy those who don the cap and gown without a job offer in hand. But don't give up and certainly don't let down in your efforts. This is not the time to take a vacation or "take time off." It's time to double your efforts and make a strong push forward. You are now truly full-time in your job search, and the quicker you make your mark the better, because the market is about to be flooded with about 400,000 other lost souls just like yourself. But with one very major difference—you have armed yourself for battle and are ready to push at the lines. Use the Napoleon Strategy— keep pushing at the lines until you see a point that is vulnerable, then put all your forces and energy into penetrating that area of possible access.

If you have not already done so, go back and read this book in its entirety. In it you will find several keys that can still unlock doors that might otherwise block your progress.

And never ever give up. This is your moment of truth and you need to push forward with every ounce of courage and tenacity.

THE RETRACING TECHNIQUE

The first thing you should do upon graduating without a job is to retrace your job search steps over the past year. You should immediately recontact all the employers you interviewed with. If you interviewed at the company-site and failed to make the final cut, you should recontact. If you interviewed on campus and received a form letter rejection, you should recontact. Even if you only went through a short interview on the phone you should recontact.

Why? Several reasons. First, most employers have a minor attrition factor at the actual start date, when some of the accepted offers do not actually start. Better offer. Decided to go back to school. Budding romance in another part of the country. Joined the Peace Corps. Whatever the reason, when there is a dropout before the start date, there is an open position. And when it is this late in the process, few companies want to begin the hiring process all over again. In larger companies there are usually a set number of entry level positions that need to be filled for a full training class. You could be the right person at the right time.

The second reason is that many employers will have made changes in their hiring demand during the intervening weeks or months. If that demand is greater, your notification of immediate availability can make you a prime candidate. Even if there is not an immediate need, any new openings that become available could have your name attached.

The third reason is that your availability has changed. Namely, you are available immediately. Since many medium-sized and smaller companies operate within shorter time frames, they may have shied away from you when your graduation (and availability) was still months away. Your present availability could put you in immediate contention for any currently open positions.

> YOUR NEW JOB IS OUT THERE WAITING FOR YOU TO FIND IT.

The final reason is that even if you come up against a "Sorry, nothing is available" dead end, you have another opportunity to ask for referrals to other companies. Most employers are willing to help you by providing contact information for other employers who may be hiring.

So retrace your steps and notify all past contacts that you are still available. If you are uncomfortable in making this approach, use the excuse of updating the employer with your new address and phone number, vital information if employers are to be able to reach you at a later date. And don't just stop with your employer contacts—recontact your whole network of contacts. There will be a renewed sense of urgency on everyone's part to assist you in your job search. Take advantage of it.

STEP NUMBER TWO AFTER GRADUATION

Contact all your friends and classmates who just graduated. If they have found a job, congratulate them. Then ask if there were any positions they turned down during the course of their job search. If the position and company are in your field, ask for employer contact information and their personal recommendation. The employer may not have filled the position yet, and the recommendation from their previously favored candidate may provide you with an immediate "in" for the position.

WHAT TO DO NEXT

Reread this book. Cover to cover. And do all the things you did not do the first time around. Job search requires a multifaceted approach to be successful. Make sure you take advantage of every avenue available to you.

YOUR JOB SEARCH SCHEDULE

Congratulations. You have just accepted a full-time job. Full-time job search, that is. Do not conduct your job search with anything less than a full-time effort. Without full-time commitment, you increase the amount of time you will be without work—which decreases your attractiveness in the job market.

Following is a simple work schedule to follow:

7:30 a.m.	Early morning callbacks to contacts you were unable to reach the previous day.
8:30 a.m.	Off to the library or Career Development office to do further research and write follow-up letters from the day before.
12:30 p.m.	Make phone calls all afternoon. Do not give up on this activity until you have contacted every potential employer and every potential contact.
4:30 p.m.	Send same-day follow-up letters to the most promising contacts of the day.
5:30 p.m.	One last attempt to reach all those who were unreachable during the day.

In looking at the above, there is one major activity missing: interviewing. Until you spend the time to make direct contact with potential employers, there will not be any interviewing. There are worse things than having your day filled with interviews. When that starts happening, you will know that your new job is within reach.

THE PUPPY DOG CLOSE TECHNIQUE

What should you do when an employer says, "I'm sorry, we don't have any job openings"? Just give up? Cross them off your list? If you do, you are overlooking a large segment of the "hidden job market" that we hear so much about. By utilizing a common sales technique, the Puppy Dog Close, you can tap into this potentially immense source of employment.

In brief, the Puppy Dog Close is a sales technique that is based (aptly) on a method that pet store salespeople use to sell puppy dogs. The idea is that while it may be difficult to get the customer to make a large commitment (buying the puppy), if we can break down the sale into smaller components with a "guaranteed/no risk" offer, the customer may be willing to make an initial commitment.

> # HIRING IS A RISK. REDUCE MY RISK AND I MAY BE WILLING TO RESPOND FAVORABLY.

For example, the pet store salesperson tells you you can take the puppy home with you and if you don't like it, just bring it back. So what happens? You take the puppy with you, you play with him and run around outside with him, he licks your nose in the morning and waits for you faithfully at the door at the end of the day. And the sale is made. Not by the salesperson, but by the puppy.

How does this apply to employment? Think about the commitment you are asking a company to make. Based solely on a phone call or brief meeting, can you reasonably expect them to create a new job opening for you where none currently exists? Obviously not. Yet these same managers, who technically do not have any job openings, still have work to get done. In fact, many companies have had to reduce their staff while completing the same amount of work. So the work is there, but they just can't hire right now—that is, they can't hire permanent employees. But these same managers can usually bring in "temps" (temporary workers) to help out when needed. Here is the key—those temp workers are often the first ones managers will look to when attempting to fill a permanent opening. Sometimes managers with no openings will go out of their way to create an opening for an outstanding temporary worker.

Working as a temp is no longer the domain of part-time secretaries. There are as many different types of temp positions out there as there are permanent—everything from office to factory to professional to management. While I worked at IBM, we often had professionals working for us as temps or contractors. And when the hiring window opened we did not begin to interview or start a full-scale candidate search to fill our open positions. We hired the temps who were already working for us, since they were known entities who had already proven themselves.

In application, the Puppy Dog Close merely requires you to get past the "no openings" response with the question, "Do you still have work that needs to be done?" By following this line of questioning, you can usually determine any potential "project needs" the company may have (which usually are not long enough to require permanent workers). Offer to work for them as a temp on these projects. Then, if hired as a temp, work like you have never worked before. Be the superstar in the department, always willing to give that extra effort managers look for in hiring new people. Keep your eyes open for other projects, in that department and others. Many such temporary assignments can turn into long-term commitments. Make it known that you would like to be considered if a permanent opportunity becomes available. Have an active application on file with Manpower, Kelly, or another low-markup agency which can be suggested as a facilitator for payroll arrangements if needed (many companies are unwilling to add temps to their own payroll for benefits and tax reasons). Note, however, that most temp firms do not actively market your professional skills to companies—they are reactive, not proactive. You need to be the one who markets your skills and suggests the arrangement (this approach is rather novel and companies will need the prompting).

The Puppy Dog Close is an excellent technique to use when you hear the "no openings" response. Does it always work? No, but it does add a unique approach that others are not taking, putting you in a position with very little competition for opportunities that may come up. You must believe in yourself and your ability to benefit the company you work for. Obviously, if you do a mediocre job, you will not be offered further work. But if you do your best to be an outstanding employee, you may find a job that is never advertised, never known to anyone outside of the company, and never known to be open until after you fill it. The Puppy Dog Close actually works better during high unemployment, since managers often have work that needs to be done but lack the ability to hire.

Try the Puppy Dog Close as an added tool in your job search. Minimally, you may find a temp job that gives you great experience and a valuable reference. On the other hand, it may provide you with a route into a company that might have otherwise ignored you. Remember, you don't need to be a salesperson to use this approach—the "puppy" (the quality of your work on the job) makes the sale in this win-win situation. Give it a try!

THE FREELANCER TECHNIQUE

Similar to the Puppy Dog Close, the Freelancer Technique works especially well in those fields where freelancing (independent contracting) is commonplace. A recent college grad used this technique very successfully in the advertising field. He put together a full portfolio of services he could provide to local advertising firms, including freelance writing, design, and voice talent. He then contacted all the area advertising agencies, said he had some materials to forward to them, and asked if they would give him the name of the owner or creative director of the agency. They all did, and his first goal was achieved: he had the names of the target contacts. He then wrote letters to those individuals, introducing himself as a freelancer. He followed up these letters a week later with a phone call and virtually every person took his call! Several set up appointments to talk about potentially working with him on a freelance contract basis. These appointments (interviews?) allowed him to show his work portfolio and open the door when future needs would arise. He then followed up with a "thank you" note.

Result? In less than two weeks, he had gone from being a total unknown in the ad business to perhaps the best-known freelancer in the area. He came up with several freelance contracts, and eventually landed a job with one of the agencies he freelanced for as an account executive and chief copywriter.

> **I MAY NOT BE ABLE TO HIRE RIGHT NOW. BUT I ALWAYS NEED HELP.**

Why does this approach work? Because most companies will only talk about "employment" when they have a current, active need. If he had sent out his material as a solicitation for employment, he likely would have gotten no response. But most companies are very willing to talk to freelancers regardless of their current needs.

The Freelancer Technique works well in all fields where independent contractors are commonplace, such as the creative fields (Advertising, Publishing, Writing, Arts), technical fields (Programming, Engineering), and specialty fields (Accounting, Legal, Medical). The side benefit is that the pay is usually quite good (anywhere from 25 to 100 percent higher than the average wage for similar in-house work), although you are on your own in the perks category.

It usually costs very little to establish yourself as a freelancer (other than a basic work portfolio and an outline of your services), and it often opens doors that would otherwise be shut. And it sure beats flipping burgers at McDonald's!

THE WORK DOWN UNDER TECHNIQUE

Not Australia, but down under the position you are seeking. Again, this is a technique best used by someone who is unemployed or underemployed. If you cannot find work at the level you desire, you might consider starting at a lower level and working your way up. The days of "starting in the mail room" are not necessarily past. But these days the "mail room" may be in administrative, clerical, or other support positions. One college graduate who couldn't find a job in advertising took a job as a receptionist with a large ad agency. Within two years, she was working in her "dream job" as an ad copywriter handling one of the agency's largest national accounts.

THE PARTIALLY EMPLOYED TECHNIQUE

When looking for companies that may have an interest in your wares, consider working for a smaller company that is unable to hire someone full-time at the going market rate, but would be willing to bring you on part-time.

By working part-time, you are often more able to gather higher-level experience than if you sought a lower-level, permanent, full-time position. And by working with a smaller company, the experience will likely be much broader, since each person often wears many different hats.

If you do outstanding work for them, they will be happy to give you an excellent reference. Or they may surprise you by offering you full-time work in some combination of duties. It's a start—and often that is all it takes.

THE TEMPORARILY EMPLOYED TECHNIQUE

If you are seeking both a way to keep busy and a way to gain valuable experience (and contacts!), temporary employment, temping, may be the solution. Most temporary help agencies are quite willing to work with new college grads, with assignments ranging from basic clerical to office administrative to para-professional.

It should be noted that general temping is different from the Puppy Dog Close selective temping in that you have little control over the assignment and company location. But it can provide you with an extra measure of experience to include on your resume and can help pay the bills until a real job comes along. Always keep your eyes open for new opportunities with the companies you work for. You are now on the inside and have access to otherwise unavailable information.

THE VOLUNTARILY EMPLOYED TECHNIQUE

Even if you are able to locate temp or part-time paid work elsewhere, you may want to consider expanding your experience by volunteering for a local school, government agency, association, or community service organization. You can often work at the same professional level you are seeking as your

> THE WORD "FREE"
> WILL ALMOST
> ALWAYS GET THEIR
> ATTENTION.

long-term goal, so the experience will serve you well both on your resume and within the interview. Plus, not-for-profits often have good connections in the business community, so you may be able to develop further network contacts.

MASTERS OF THE UNIVERSITY

Probably the most popular option for the perpetually unemployed is further schooling. But unless graduate study truly enhances your job search opportunities, you are only delaying the inevitable.

Why do so many students head off to grad school? Is it because they are so much more employable with the advanced degree (as most grad schools would have you believe)? Or is it to further enhance the academic and professional understanding of the field of interest? Unfortunately, no. The majority of college students (over 60 percent by a recent poll) choose grad school not for the educational opportunities offered, but because it is preferable to having to go out and find a job.

Yes, it does look much better to go on to grad school than to spend two years watching *Oprah* and eating Cheetos. If that is truly your only alternative, go hide from reality for a couple more years in hopes of a better job search later.

> GRAD SCHOOL IS
> MUCH LESS PAINFUL
> THAN THE REALITY
> OF UNEMPLOYMENT.

But next time, do your job search right from the start. In fact, begin to plan now so that you will be ahead of the game instead of behind it. Plan ahead for your spring thaw early in your hibernation cycle.

DON'T QUIT!

Following is a piece of poetry that I have framed on the wall in my office. I look to it when I need inspiration. I hope it will inspire you as well.

Don't Quit!

When things go wrong, as they sometimes will,
When the road you're trudging seems all uphill,
When the funds are low and the debts are high,
And you want to smile, but you have to sigh,
When care is pressing you down a bit,

Rest, if you must, but do not quit.
Life is queer with its twists and turns,
As every one of us sometimes learns,
And many a failure turns about,
When he might have won had he stuck it out;
Don't give up though the pace seems slow-
You may succeed with another blow.

Often the goal is nearer than,
It seems to a faint and faltering man,
Often the struggler has given up,
When he might have captured the victor's cup,
And he learned too late when the night slipped down,
How close he was to the golden crown.

Success is failure turned inside out—
The silver tint of the clouds of doubt,
And you never can tell how close you are,
It may be near when it seems so far,
So stick to the fight when you're hardest hit—
It's when things seem worst that you must not quit.

—Anonymous

Your job is just around the corner. Stay with it. Don't be afraid to work hard at finding work. In the end, you will succeed. I know you will. My thoughts and prayers are with you.

Chapter 25

NEW JOB PREPARATION

Trust men and they will be true to you;
treat them greatly, and they will show themselves great.
—Ralph Waldo Emerson

Congratulations! Your hard work has finally paid off! Now what? First of all, get ready for one of the most enjoyable parties you have ever attended—and you are the guest of honor. It doesn't matter if it's two hundred people at Mom and Dad's or just a celebration night out with a few friends or a loved one. Splurge! Spend a few bucks. Buy a bottle of nice champagne! After all, this is a pivotal event in your life and should be welcomed with a bang!

FIRST THINGS FIRST

Make sure you take the time to get all of your paperwork in order. If the offer was made to you verbally, make *certain* you also get a written offer. The basic information you are looking for is the salary (plus any promised bonuses and/or commissions), benefits, start date, and who to report to and when. Treat it like gold since that letter is an actual contract—but remember, not until you accept it. Make sure you put your acceptance in writing and keep a copy for your files.

Ask if there is any employment paperwork you can fill out before you actually report to work. Taking care of your paperwork now will avoid confusion later. Make sure everything is in order now and don't put it off.

P.S. Most banks will acknowledge your offer letter as sufficient for securing a car loan. So if you have been waiting to buy that new car, you now have the necessary document in hand.

DRUG TESTING AND OTHER POSSIBLE CONDITIONS OF EMPLOYMENT

Some may consider drug testing, credit checks, reference checks, and other pre-employment checks to be Gestapo tactics, but they are a requirement of many companies. And, yes, in most cases they are legal. Remember that little section of legalese at the end of the employment application you didn't really read? Your signature on that document is what gives them the right. So be ready to live up to the terms you have already agreed to. By the way, if you look closely at your acceptance letter, you may notice that the offer is contingent on your passing whatever pre-employment checks and/or tests they may have. Even if it isn't in the letter, it was probably contained within the application you signed earlier. Most employers consider these tests to be "conditions of employment," and these conditions can be in effect even after you have started with the company.

> IT'S NOT A REAL JOB UNTIL THE FIRST PAYCHECK CLEARS THE BANK.

An example of this "condition of employment" clause being invoked occurred when a recently hired grad was found to have lied about some information on the employment application. There have been numerous cases of graduates who have been hired and then fired by the new employer based solely on the conditions of that document. As long as you have been straight and honest, this should not be a problem for you.

On the other hand, the pre-employment check that many college students fear most is the pre-employment drug screening—and rightly so. A strong note of caution: if you have in the past or are presently using illegal drugs, you are strongly advised to stop using them—immediately! The day before—or even the week before—the test will likely be too late to achieve "clean" results. But if you make a commitment to steer clear far enough in advance, you may give your body enough time to flush out. While many substances can clear in under a week, there are some—such as marijuana, PCP, cocaine, and Valium—that will stay with you much longer. I recently spoke with a graduate who had accepted employment, only to fail the drug test. Reason? He had used marijuana thirty-one days before the drug test. So if you have been exposed to illegal drugs, again, your best insurance for a clean drug test is to stop using them immediately. And not just temporarily—permanently. Drug test or no drug test, using illegal drugs (and excesses of alcohol) will eventually catch up with you—sooner (if you are foolish enough to use them during work hours) or later (if you obliterate the rest of your life outside work).

Please note: this is not a lecture from Mom and Dad on the evils of drugs. This is a straightforward and honest warning from someone who has seen the negative effects that drugs can have in the workplace. Drugs have *no place* in work society today and *never will*.

If you are not a drug user and you fail the drug screening (it does happen), be as straightforward with the employer as possible. Let them know you are not a drug user and ask them if they would please do a confirmation test. Recent estimates from the *Journal of Analytic Toxicology* showed error rates of 5 to 14 percent on this initial test. Most employers do not automatically perform the confirmation test since it is significantly more expensive than the initial test. If they refuse, offer to pay the expense on your own and then use a different testing service—ideally a secondary testing provider recommended by the employer so that you won't have a credibility problem with the second test. If you are turned down in your request or you have additional problems, you may want to seek the advice of a competent attorney for further counsel on your available options.

THE VERY BEST QUESTION TO ASK BEFORE YOU START WORK

Want to really impress your new employer? Ask if there are any materials that you can read or study before you start work. Not only will it give you a jump start on the work at hand, it will place you very favorably with your future employer. Of all the people I have been involved in hiring over the years, this request was made only twice—and both times it was made known to everyone in the department, from line management on up to VP, that this person truly had "the kind of attitude that will go far in our company."

Even if you will be part of a formal training program, just the fact that you requested to go above and beyond will place you in good standing. And if they don't have any work-related materials, you might ask for a recommendation of outside reading (books, articles, etc.). It will be duly noted that you are a potential superstar in the making.

THE ANNOUNCEMENT LETTER TECHNIQUE

Remember all the hard work you put in to develop your personal network? Now is an excellent time to show them your gratitude. Send out an announcement letter about your new job to all of your network contacts. Let them know your new address (if you have it), both home and work. Yes, you have now entered the life of dual phone numbers and addresses.

By keeping in touch with your network, you have planted the seeds for future contact. And now that you will also be well connected in the field, be sure to offer your support to anyone in need in the future. Once you have reached your initial goal, do not forget to extend a helping hand to others.

If your new job came directly through a network connection, it would be entirely appropriate to send a small gift, such as a box of chocolates, along with a personal note of gratitude.

And, if you still have time for one more letter, I would appreciate hearing your personal success story. You can reach me at:

Brian Krueger
c/o Adams Media Corporation
260 Center Street
Holbrook, MA 02343

NEW JOB PROVERBS

Following is a collection of "new job proverbs": for the sometimes difficult world of work:

Your first few days:

➤ Know what your company does. Be ready to give a thirty-second overview to anyone who asks, from your friends to your grandma to your next-door neighbor.

➤ Understand your role in contributing to the bottom line of the company. Keep your eyes (and your career) focused on the big picture rather than your own little cube.

➤ Get a copy of your company's most recent annual report and read it cover to cover.

➤ Dress conservatively—at or above the conservative median within the company. You should always speak louder than your clothes.

➤ Remember the names of those you are introduced to. In your first few days on the job, jot down names until you remember them. They only have to remember one new name, while you have scores.

➤ Take the time to understand your company benefits plan. Don't wait until you need to use one of the benefits to understand it.

➤ Watch and emulate those who are successful in the company. Allow them to be your mentors from afar.

➤ Personalize your work area, but not too personal. Frame your degree and hang it on the wall. Put a small picture on your desk. Get a nameplate so everyone will know who you are.

➤ If your employer provides the option, have your paycheck set up for direct deposit. It will save you the time and hassle of depositing each paycheck and will give you quicker access to your money.

The daily routine:

➤ Rehearse what you need to accomplish that day during your morning commute.

➤ If you can take public transportation to work, do it. It not only saves energy, but gives you time to read. Always have profitable reading materials with you. And no, the daily paper does not qualify.

➤ If you drive to work, get in the habit of "reading" books on tape. It's amazing how much reading you can accomplish over the course of a year.

➤ Always carry a notepad or pocket organizer with you. If you drive, get a windshield-attached notepad. Get in the habit of writing down both your brilliant thoughts and daily reminders as they occur to you. Or you may lose them forever.

➤ Be a morning person. Always be on time.

➤ Plan your day. Ten to fifteen minutes in the morning will equal an extra hour or more of productivity throughout the day.

➤ Develop a routine only where it increases personal productivity; don't get into the rut of doing something only as part of a routine.

➤ Be the first person to say "Hello" to others in the morning. And say it with a smile.

➤ Never leave a half cup of coffee in the coffee maker for the next person. Always make a fresh pot.

➤ Keep a toothbrush and breath mints in your desk for bad breath emergencies. And remember, just because you can't smell your breath doesn't mean it's sweet and clean.

➤ Keep an extra shirt or blouse, pressed and boxed, in your car. Also consider having an extra tie or an extra pair of nylons available at the ready.

➤ Always check your appearance in the mirror before leaving the washroom.

➤ Arrive at meetings on time. Bring extra work that you can pass the time with while you are waiting for others.

➤ Don't doodle or daydream at meetings. If topics being covered are outside of your area, take out your pocket planner and review what you need to accomplish that day.

➤ Eat lunch in. You will save both time and money. Even just $5 per lunch eating out (and it can easily be quite a bit more) adds up to $2500 per year. Plus it's healthier to bring your own. Use a resealable lunch container and bring last night's leftovers or soup or pasta. And as a by-product, you will often be viewed as a hard worker for consistently staying in when others are going out.

➤ Go for a brisk walk each day. Park at the far end of the lot in the morning. Or stretch your legs during lunch. It will clear your mind and make you more productive for the remainder of the day.

Work ethics:

➤ Draw a solid ethical line and never cross it. Especially when others are encouraging you to do so.

➤ Integrity sold cannot be repurchased. Do not allow yours to go on the trading block, for there will always be a ready buyer.

➤ Integrity means doing what is right, even if it is unpopular, unfashionable, and unprofitable.

➤ Develop a reputation for honesty and integrity. If you have failed in these areas in the past, your new job is an opportunity to start fresh. It is a reputation you must earn over time. And live up to that reputation at all times, at work and everywhere else.

➤ Don't use profanity, even when others do.

➤ Never tell dirty jokes, racist jokes, or sexist jokes. And ignore those who attempt to share them with you.

> ### TRUE ETHICS ARE NOT SITUATIONAL.

➤ Don't lie, cheat, or steal, even when the temptation is great—stand for honesty and integrity in all you do, and you will be amazed how far it sets you above your peers.

➤ Make good on your promises. If you are not sure you can deliver, don't promise.

➤ If you are not sure, don't do it. That's your conscience talking. Listen closely.

➤ Always seek the good in others, and they will be more likely to find it in you.

Interpersonal skills:

➤ Talk 20 percent and listen 80 percent. And avoid those who talk 100 percent.

➤ Always take the opportunity to praise others who are worthy of praise. If someone has done well, take the time to compliment them.

➤ When someone is telling you a story, don't interrupt. And don't try to upstage them with a better story of your own.

➤ Smile. A lot. Even when you feel like frowning.

➤ If someone is confrontational with you, avoid the confrontation. Take time to cool off before you respond.

➤ Be the person in your office who makes everyone else smile. Everyone loves a cheerful person.

➤ Look for solutions, not problems. Anyone can identify problems.

➤ When someone compliments you for your work, don't say "It was nothing" or try to talk them out of it. Just say "Thank you" with a smile and move on. Nothing more, nothing less.

➤ Life isn't fair. And sometimes work isn't either. There will be some days when just getting through is the best you can do. Wait until tomorrow to see if things clear up. They usually do.

➤ Don't be a complainer. Every work environment has a person who feels responsible for the role of office complainer. Let someone else fill that role. And ignore them when they attempt to practice their art upon you.

➤ When you are unhappy on the inside, do your best to stay happy on the outside. Your inside will eventually get the point and come around.

Office politics:

➤ Show respect for your boss in everything you do. Don't join in when others are boss bashing. It can be contagious.

➤ While you are subordinate, you must be willing to submit to the plans of others. Submission is not found in obeying the commands of those you are in agreement with. True submission is found in obeying another when you are not in agreement.

➤ Never discuss your salary with your coworkers. Your refusal to discuss will drive them crazy wondering why you are making so much more than they are.

> YOUR REAL EDUCATION BEGINS NOW.

➤ The work washroom is located at work. Don't let your conversation change to match the surroundings.

➤ When you are personally complimented for something that was a team effort, always give proper credit to the team.

➤ When others begin to criticize, fight the urge to join in the slaughter.

➤ Be a builder, not a destroyer.

Education and training:

➤ Know and understand the company training program. And take advantage of it.

➤ Learn to match your training with application of what you have learned. Apply it and it's yours forever. Don't apply it and it's lost.

➤ Continue your education. Even if you do not pursue a formal degree, make learning a lifelong vocation. What you learn will affect what you earn.

➤ If you are a "hunt and peck" typist, learn to type properly. It will save you immeasurable time over the course of your career. And keep you from looking silly.

➤ Become fully computer literate. You don't have to be a computer wizard, but you do need to become proficient in the use of technology in your work. Stay ahead of the technology curve.

➤ Learn to become a team player. College rewards individual performance. Employers reward team performance.

➤ You probably don't know nearly as much as you think you know. It often takes the maturity of a lifetime to come to this realization, but if you are willing to acknowledge this fact early in life, you will capture a lifetime of learning and growth.

Financial:
➤ There is more to life than the endless accumulation of wealth. There will never be enough money. You must find your wealth elsewhere in your life.
➤ Wealth and happiness are not the same thing.
➤ Buy stock in your company. If you are not willing to invest financially in your company, why are you investing your entire career with them?
➤ Read your company's annual report every year. And study the President's Message to the Shareholders. That's both the history of the past year and the next year's vision. Keep your career focused on doing your part in reaching that vision.
➤ Sign up for your 401(k) plan as soon as possible and have 10-15 percent automatically deducted from your paycheck. You will never have it, so you will never miss it. And you will be well taken care of later in life while others continue to struggle just to survive.
➤ Always pay your bills on time. Especially credit cards. And student loans. An unblemished credit record is an asset that should be cherished and protected.
➤ When someone offers you "the opportunity of a lifetime" in the form of multi-level marketing (a/k/a MLM, a/k/a network marketing), save your time and professional reputation with a polite yet firm "No thanks."
➤ Don't run a monthly balance on your credit card. If you can't pay it off, don't buy it.

Extracurricular:
➤ Limit yourself to one glass of beer or wine when dining out with coworkers or clients. And wait for someone else to order liquor first—don't be the only one.
➤ Don't drink at all at the Christmas Party or other company social activity-it's much more fun to watch others who are drinking.
➤ Don't do drugs and avoid those who do.
➤ Beware of office romances. Keep personal matters outside the work environment.
➤ Listen to your home answering machine message from the perspective of your boss. If you don't want the office to hear it, change it. Cutesy messages usually don't sound cute when played over a speakerphone at the office. And if it's real cutesy, they will probably tell others to call and listen to it.
➤ Join a health club. Go before work, during lunch, or after work. It will increase your level of energy in your life. You will look better and feel better.

Career progression:
➤ Know who your boss's boss is. This is the person who may either recommend or authorize your promotion in the future.

➤ Ask your boss to point out areas for continuous improvement.

➤ Become known either as the person who is the first in to work or as the person who is the last to leave. Or both. But don't do both forever. It's a good start in your career, but it's not a good life in the end.

➤ Develop a reputation as a problem-solver. If a problem lands on your desk, don't pass it on to someone else.

➤ Even if you receive a good performance review, ask what you can do to improve your future performance.

➤ Be aware of the work that is going on around you. These are your areas of potential future growth.

➤ Get copies of your competitor's annual reports. It will keep you in tune with your industry and help you to better understand and appreciate your company's competitive edge.

➤ If you love doing what you do, success will follow.

➤ If you go out for lunch, make it business. Take others in your company out to lunch to learn more about their jobs and their departments. Let them do the talking. You do the listening.

➤ Learn to tap into the Web network. Career progression is more like climbing a web than climbing a ladder. Make sure you web into as many connections as possible.

➤ No one owes you a living. No one owes you a job. You earn it, each and every day, all over again. And when you cease to earn your job on a daily basis, you will cease in your career progression.

➤ If you do more than what you are paid to do, you will eventually be paid more for what you do.

➤ Don't ask for a raise because you need more money. Ask for a raise because you are worth more money.

➤ When faced with earning $20,000 and loving what you do versus earning $50,000 and hating what you do, take the $20,000 job and sleep well at night. Your life will be much richer than if you had taken the other job.

➤ Take the pillow test to assess your career satisfaction. When you take your head up off the pillow in the morning, are you excited about going to work? And when you lay your head down on the pillow at night, are you happy about what you have accomplished? The answer will not always be "Yes," but if it is consistently "No," it may be time to move on.

Skills for a lifetime:

➤ Life is never exactly what we want it to be. Life just is. It is what we make of life that will bring it nearer to what we want it to be.

➤ You are the best investment you will ever have. The dividends received on this investment will pay you back for the rest of your life.

➤ Be proactive in planning for the future. To get things in the future, you have to pursue them today.

➤ Expect great things from yourself and hope for great things in others.

➤ Set goals in your life. Break down your long-term goals into short-term goals. Then break down your short-term goals into annual goals. Then break down your annual goals into monthly goals. Then break down your monthly goals into weekly goals. Then break down your weekly goals into daily goals. Then break down your daily goals into tasks. And make sure it is all down on paper. Then do it. You are on your way to accomplishing all the goals in your life.

➤ Begin to use a Day-Timer, Franklin Planner, or other pocket planner religiously. It will quickly become your daily guide to accomplishing your goals in life.

➤ Be observant—learn from the mistakes of others so that they are not repeated in your life.

➤ When you do make mistakes, take responsibility for them immediately. Denial will only prolong and intensify the error. Acknowledge you were wrong and move on. And don't make the same mistake again.

➤ Every journey begins with a single step. And with each new step, the objective comes into clearer view.

➤ Don't put your ballet shoes in the attic. Do your best to keep your life multifaceted.

➤ It's not where you start out in life; it's where you end up.

➤ Always give back to those who are less fortunate than you. No matter how hard you have worked to get where you are now, there is always someone who has not had the same opportunities that you have had in life. Do your best to give something back.

➤ Stop to smell the roses. And listen when children speak to you.

And finally, always remember that work should never be your sole purpose in life. No one ever said on their death bed, "I wish I would have spent more time at the office."

I wish you all the best in your new life after college!

Appendix A

GUIDELINES FOR SUCCESSFUL INTERVIEW DRESS

MEN AND WOMEN
- ➤ Conservative two-piece business suit (solid dark blue or grey is best)
- ➤ Conservative long-sleeved shirt/blouse (white is best, pastel is next best)
- ➤ Clean, polished conservative shoes
- ➤ Well-groomed hairstyle
- ➤ Clean, trimmed fingernails
- ➤ Minimal cologne or perfume
- ➤ Empty pockets—no bulges or tinkling coins
- ➤ No gum, candy, or cigarettes
- ➤ Light briefcase or portfolio case
- ➤ No visible body piercing (nose rings, eyebrow rings, etc.)

MEN
- ➤ Necktie should be silk with a conservative pattern
- ➤ Dark shoes (black lace-ups are best)
- ➤ Dark socks (black is best)
- ➤ Get a haircut; short hair always fares best in interviews
- ➤ Fresh shave; mustaches are a possible negative, but if you must, make sure it is neat and trimmed
- ➤ No beards (unless you are interviewing for a job as a lumberjack!)
- ➤ No rings other than wedding ring or college ring
- ➤ No earrings (if you normally wear one, take it out)

WOMEN

➤Always wear a suit with a jacket; no dresses

➤No high heels

➤Conservative hosiery at or near skin color (and no runs!)

➤No purses, small or large; carry a briefcase instead

➤If you wear nail polish, use clear or a conservative color

➤Minimal use of makeup (it should not be too noticeable)

➤No more than one ring on each hand

➤One set of earrings only

Appendix B

FIFTY STANDARD ENTRY LEVEL INTERVIEW QUESTIONS

1. Tell me about yourself.
2. What do you want to do with your life?
3. Do you have any actual work experience?
4. How would you describe your ideal job?
5. Why did you choose this career?
6. When did you decide on this career?
7. What goals do you have in your career?
8. How do you plan to achieve these goals?
9. How do you evaluate success?
10. Describe a situation in which you were successful.
11. What do you think it takes to be successful in this career?
12. What accomplishments have given you the most satisfaction in your life?
13. If you had to live your life over again, what would you change?
14. Would you rather work with information or with people?
15. Are you a team player?
16. What motivates you?
17. Why should I hire you?
18. Are you a goal-oriented person?
19. Tell me about some of your recent goals and what you did to achieve them.
20. What are your short-term goals?
21. What is your long-range objective?

22. What do you see yourself doing five years from now?

23. Where do you want to be ten years from now?

24. Do you handle conflict well?

25. Have you ever had a conflict with a boss or professor? How did you resolve it?

26. What major problem have you had to deal with recently?

27. Do you handle pressure well?

28. What is your greatest strength?

29 What is your greatest weakness?

30. If I were to ask one of your professors to describe you, what would he or she say?

31. Why did you choose to attend your college?

32. What changes would you make at your college?

33. How has your education prepared you for your career?

34. What were your favorite classes? Why?

35. Do you enjoy doing independent research?

36. Who were your favorite professors? Why?

37. Why is your GPA not higher?

38. Do you have any plans for further education?

39. How much training do you think you'll need to become a productive employee?

40. What qualities do you feel a successful manager should have?

41. Why do you want to work in the _____ industry?

42. What do you know about our company?

43. Why are you interested in our company?

44. Do you have any location preferences?

45. How familiar are you with the community that we're located in?

46. Will you relocate? In the future?

47. Are you willing to travel? How much?

48. Is money important to you?

49. How much money do you need to make to be happy?

50. What kind of salary are you looking for?

Appendix C

ILLEGAL INTERVIEW QUESTIONS

While laws vary from state to state, there are some definite taboo areas with regard to interview questions that employers should be avoiding. Following are some of the basic subject areas and questions that, if asked during the course of the interview, might be viewed as illegal questions or intention to discriminate:

➤ Questions related to birthplace, nationality, ancestry, or descent of applicant, applicant's spouse, or parents
(Example: "Pasquale—is that a Spanish name?")

➤ Questions related to applicant's sex or marital status
(Example: "Is that your maiden name?")

➤ Questions related to race or color
(Example: "Are you considered to be part of a minority group?")

➤ Questions related to religion or religious days observed
(Example: "Does your religion prevent you from working weekends or holidays?")

➤ Questions related to physical disabilities or handicaps
(Example: "Do you have any use of your legs at all?")

➤ Questions related to health or medical history
(Example: "Do you have any pre-existing health conditions?")

➤ Questions related to pregnancy, birth control, and child care
(Example: "Are you planning on having children?")

It should be noted that just because an illegal question has been asked does not necessarily mean a crime has been committed. It is up to a court of law to determine whether the information was used in a discriminatory manner.

INDEX

A

Academic projects, 23
Accidental death insurance in job offer negotiations, 279
Accountants, audit certification statements for, 193
ACT!, 63
Adams Media Corporation, 101–2
Advice, requesting, 81
Alta Vista, 123–24
Alternative choice technique to getting off-campus interviews, 171–72
America Online (AOL), 128
Announcement letter, sending out, on accepting new job, 315–16
Annual report as source of company information, 105–6, 150
Answering machine. *See also* Voice mail
proper use of, 61–62
Articulation factor in interviews, 237–38
Attitude, importance of, in successful interview, 198
Audio tape
recording references on, 56–57
recording resumes on, 189
Audit certification statements, 193
Availability of materials at telephone interview, 252–53
Avery's Laser Index & Postcard form, 51

B

Behavioral answering technique in interviews, 221
Behavioral questions in interviews, 220
Believability in interviewing, 209
Benefits, evaluating in job offer negotiations, 277–83
Bidding technique for interviews, 151–52
Bid points, buying graduate students, 152
Birth announcements, as style of communication, 192–93
biz.jobs.offered, 126
Blind box ads, responding to, 112–13
Books as service offered by career development office, 71
Briefcase
at job fair, 139
in job search, 64–65
Business Periodicals Index (BPI), 104
Business travel insurance in job offer negotiations, 279
Buzzword resume, 34–35

C

Campus-sponsored career days, 136
Campus-sponsored job fairs, 136
Career development office, 69–74
benefits of, 71
calling at other schools, 180
dropping by in person, 182
getting list of companies holding closed interviews from, 153–54
maximizing relationship with, 73–74
organization of, 69–70
services of, 71–72
signing up with, 72–73
Career Guide: Dun's Employment Opportunities Directory, 102
Career mission statement, developing personal, 9–10
CareerMosaic, 117–18, 120
CareerPath, 118–19
Career planning, 5–6
Career progression in new job preparation, 320–21
Career Search on CD-ROM, 104
CD-ROM research guides, 103–5
Cellular phone in job search, 65–66
Classified advertisements
choosing old, 110–12
responding to, 109–10, 111
Class schedule, modifying to your advantage, 12
Close in interviews, 216
College Grad Job Hunter WebSite, 115, 116
College recruiters, 156
Commercial entry level job fairs, 136–37
Commercial professional job fairs, 137
Commercial specialty job fairs, 137
Commitments
making final, in job offer negotiations, 291
trying to get small, 305–7
Community job fairs, 137
Commuting cost reimbursement in job offer negotiations, 282
Companies. *See also* Hiring companies
identifying top five, 83
interviewing process of, 245–46
interviewing techniques at, 26–27
reviewing information on, before interviewing at, 200–201
talking with employees at, before interview, 200
Company-site interviews, 255–65
process of, 259
securing, 249–50
taking exams and tests at, 259–61
Compelling stories, telling at interviews, 221–23
Competition
knowing, at on-campus interview, 246
talking about, in interviews, 238–39
Competitive posture, maintaining at interviews, 240

Complaints, avoiding, in interviews, 238
Comp time in job offer negotiations, 282
CompuServe, 128
Computer databases as service offered by career development office, 72
Computers
in job search, 65
using experience to your advantage, 27
Confidence, in interviews, 205, 226
Connexion, 130
Contacts as choice when interviewing, 202
Corporate Yellow Book, 102
Counseling as service offered by career development office, 72
Counteroffers in job offer negotiations, 291–94
Cover letters, 45–52
basic formula for, 47
best use of, 46–47, 49
checklist for, 52
contents of, 45–46
poor use of, 49–50
postscript technique for, 49
reality of, 45–46
reply postcard technique for, 50–51
sample, 48
testimonial technique for, 50
Credential questions in interviews, 220

D
Database searching
off-line, 133
on-line, 132–33
Day-Timer, 60, 63
D&B Marketplace on CD-ROM, 104
Defensiveness in interviews, 205
DejaNews, 125
Dental insurance in job offer negotiations, 278
Dependent care in job offer negotiations, 281–82
Direct approach to getting off-campus interviews, 169–70
Directories as service offered by career development office, 71
Directory of American Firms Operating in Foreign Countries, 102
Disk, resume on, 42–43
Dress
for interview, 201–2
guidelines for successful, 323–24
for job fair, 139
in job search, 64
Drug testing and other possible conditions of employment, 313–15
Dumb questions in interviews, 220
Dun & Bradstreet, 102
Dun & Bradstreet's Million Dollar Directory, 103

E
Education in new job preparation, 319
Electronic Job Matching, 131
E-mail
aliasing services, 119
mailing resumes via, 122
sending, in response to ads, 119
sending your resume via, 121–22
special interest group technique in, 130

Employee assistance programs in job offer negotiations, 282
Employer information
as service offered by career development office, 72
sources of, 106–7
Employer listings as service offered by career development office, 71
Employer research
purpose of, 99–100
strategies in, 99–113
annual reports as, 105–6, 150
blind box ads as, 112–13
CD-ROM guides as, 103–5
choosing last listed individual in responding, 112
choosing old ads in, 110–12
contacting employers on Monday, 112
employment opportunities as, 106
hard copy guides in, 100–103
marketing information in, 107
responding to classified advertising, 109–10, 111
sources of, 106–7
stockbroker information in, 108–9
using news to advantage, 109
Yellow Pages as list of potential, 105
Employers
attrition factor of, 303–4
avoiding burning of bridges at previous, 294–95
dreaming about potential, 187–88
giving proper notice to old, 294
Employment agencies, successful use of, 96–98
Employment marketplace, marketing you in, 8–9
Employment Opportunities with..., 106
Encyclopedia of Associations, 103
Enthusiasm, projecting, in telephone interviews, 253
Entry level hiring process, 77–78
steps in, 245–46
ESOPS in job offer negotiations, 281
E-span, 117, 120
Executive recruiters, 96–97
Executive/retained search, 96–97
Expense reimbursement in job offer negotiations, 282–83
Experience
questions on, in interviews, 220
talking about experience in, 236–37
Extracurricular activities, 16
in new job preparation, 320
Eye care insurance in job offer negotiations, 278
Eye contacts, in interviews, 203, 204, 205
Eyewear, choice of, for interview, 202–3

F
Facial expressions in interview, 203–4
Fair enough technique to getting off-campus interviews, 172
Fifteen-second proof technique for resume, 39
Final arrangements, making, for company-site interviews, 256–58
Final impression, leaving, in on-campus interviews, 250

Financial activities in new job preparation, 320
First impressions
    importance of, 213–14
    at on-campus interviews, 247–48
Five minutes, getting for off-campus interviews, 173
Follow-up for job fairs, 147
401(k) plans in job offer negotiations, 280
Franklin Planner, 60, 63
Full interview, 143

G
Gale Research, Inc., 102, 103
Gap analysis technique, 10
geo.jobs newsgroups, 126
Gestures in interviews, 204
Government Job Finder, 101
Grade point average (GPA), listing, on resume, 36–37
Graduate students, buying bid points from, 152
Graduate study, 310
Guerrilla insider techniques, 179–93

H
Handshakes, effectiveness of, in interviewing, 219
Health clubs in job offer negotiations, 281
Hero stories in interviews, 224–25
Higher calling technique, 183–84
Highlighting points on resume, 183
Hiring companies, 155–65
    ad infinitum call-waiting technique, 161
    aiming for right target in, 155–56
    best time to call technique, 160, 163–64
    better than leaving message technique, 163
    everyone-loves-to-hear-their-own-name
        technique, 160
    finding your target contact, 158–59
    getting past guardian of the gate at, 159
    importance-of-this-call technique, 161–62
    instant best friends technique, 163
    mailing list update technique, 158
    spelled name technique, 161
    three strikes and you're out, 165
    two-step targeted contact process, 157
    unanswerable question technique, 162–63
    voice mail messaging technique, 164–65
Hiring managers, 156. See also Off-campus
    interviews
Holidays in job offer negotiations, 279–80
Honesty in interview, 206, 260
How to Find Information about Companies, 103
HTML (hypertext markup language) resume
    developing personal, 124
    format for, 120, 121
    posting technique, 124–25
Hybrid approach to getting off-campus
    interviews, 171

I
Impassioned plea technique, 152–53
Impressions
    importance of
        first, 213–14
        at on-campus interviews, 247–48
    leaving final, in on-campus interviews, 250
    with on-campus interviewer, 248–49

at post-interviews, 269
Independent contracting, 307–8
Indirect approach to getting off-campus
    interviews, 170–71
Industry proofing technique for resume, 39
Information, gathering, in interviewing, 216–17
Informational interviewing, 25–26
Intelligence tests at company-site interviews, 260
International Job Finder, 101
Internet-based Employer Information, 104–5
Internet job search strategies, 115–33
    developing your personal HTML resume, 124
    extreme resume drop technique, 122
    HTML resume posting technique, 124–25
    off-line database searching, 133
    on-line database searching, 132–33
    on-line services, 128–29
    resume database technique, 130–32
    search engine keyword technique, 124
    search engine research technique, 122–24
    before sending e-mail, 119
    special interest group e-mail technique, 130
    special interest group posting technique,
        129–30
    Usenet Newsgroups, 125–27
    websites, 116–19
Internet resumes, 120–22
Internships, 19–20
    unknown information about, 20–21
Interpersonal skills in new job preparation,
    318–19
Interviewer, questions to ask, 240–41
Interviewing lottery, beating, 151
Interview questions
    answers for tough, 229–32
    college student's failure to answer, 232–33
    fifty standard, 232
    types of, 220–21
Interviews. See also Company-site interviews; Off-
    campus interviews; Telephone interviews
    articulation factor in, 237–38
    avoiding complaints in, 238
    behavioral answering techniques in, 221
    behavioral questions in, 220
    believability in, 209
    body language in, 205–6
    bringing work samples to, 206–7
    choice of eyewear for, 202–3
    close in, 216, 217
    company-site, 249–50
    company technique, 26–27
    compelling story technique in, 221–23
    competitive posture technique in, 240
    confidence in, 205
    credential questions in, 220
    critical success factors in, 214–15
    defensiveness in, 205
    demonstrating skills in, 207–8
    dressing for, 201–2, 323–24
    dumb questions in, 220
    effectiveness of handshakes in, 219
    establishing rapport in, 215–16
    experience questions in, 220
    eye contact in, 203, 204, 205
    facial expressions in, 203–4

full, 143
gathering information in, 216–17
gestures in, 204, 205
hero stories in, 224–25
honesty in, 206
illegal questions in, 243–44, 327
informational, 25–26
at job fairs, 142–43, 144, 145–46
key element to successful, 197–98
maintaining competitive posture at, 240
making personal connection in, 214
meal, 261–62
mental preparation for, 210
mini-, 143
mock, 199, 206
money response technique in, 241–43
multiple techniques in, 177
nervousness in, 205, 227–29
nonverbal, 206
on-campus, 149–54
openness in, 205
opinion questions in, 220
out-of-state, 177–78
parroting technique in, 234
personal space in, 204, 205
posture in, 204, 205
pregnant pause technique in, 223–24
preparing for, 197–211
pride of ownership technique in, 239
psyching up before, 209
quotable quotes technique in, 224
recaps in, 243
reframing technique in, 235–36
safety valve technique in, 234–35
screening, 142–43
and self-evaluation, 208–9
showing confidence in, 226
showing proficiency in, 208
sins committed in, 233–34
small talk in, 216
standard entry level questions, 325–26
steps in, 215–17
successful vagabond technique in, 226
talking about competition in, 238–39
talking about experience in, 236–37
truth about, 213–14
untrustworthiness in, 205
visualization technique in preparing for, 211
warmth in, 205
Investment, preparing to make, 10–12

J
Job Bank USA, 131
Job fairs, 135–48
    attending, 181
        at other colleges, 147–48
    bypassing long interview lines, 145–46
    critical last step of, 147
    gaining favor with busy job fair recruiters, 145
    gaining favor with recruiters, 145
    gaining instant rapport in interview, 144
    introduction question at, 144
    key to treasure room technique, 144
    lasting impression technique, 146–47
    lineage mileage technique, 142
    making most of time allotted, 144
    mistakes made at, 139
    most popular jobs at, 146
    no-show technique, 148
    portfolio for, 138–39
    recruiters at, 137–38
    types of, 135–37
    types of interviews at, 142–43
    walkabout technique at, 140–42
Job market, reality of, 77
Job offer negotiations
    balancing items in, 284–85
    communicating acceptability in, 286–88
    communicating unacceptability in, 285–86
    counteroffers in, 291–94
    getting advice in, 290–91
    items in, 283–84
    making final commitment in, 291
    negotiations in, 288–89
    relocation expenses in, 291
    salary comparison in, 283
    salary negotiation in, 289–90
Job offers, 303–11
    communicating acceptability, 286–88
    communicating unacceptable, 285–86
    contacting companies who received
        refused, 273
    early, 271
    generating, 271
    making other companies aware of, 271–72
    multiple, 272–73
    non receipt of, 303–11
    strategies for nonreceipt of, 297–301
    successful negotiations, 275–95
        evaluating benefits package, 277–83
        evaluating total package, 277
        outstanding questions in, 276
        timing in, 275
Job Opportunities in..., 100–101
Job postings as service offered by career
    development office, 72
Job prep proverbs, 16–17
Jobs bulletin board, 181
Job search
    college course in preparing for, 13
    four D's of getting things done in, 62–63
    personal information managers in, 63–64
    as priority in final year of college, xi–xii
    Quickstart Job Search™ Software in, 67
    reality of successful, 6
    retracing steps in, 303–4
    sales manager technique in, 66
    schedule in, 305
    steps in process, 3–5
    timetable for, 13–15
    tool kit in, 64–66
    tracking system in, 63
Job Search Control Center
    proper use of answering machine, 61–62
    setting up your, 59–60
    telephone etiquette, 61
Job Seeker's Guide to Private and Public Companies, 102
Jobs hotline, 181–82
JOBTRAK, 118
JobWeb, 118

K
Kiersey Temperament Sorter, 5

L
Lasting impression technique, 146–47
Law of 250, 79
Law of Network Gravity, 85
Law of Seven, 84–85
Leadership Directories, 102
Letters of recommendation for job fair, 139
Life insurance in job offer negotiations, 278
Lifetime skills in new job preparation, 321–22
Lines, networking in, 142
Lobby, waiting in preparing for on-site interviews, 258–59
Lottery points, buying, 152
Lotus Organizer, 63
Lunch, taking interviewer to, 173

M
MainQuad, 122
Managers, calling on unannounced, 184–85
Marketing flyer technique, 190–91
Marketing information, 107
Marketing strategy, developing your, 7–8
Materials, availability of, at telephone interview, 252–53
Maximizer, 63
Meal interview, 261–62
Medical insurance in job offer negotiations, 278
Mental ability tests at company-site interviews, 260
Mental preparation for interview, 210
MIME format for sending resume, 121
Mini-interview, 143
Mini-resume card technique, 88
Mirror, looking in, during telephone interview, 253
misc.jobs.offered, 126
misc.jobs.offered.entry, 126
misc.jobs.resumes, 126
Mistakes, making best of, at company-site interviews, 263–64
Mock interview, 199, 206
Monday, contacting potential employers on, 110–12
Money response technique in interviews, 241–43
Monster Board, 118, 120
Multiple interviews technique, 177
Myers-Briggs Type Indicator (MBTI), 5

N
NAPA Computerized Job Matching Service, 130
National Career Services, 131
National Career Services (NCS) Jobline, 131
National Job Bank, 101–2
National Resume Network, 131
Nervousness in interviews, 205, 227–29
Networking
    advice request technique, 81
    by association, 93–94
    business cards in, 87–88
    consistency in, 84
    elevator pitch in, 82
    employment agencies in, 96–98
    expanding contacts in, 86
    explaining opportunities in, 86

getting assistance in, 86–87, 90–91
    intelligence gathering in, 77–98
    Law of 250, 79
    Law of Network Gravity, 85
    Law of Seven, 84–85
    levels in, 79–80
    in lines, 142
    making contacts in, 80–81
    mini-resume card technique in, 88
    personal contacts in, 88–89
    political network in, 95–96
    professional contacts in, 91–93
    purpose of, 78–79
    saying magic word in, 83
    technique in, 95
    ten-second sound bites in, 81
    top five technique in, 83
    tracking down information in, 86–87
    turning contacts into network contacts, 82
New job preparation, 313–22
    drug testing and other possible conditions of employment, 313–15
    proverbs on, 316–22
    questions to ask in, 315
    sending out announcement letters, 315–16
Newspaper, creating one-page about yourself, 191–92
Non-Profits & Education Job Finder, 101
Nonverbal communication in interviews, 203–4
Nonverbal interview, 206
Notables techniques for resumes, 36
Notice, giving proper, to employer, 294

O
Occupational listings as service offered by career development office, 71
Occupational Outlook Handbook, The, 6
Off-campus interviews, 167–78
    alternative choice technique, 171–72
    company logo technique, 176
    direct approach, 169–70
    fair enough technique, 172
    fax yourself technique, 174–75
    five minutes and counting technique in, 173
    ground zero resume technique, 175–76
    handling stalls in, 173–74
    hybrid approach, 171
    improving your out-of-state search, 177
    indirect approach, 170–71
    I-only-love-you technique, 176
    limited time offer technique, 176–77
    making yourself irresistible, 167–68
    multiple interviews technique, 177
    out-of-state, 177–78
    solution suggestion technique, 172
    trashproof resume technique, 175
    we-all-have-to-eat technique, 173
    what to say to get, 168–69
Office politics in new job preparation, 319
Off-line database searching, 133
Old is new technique, 110–11
On-campus interviews, 149–54, 245–50
    asking for schedule for, 181
    beating lottery, 151
    bid technique, 151–52

choosing best employers, 149
company's process of, 245–46
efficient market technique, 152
impassioned plea technique, 152–53
increasing your hit rate with invitational, 153–54
knowing competition in, 246
leaving final impression in, 250
materials needed at, 246
next steps, 154
personal investment decision technique, 150
securing company-site, 249–50
signing up for, 155
timing, 154
waiting room at, 247
One-a-day technique, 84
Online Career Center, 116–17, 120
On-line database searching, 132–33
On-line services, 128–29
Openness in interviews, 205
Opinion questions in interviews, 220
Other alma mater technique, 179–82
Out-of-state interviews, 177–78
Out-of-state search, improving, 177
Overtime in job offer negotiations, 282

P
Pager in job search, 65
Parking reimbursement in job offer negotiations, 282
Parroting technique in interviews, 234
Part-time employment, 309
Pen in job search, 65
Pension plans in job offer negotiations, 280
Personal connection, making with interviewer, 214
Personal Information Managers (PIMs), 63–64
Personal investment decision technique, 150
Personality
    matching, with telephone interviewer, 252
    mirroring of interviewer, 217–19
Personality tests at company-site interviews, 260
Personal space in interviews, 204
Petersen's Guides, 100–101
Picture perfect technique, 186
Pocket organizer in job search, 65
Political network, tapping into, 95–96
Portfolio
    at job fair, 139
    in job search, 64
Positive attribute development, 30
Positive image, projecting, in telephone interviews, 253
Post-interview
    making good impression, 269–70
    recommendations from technique, 270–71
Post-it note technique, 182
Postscript technique for cover letters, 49
Posture in interviews, 204
Pregnant pause technique in interviews, 223–24
Pride of ownership technique in interviews, 239
Procrastination, 66
Product advertising technique, 192
Product introduction technique, 192
Professional contacts, finding best, 91–93
Professional's Job Finder, 101

Professors, getting assistance from, 90–91
Proficiency, showing, in interview, 208
Profit sharing in job offer negotiations, 280
Psyching up before interviews, 209

Q
Qualitative tests at company-site interviews, 261
Quantitative tests at company-site interviews, 261
Questions
    illegal, in interviews, 243–44
    outstanding, in job negotiations, 276
Quickstart Job Search™ Software, 67
Quickstart Résumé Software, 31
Quotable quotes technique in interviews, 224

R
Rapport, establishing
    in interviews, 215–16
    in on-campus interviewer, 248
Real-world experience, 19–28
Recaps in interviews, 243
Reference referral technique of cover letters, 57–58
References, 53–58
    getting recommendation from, 270–71
    making sure of, 57
    and post-it note technique, 182
    presentation of, 54–55
    recording, for cover letters, 56–57
    referral technique of cover letters, 57–58
    sources of outstanding, 53–54
    talking technique in writing cover letters, 56
    using letters of, 56
Reframing technique in interviews, 235–36
Rejection letter, 297–98
    requesting feedback after receipt of, 297–301
Relocation expenses in job offer negotiations, 291
Reply postcard technique for cover letters, 50–51
Resumes, 29–44
    audio, 189
    buzzword, 34–35
    checklist, 44
    database technique, 130–32
    delivering first copy of finished, 40
    on disk, 42–43
    faxing, 174–75
    fifteen-second proof technique, 39
    getting noticed, 38
    handling stall involving sending, 174
    highlighting points on, 183
    HTML (hypertext markup language), 120, 121, 124–25
    important features of, 33–34
    industry proofing technique, 39
    as initial marketing brochure, 29
    Internet, 120–22
    for job fairs, 138–39
    listing your grade point average (GPA) on, 36–37
    making irresistible, 41–43
    mistakes on, 38
    need for specific objective, 33–34
    as never complete, 40
    notables techniques, 36
    and off-campus interviews, 175–76

and picture perfect technique, 186
presentation of, 40–41
sending to job fair sponsors, 148
steps in creating, 30–33
summary section in, 34
and time is money technique, 186–87
using services for, 37
verbal proofing technique, 38
video, 188–89
voice mail, 189
web, 190
Ripple effect, 78
Rowboat technique, 227–29

S
Safety valve technique in interviews, 234–35
Salary comparison in job offer negotiations, 283
Salary negotiation in job offer negotiations, 289–90
Sales manager technique, 66
Scarlett O'Hara syndrome, 16
Screening interview, 142–43
Search engine keyword technique, 124
Search engine research technique, 122–24
Search engines in job search, 122–24
Second place candidate, negotiations by, 300
Secretary, importance of, in company-site interviews, 264–65
Self-evaluation and interviewing, 208–9
Seminars as service offered by career development office, 72
Shadowing technique, 24–25
Sick/personal days in job offer negotiations, 280
Skills, demonstrating, in interview, 207–8
Skills tests at company-site interviews, 260
Small talk in interview, 216
Smoking at company-site interviews, 262–63
Sneak preview technique, 207–8
Solution suggestion technique to getting off-campus interviews, 172
Special interest groups e-mail technique, 130
Special interest groups posting technique, 129–30
Special project technique, 22–23
Sponsors in company-site interviews, 255–65
Squeaky wheel theory, 46
Standard and Poor's Register of Corporations, 103
Stockbroker, getting company information from, 108–9
Stock options in job offer negotiations, 281
Strategic Résumés, 37
Strong Interest Inventory (SII), 6
Structure of Intellect (SOI), 6
Subscriptions as service offered by career development office, 72
Successful vagabond technique in interviews, 226
Success signals at company-site interviews, 265
Summer work, finding, 20
System for Interactive Guidance and Information (SIGI), 6

T
"Take Your Daughter/Son to Work Day," 25

Talking reference technique in writing cover letters, 56
Telephone interviews
etiquette at, 61
preparation for, 251–52
types of, 251
Temporary employment, 309
Temporary help agencies, 98
Ten-second sound bite technique, 81
Testimonial cover letter technique for cover letters, 50
Tests at company-site interviews, 259–61
Thank you, saying, for interviews, 269–70
Thirty-second elevator pitch technique, 82
Time is money technique, 186–87
Toastmasters International club, joining, 13
Tombstone technique, 193
Training in new job preparation, 319
Travel premiums in job offer negotiations, 282
Trying-on-for-size technique, 23–24
Tuition reimbursement in job offer negotiations, 281

U
Underemployment, 308–9
Uniworld Business Publications, 102
Untrustworthiness in interviews, 205
Upgrade your staff technique, 184
Usenet newsgroups, 120, 125–27

V
Vacation in job offer negotiations, 279
Verbal proofing technique for resumes, 38
Video tape
recording references on, 56–57
resume on, 188–89
Video teleconferencing interview technique, 190
Vision insurance in job offer negotiations, 278
Visualization technique in preparing for interview, 211
Voice, warming-up for on-site company interview, 258
Voice mail. *See also* Answering machine
leaving brief resumes on, 189
leaving messages on, 164–65
Volunteer employment, 309–10
Volunteer interning, 21–22

W
Walkabout technique, 140–42
Warmth in interviews, 205
Washington Researchers Publishing, 103
Web resumes, 190
Websites, 116–19
"Who-do-you-know" network, 78
Work ethics in new job preparation, 318
Work samples, bringing to interviews, 206–7
Work simulation tests at company-site interviews, 260

Y
Yahoo!, 123
Yellow Pages, 105

From:

_____

_____

_____

College Grad Jobs Hunter
6910 W. Brown Deer Road, Suite 201
Milwaukee, WI 53223-2104

SOFTWARE OFFERS

As the purchaser of this book, you are entitled to a free copy of Quickstart Job Search™ Software and/or a copy of Quickstart Résumé™ Software.

Just send this coupon along with cash, check, or money order (to cover shipping and handling) to:

**College Grad Job Hunter
6910 W. Brown Deer Road
Suite 201
Milwaukee, WI 53223-2104**

By the way, what do you think of the book so far?

"I think it is...

Or just fold over this form, enclose $3 or $5 cash, check, or money order, seal securely on all sides, and mail with the appropriate postage. Please send:

❏ Quickstart Job Search™

$3 3.5″ IBM disk
S/H Requires ability to import ASCII database data.

❏ Quickstart Resume™

$3 3.5″ IBM disk.
S/H Requires ability to import MS Word files.

❏ Both Programs

Just $5 for both 3.5″ IBM disk.

Print Name address/address in the box below. Print clearly, as this will be used in your shipping label:

Note: this limited offer is valid for 90 days from date of purchase and may only be redeemed by mail. No phone orders will be accepted for this offer. Library patrons are permitted to copy this form.

ABOUT THE AUTHOR

Brian Krueger, the author of this book, is an active Hiring Manager. Brian currently serves as a Hiring Manager for Keane, Inc., the largest Information Systems Consulting Firm in the United States, with more than seven thousand employees worldwide and $600 million in sales. Keane, based in Boston, currently hires eight hundred to nine hundred new entry level hires each year. Previously, Brian was with IBM Corporation and Data Professionals International. He is a Certified Personnel Consultant and an honors graduate of the University of Notre Dame.

Brian works in the hiring trenches each and every day, sitting on the other side of the hiring desk. He knows what techniques and tactics work. And those that don't. He has reviewed more than thirty thousand resumes and interviewed more than six thousand candidates in his fifteen-year career.

This book is the compilation of all Brian has learned (and now willingly shares with his readers) from the other side of the hiring desk.

In addition to his work responsibilities with Keane, Brian writes the *Job Hunter* nationally syndicated college newspaper column (syndicated through UWire at www.uwire.com) and serves as Webmaster for the College Grad Job Hunter Website (www.collegegrad.com), which has won more Web awards than any other career site. He is also an active speaker at college campuses and job fairs throughout North America. If you are interested in having Brian speak at your college or university, please contact him at bkrueger@collegegrad.com.

Brian shares with you, in the pages of this book, what you need to know about how you really get hired. How to prepare. What to do. And say. And not do. And not say. Taking you all the way through the hiring process to the final step of job offer negotiation and acceptance.

It's all here, in the pages of this book. Welcome to the first major step on the journey to your new life after college.